Who's Watching the

the

Spies?

Who's Watching the Spies?

Establishing Intelligence Service Accountability

Edited by

HANS BORN, LOCH K. JOHNSON, IAN LEIGH

Foreword by
Ambassador Theodor H. Winkler
and Ambassador Leif Mevik

Potomac Books, Inc.
Washington, D.C.

Library of Congress Cataloging-in-Publication Data

Born, H. (Hans), 1964–
   Who's watching the spies : establishing intelligence service accountability / Hans Born, Loch K. Johnson,
   Ian Leigh ; with a foreword by Theodor H. Winkler and Leif Mevik.
      p.   cm.
   Includes bibliographical references and index.
   ISBN 1-57488-896-X (hc : alk. paper)—ISBN 1-57488-897-8 (pbk. : alk. paper)
      1. Intelligence service.   I. Johnson, Loch K., 1942–   II. Leigh, I. (Ian)   III. Title.
   JF1525.I6B67   2005
   353.1′7235—dc22   2004027143

Printed in Canada on acid free paper that meets the
American National Standards Institute Z39-48 Standard.

Potomac Books, Inc.
22841 Quicksilver Drive
Dulles, Virginia 20166

First Edition

10   9   8   7   6   5   4   3   2   1

Contents

PART 1
Introduction to Intelligence Accountability

PART 2
The Revolution in Intelligence Accountability

Tables and Figures

Foreword

Ambassador Theodor H. Winkler
and Ambassador Leif Mevik

INTELLIGENCE SERVICES play an indispensable role in democratic societies. By providing timely and effective intelligence, they shield a country from dangerous threats to its vital security interests. Notably, after September 11, 2001, it became widely acknowledged that a legitimate requirement for secrecy exists; that is, the operational details of intelligence agencies may have to be restricted from public knowledge. Yet the imperative for secrecy can also be abused and may lead to unauthorized actions, inefficiencies, the misuse of power, or—as widely charged in the United States and the United Kingdom during the second Persian Gulf War—the politicization of intelligence agencies. Finding the right balance between the need for secrecy, on the one hand, and the protection of the rule of law, on the other hand, is a formidable challenge to all countries irrespective of their constitutional differences.

Little systematic international comparison of democratic accountability over intelligence services has been carried out, especially concerning the role of lawmakers in parliaments and other legislative institutions; as a result, no set of international standards for democratic oversight of intelligence have evolved. The Geneva Centre for the Democratic Control of Armed Forces, in close cooperation with the Norwegian Parliamentary Intelligence Oversight Committee and the Human Rights Centre of the University of Durham, teamed up to initiate a project which seeks to enhance understanding about this important subject by providing insights into tried and tested legal and institutional arrangements for effective intelligence accountability in eight different countries. This book, the first result of this collaboration, addresses the central criteria that must be taken into account by any nation or international organization that hopes to place intelligence agencies under democratic supervision—a shared responsibility of the executive, the legislative, and the judiciary. A sound system of checks and balances is necessary, rather than an approach that makes the executive the exclusive overseer of a nation's secret agencies. Parliament and, to some extent, the judiciary must play vital roles in any serious attempt to balance the values of security and liberty.

As an introduction to the country case studies, three thematic chapters lay out an overview of the essential challenges facing the democratic governance of secret agencies. By drawing upon the knowledge and expertise of established scholars and practitioners in a wide range of nations around the world, including Argentina, Canada, Norway, Poland, South Africa, South Korea, the United Kingdom, and the United States, this volume brings together the rich experience of three decades of intelligence accountability. The reader can benefit from a combination of best practices and legal procedures from countries with a variety of constitutional and political backgrounds. This volume demonstrates that not only do transition states face problems with the democratic accountability of intelligence but also that many problems are common to established western democracies as well.

By supporting this research, the Geneva Centre for the Democratic Control of Armed Forces and the Norwegian Parliamentary Intelligence Oversight Committee hope to contribute to a substantive and informed debate among lawmakers, administration officials, journalists, and academic experts on the role and reformed nature of intelligence agencies in today's democratic societies.

Ambassador Theodor H. Winkler
Director of the Geneva Centre for the Democratic
    Control of Armed Forces
Geneva, April 2005

Ambassador Leif Mevik
Chairman of the Norwegian Parliamentary Intelligence
    Oversight Committee
Oslo, April 2005

Acknowledgments

THE STUDY OF intelligence oversight calls for connecting the seemingly divergent worlds of democracy and security. From an academic point of view, it necessitates an interdisciplinary research that combines political science, law, security studies, and perhaps the understanding of human behavior as well. From an institutional point of view, the parliament is a public forum of open debates and discussion, while the intelligence and security agencies are often regarded as secretive organizations. This volume presents the findings of comparative research into the intelligence oversight trends, frameworks, and practices in various democracies.

Many people supported us in bringing these worlds together and we are delighted to acknowledge them here. In particular, we are grateful to Amb. Theodor H. Winkler, director of the Geneva Centre for the Democratic Control of Armed Forces (DCAF) and Amb. Leif Mevik, chairman of the Norwegian Parliamentary Intelligence Oversight Committee. They provided us with the opportunity and resources to undertake this research project. We greatly appreciated the cordial and warm welcome of the Norwegian Parliamentary Oversight Committee at the international workshop "Making Intelligence Accountable" in September 2003.

We are very much indebted to Thorsten Wetzling, our main editorial assistant who was part of the project from the very beginning, and to Ingrid Thorburn for her efficient and timely help. Furthermore, we welcome the assistance of Wendy Robinson and Eden Cole in the realization of the manuscript. We would like to thank all of them and to express our special gratitude to the book's contributors, who did a wonderful job in meeting the great many demands the editors placed on them.

April 2005
Hans Born, Geneva, Switzerland
Loch K. Johnson, Athens, USA
Ian Leigh, Durham, UK

Acronyms

ABW	Agencja Bezpieczenstwa Wewnetrznego (Agency for Internal Security) (Poland)
AMIA	*Asociación Mutual Israelita Argentina* (Argentina)
ANC	African National Congress (South Africa)
ANSP	Agency for National Security Planning (South Korea)
ASIO	Australian Security Intelligence Organisation (Australia)
ASIS	Australian Secret Intelligence Services (Australia)
AW	Agencja Wywiadu (Foreign Intelligence Agency) (Poland)
BAI	Bureau of Audit and Inspection (South Korea)
BCW	Binary Chemical Warhead
BOR	Biuro Ochrony Rzadu (Government's Bureau for Protection) (Poland)
BOSS	Bureau of State Security (South Africa)
BverfG	Bundesverfassungsgericht (Federal Constitutional Court) (Germany)
CCSI	Cabinet Committee on Security and Intelligence (South Africa)
CIA	Central Intelligence Agency (USA)
CODESA	Conference on a Democratic South Africa (South Africa)
COE	Council of Europe
CSE	Communications Security Establishment (Canada)
CSIS	Canadian Security Intelligence Service (Canada)
DCI	Director of Central Intelligence (USA)
DIS	Defence Intelligence Staff (UK)
DMI	Directorate of Military Intelligence (South Africa)
DPRK	Democratic Peoples Republic of Korea
DSC	Defence Security Command (South Korea)
DSD	Defense Signals Directorate (Australia)
ECHR	European Convention on Human Rights
ECtHR	European Court of Human Rights
ETS	European Treaty System
EU	European Union
FAC	Foreign Affairs Committee (UK)

FBI	Federal Bureau of Investigation (USA)
FISA	Foreign Intelligence Surveillance Act (USA)
GCHQ	Government Communications Headquarters (UK)
GNU	Government of National Unity (South Africa)
GOP	Grand Old Party (USA)
HPSCI	House Permanent Select Committee on Intelligence (USA)
IFP	Inkatha Freedom Party (South Africa)
IG	Inspector-General
INR	Bureau of Intelligence and Research (US)
IOB	Intelligence Oversight Board (USA)
IOC	Interception of Communications Act (UK)
ISA	Intelligence Services Act (UK)
ISC	Intelligence and Security Committee (UK)
JCIC	Joint Co-coordinating Intelligence Committee (South Africa)
JSCI	Joint Standing Committee on Intelligence (South Africa)
JIC	Joint Intelligence Committee (UK)
KCIA	Korean Central Intelligence Agency (South Korea)
MEC	Members of Executive Councils (South Africa)
MI5	Security Service (UK)
MI6 or SIS	Secret Intelligence Service (UK)
NCIS	National Crime Investigation Service (South Africa)
NCPS	National Crime Prevention Strategy (South Africa)
NGA	National Geo-Spatial Agency (USA)
NIA	National Intelligence Agency (South Africa)
NICOC	National Intelligence Co-ordinating Committee (South Africa)
NIE	National Intelligence Estimates (USA)
NIK	Najwyzsza Izba Kontroli (Chamber of Control) (Poland)
NIS	National Intelligence Service (South Korea)
NPA	National Police Agency (South Korea)
NRO	National Reconnaissance Office (USA)
NSA	National Security Agency (USA)
NSL	National Security Law (South Korea)
ONTA	Office of National Tax Administration (South Korea)
OSP	Office of Special Plans (USA)
PAC	Pan African Congress (South Africa)
PASS	Pan African Security Service (South Africa)
PCO	Privy Council Office (Canada)
PFIAB	President's Foreign Intelligence Advisory Board (USA)
PSPD	Peoples Solidarity for Participatory Democracy (South Korea)
RCMP	Royal Canadian Mounted Police (Canada)
RIPA Act	Regulation of Investigative Powers Act (UK)

RSA	Republic of South Africa
SACP	South African Communist Party (South Africa)
SANDF	South African National Defence Force (South Africa)
SASS	South African Secret Service (South Africa)
SB	Sluzba Bezpieczenstwa (Civilian Security Service) (Poland)
SIRC	Security Intelligence Review Committee (Canada)
SSC	State Security Council (South Africa)
SSCI	Senate Select Committee on Intelligence (USA)
TEC	Transitional Executive Council (South Africa)
UAV	Unmanned Aerial Vehicle
UK	United Kingdom
UOP	Urzad Ochrony Panstwa (Office of State Protection) (Poland)
USA	United States of America
WMD	Weapons of Mass Destruction
WSI	Wojskowe Sluzby Informacyjne (Military Information Services) (Poland)

PART 1

Introduction to Intelligence Accountability

More Closely Watching the Spies: Three Decades of Experiences

Ian Leigh

This chapter introduces the studies that follow on specific themes in intelligence oversight and how it operates in different countries. The aim is to provide a framework for thinking about oversight by looking at some of the major causes of reform and at some recurring issues addressed by reforms of intelligence oversight.

There could scarcely be a more appropriate time to consider the oversight of security and intelligence. The debate about oversight of intelligence agencies by governments and legislatures began in the 1970s and is now in its third decade. A body of comparative experience has amassed that can yield more general lessons, especially for states now embarking on the process of reform. Moreover, the changed climate since September 11, 2001, has underlined the urgent need to somehow balance our simultaneous commitments to security and democracy. This can be achieved only if new powers to meet the new security challenges are accompanied by a renewed emphasis on the oversight of security and intelligence agencies.

A Brief History: From 1975 to 9/11

The choice of 1975 as the beginning of intelligence oversight might seem arbitrary. Certainly there was legislation earlier, notably in the United States and Germany (and a parliamentary committee in the Netherlands since 1952). The mid-1970s, however, mark the beginning in liberal democratic systems of exposures concerning abuses by security and intelligence agencies, which have proved to be a major catalyst for reform across the globe. Following the United States, Australia and Canada legislated for intelligence oversight in 1979 and 1984.[1] Having commenced in the Anglo-Saxon world (though reform would not reach the UK until 1989; see chapter 5), a wave of reform spread to Europe in the 1980s and 1990s, with reforms in Denmark in 1988, Austria in 1991, Romania in 1993, Greece in 1994, Norway in 1996, and Italy in 1997.[2] These developments have attracted support from the Parliamentary Assemblies of the Council of Europe and of the Western European Union.[3] Progress outside Europe has been slower, although there are exceptions, as the chapters in this volume dealing with oversight in Argentina, South Africa, and South Korea demonstrate.

The congressional investigations by the Church and Pike Committees, which documented systematic abuses both in the United States and abroad by that country's intelligence agencies, began a pattern of exposure, report, and strengthening of oversight that has been repeated in many countries since.[4] These include the McDonald Commission in Canada (1977–80), the Royal Commission under Justice Hope in Australia, and the Lund Commission in Norway (1996).[5] A common theme was the growing recognition among the public and legislators that security and intelligence agencies not only protect but can also threaten democracy. The threat may come from invasions of privacy by information gathering and surveillance and direct attempts to manipulate the political process; in the extreme, by assignations and coups in foreign countries; but also by control of information, infiltration of political movements, pressure groups, trades unions, and so on.

Apart from scandal, three other recurring causes of reform can be identified, in some instances overlapping: constitutional reform (e.g., Canada and the Republic of South Africa, described in this volume), transition from military to civilian rule (e.g., Argentina and South Korea, represented in this volume), and legal challenges (UK, Netherlands, and Romania).

Constitutional reform is perhaps most marked as a cause of reform in the case of post-apartheid South Africa (see chapter 11) and in the transitional states in Southern and Eastern Europe following the collapse of the Soviet bloc from 1989 onwards. Civil-military relations are a recurring theme of these new European constitutions.[6] A key feature of democratization in Eastern Europe has been the vesting of key decisions in defense and security with parliaments, such as the budget approval, declaring or confirming states of emergency, the declaration of war and peace, and control over the appointment of defense chiefs. As a part of the civilianization process it is common also to find the president (chief executive) designated as commander in chief of the armed forces.[7]

In transitional states the domestic security agency has often been tainted by a repressive past, and many of these states codified in law the constitutions of their security forces as part of a package of constitutional reforms. Some recent examples include legislation in Slovenia, Lithuania, Estonia, and South Africa[8] and, most recently, Bosnia-Herzegovina.[9]

The absence of an explicit legal basis for the work of its security and intelligence agencies may bring a state into conflict with constitutional or human rights norms, especially in the case of powers affecting individuals, such as surveillance. This has been of particular importance in leading to reform in European states that are parties to the European Convention on Human Rights (see chapter 3). In several states aspects of the legal basis have been found to be inadequate.[10] The European Court of Human Rights refers additionally to the "quality of law" test—this requires the legal regime to be clear, foreseeable, and accessible. This test puts a particular responsibility on legislatures when establishing the legal framework for security and intelligence agencies.

Finally, after 9/11 the phenomenon described as "superterrorism"[11] is producing some important changes. There are two discernible legal and administrative responses. First, there has been the blurring of the legal boundaries between war and peace, with resort to wartime powers, for instance the detention of "unlawful combatants" at the Guantanamo Naval Base and detention of foreign nationals under the UK Anti-Terrorism Crime and Security Act 2001. Second is the creation of new institutions to combat the threat. In the United States a single Department of Homeland Security and the Homeland Security Council have been created.[12] In the UK the Joint Terrorism Analysis Centre, an interagency joint working group on terrorism and threat assessment, has been established.[13] Following the Madrid bombing in March 2004, EU ministers have discussed the establishment of a European Intelligence Coordinator to facilitate the sharing of counterterrorist intelligence among states.[14]

This combination of wartime responses and organizational reform is potentially dangerous since it undermines institutional barriers put in place over the last three decades in many countries to protect against the abuse of security powers. It is vital that responses to "superterrorism" are accompanied by attendant reforms in the oversight regime to prevent black holes emerging in which the democratic writ does not pertain.[15]

Common Concerns

Three common concerns in the design of oversight procedures can be mentioned: the need to establish mechanisms to prevent political abuse while providing for effective governance of the agencies; upholding the rule of law; and ensuring the proportionate use of exceptional powers in order to protect civil rights.

So far as the first point is concerned, there are twin and opposing dangers here—both of too much or too little executive control. Too little control by the executive may be antidemocratic: intelligence becomes a law unto itself—a "no go" zone. Moreover, without information or control ministers cannot be properly accountable to the public for this area of work. Where there is too much executive control the risk is that governments may be tempted to use security agencies or their exceptional powers or capacities to gather information for the purposes of domestic politics—for instance, to discredit domestic political opponents.

There is a delicate balance between ensuring proper democratic control of the security sector and preventing political manipulation. One method is to provide legal safeguards for agency heads through security of tenure, to set legal limits on what the agencies can be asked to do, and to establish independent mechanisms for raising concerns about abuses. Where staff from security agencies fear improper political manipulation it is vital that they have available procedures with which to raise these concerns outside the organization. Whistle-blowing or grievance procedures are therefore significant.

Overall, the objective is that security and intelligence agencies should be insulated from political abuse without being isolated from executive governance.

A second common theme of much legislation in this field has been to curb lawlessness—both in the sense of the lack of a legal basis for the agencies' work and also of lawbreaking by the agencies. Legislation gives security and intelligence agencies legitimacy and enables democratic representatives to address the principles that should govern this important area of state activity and to lay down limits to the work of such agencies. As in other areas, one key task of the legislature is to delegate authority to the administration but also to structure and confine discretionary powers in law.

A third recurring issue concerns the appropriate and graduated use of the exceptional powers with which these agencies are often entrusted, such as surveillance and the gathering of personal data. Proportionality is the name given in European law to a principle that is recognized more widely—the reasonable relation of "means" to "end" (see the discussion by Cameron in chapter 3). North Americans, for example, talk of the "least restrictive alternative" in relation to laws interfering with individual rights. Incursions on rights can be justified by public interests such as national security—but only to the extent necessary. "National security" should not be a carte blanche.

Practical guidance on what proportionality means was given by the Canadian McDonald Commission, which proposed that investigative techniques should be proportionate to the security threat under investigation and weighed against the possible damage to civil liberties and democratic structures; less intrusive alternatives should be used wherever possible; and control of discretion should be layered so that the greater the invasion of privacy, the higher the level of necessary authorization.[16]

Oversight Issues

"Oversight" is a means of ensuring public accountability for the decisions and actions of security and intelligence agencies. It suggests something looser than control in the sense of day-to-day management of the operations of the agencies. The form varies according to the body involved in oversight, particularly whether it is exercised by the government (executive) or the legislature (parliament). Parliamentarians typically exercise oversight by critical analysis of policy, often ex post facto. Although governments should have more direct involvement in authorizing and setting the policy context for the actions of security and intelligence agencies, it is nevertheless appropriate to refer to this also as "oversight." Doing so emphasizes that agencies in this sphere should owe their allegiance to the state or the constitution and so should have a certain distance from everyday party politics.

In considering oversight, a number of initial questions of design arise: To whom should the agency be accountable (the government, the legislature, or some independent body or person)? For what (expenditure, policy, and operations)? And when (before carrying out operations or after)? Operations are plainly highly sensitive and yet may raise policy questions that are areas of legitimate oversight concern. If an oversight body has foreknowledge of sensitive or controversial operations this will hamper its ability to dispassionately review them later. The long-term nature of security operations makes a separation of review and current activities difficult in practice, however.

Further choices concern the objective or standard of oversight, whether it is to check efficiency or effectiveness, legality or proportionality. This in turn will color the procedures involved: policy analysis or factual investigation, whether the oversight body is self-tasking, commissioned by the executive or the legislature, or has jurisdiction to receive complaints. Parliamentarians are perhaps best employed in policy oversight, rather than detective work. More investigative processes are undertaken in some countries by independent inspectors-general or commissioners.

Constitutional traditions, of course vary. Among the country studies represented in this volume are parliamentary systems (Canada, Norway, and the UK), presidential systems (such as the United States, Argentina, and South Korea) and mixed systems (for example, Poland). Whatever the tradition, it is now commonplace to find a mix of legislative and executive oversight. Providing more than one device for oversight—for example, a parliamentary committee and an inspector-general or a judicial commissioner—institutionalizes checks and balances.

A mix of oversight methods may also act as a guarantee where parts of the machinery oversee specific institutions, such as the security service, and other parts oversee specific functions, such as telephone tapping. Whereas agency oversight can be sidestepped if intelligence work is undertaken by other bodies, oversight that is purely functional runs the risk of being seen out of context. Where there is a mix of the two methods mistakes are less likely to go undetected.

Scrutiny of the security sector cannot remain the exclusive preserve of the government without inviting potential abuse. It is commonplace, aside from their role in setting the legal framework, for parliaments to take on the task of scrutinizing governmental activity. In a democracy no area of state activity should be a "no-go" zone for the legislature, including the security sectors. Parliamentary involvement gives legitimacy and direct democratic accountability. It can help to ensure that the security organizations are serving the state as a whole and protecting the constitution rather than narrower political or sectional interests. Proper control ensures a stable, politically bipartisan approach to security that is good for the state and the agencies themselves. The involvement of parliamentarians can also help ensure that the use of public money is properly authorized and accounted for.

There are dangers, however, in legislative scrutiny. The security sector may be drawn into party political controversy—an immature approach by parliamentarians may lead to sensationalism in public debate and to wild accusations and conspiracy theories being aired under parliamentary privilege. As a consequence the press and public may form an inaccurate impression and a corresponding distrust of parliamentarians by security officials may develop. Where leaks occur of sensitive material to which legislators have been given privileged access these may compromise the effectiveness of military or security operations and discourage officials from being candid.

Effective scrutiny of security is painstaking and unglamorous work for politicians, necessarily conducted almost entirely behind the scenes. Sensitive parliamentary investigations require in effect a parallel secure environment for witnesses and papers. The preservation of secrecy may create a barrier between those parliamentarians involved and the remainder. They may be envied or distrusted by colleagues because of privileged access to secret material. It is therefore essential to involve a cross-section who can command widespread trust and public credibility.

Agencies: Design and Accountability

Few states have the luxury of starting with an entirely clean page on which to write security sector reform. Even in those countries where there has been dramatic constitutional change, such as South Africa or Eastern European states, there may be strong reasons to maintain some continuity with the security apparatus of an earlier regime. To speak therefore of questions of "agency design" is somewhat misleading.

Nevertheless, there are some important questions—about how many security and intelligence agencies exist, and the relationships between them and with the military and the police—that are rarely confronted publicly.

It is clear that the greater the number of agencies, the harder effective oversight will be. Moreover, where some agencies are under close democratic scrutiny and others are not there may be a natural tendency for dubious activities to gravitate towards the less-regulated part of the sector. Many states have now legislated for their domestic security agencies, mostly in the last two decades. There are fewer reasons to place a country's own intelligence agency on a legal basis—the UK was unusual in doing so in the case of the Secret Intelligence Service (MI6) in the Intelligence Services Act 1994. Again, only a few states have legislated for military intelligence (see, for example the Netherlands, Intelligence and Security Services Act 2002, Art. 7) or intelligence coordination (Article 5 of the Netherlands Act; National Strategic Intelligence Act 1994 of the Republic of South Africa).

Whether security and intelligence or espionage are treated as discrete functions has important consequences, as does whether they are distinct from policing. The boundary between intelligence and security is significant because traditionally security agencies have been subject to greater controls for the protection of the state's own citizens and because they operate within domestic borders. The activities of an intelligence agency, on the other hand, are frequently illegal when it is operating in foreign territory. Where security and intelligence are combined in a single agency there is a fear that questionable techniques or operations may be undertaken domestically because much intelligence-related work is outside the law in any event. A similar difficulty arises from combining policing and security—that "ordinary" policing will be affected by the exceptional methods; for instance, use of agents employed by security agencies. The point is even stronger concerning separation of military intelligence.

A further question is whether or not the agency is to be given executive powers—for example, to search premises or to carry out arrests and questioning of suspects—or whether its function should be purely advisory. A body that gathers evidence in preparation for court proceedings is likely to behave quite differently from one that is concerned merely with obtaining the best available intelligence, regardless of the means. This is particularly significant in the realm of counterterrorism.

Conclusion

In modern states the security sector plays a vital role in serving and supporting government in its domestic, defense, and foreign policy by supplying and analyzing relevant intelligence and countering specified threats. It is essential, however, that the agencies and officials who carry out these roles are under democratic control through elected politicians, rather than accountable only to themselves: it is elected politicians who are the visible custodians of public office in a democracy.

The chapters that follow are on specific themes in oversight and how it operates in a variety of countries, representing different backgrounds and constitutional traditions. The remainder of Part 1 considers two important themes: the growing politicization of intelligence and supranational influences on accountability. Part 2 comprises a series of studies of the operation of intelligence oversight in what can be termed "old" democracies—the United States, UK, Canada, and Norway. Part 3 looks at the spread of oversight to a range of transitional and new democracies: Poland, Argentina, South Africa, and South Korea. The concluding chapter draws together lessons from this comparative survey in readiness for a fourth decade of intelligence oversight.

Notes

1. Australian Security Intelligence Organization Act 1979 (Cth) and Canadian Security Intelligence Service Act 1984, respectively. L. Lustgarten and I. Leigh, *In from the Cold: National Security and Parliamentary Democracy* (Oxford: Clarendon Press, 1994) is a survey of accountability in Australia, Canada, and the UK.

2. For other comparative reviews see: Jean-Paul Brodeur, Peter Gill, and Dennis Töllborg, *Democracy, Law, and Security: Internal Security Services in Contemporary Europe* (Aldershot: Ashgate, 2003); Assembly of the WEU, *Parliamentary oversight of the intelligence services in the WEU countries—current situation and prospects for reform* (Document A/1801, 4 December 2002). Available at: http://assembly-weu.itnetwork.fr/en/documents/sessions_ordinaires/rpt/2002/1 801.html (searched on March 25, 2004).

3. Recommendation 1402/1999 of the Council of Europe Parliamentary Assembly; and Western European Union Assembly Resolution 113, adopted on December 4, 2002 (ninth sitting).

4. U.S. Senate, 1976. *Final Report*. Select Committee to Study Governmental Operations with Respect to Intelligence Activities (the Church Committee), 94th Cong., 2d Sess., Rept. 94–755 (May). Loch K. Johnson, *A Season of Inquiry* (Lexington: University Press of Kentucky, 1985).

5. Respectively, Government of Canada, Commission of Inquiry Concerning Certain Activities of the Royal Canadian Mounted Police, Second Report, *Freedom and Security under the Law* (2 Volumes, Hull: Ministry of Supply and Services Canada, August 1981) [*The McDonald Commission Report*]; Royal Commission on Intelligence and Security, *Fourth Report* (Canberra, 1977) [*The Hope Report*]; Dok. nr. 15 (1995–96) [*The Lund Report*].

6. See Biljana Vankovska, ed., *Legal Framing of the Democratic Control of Armed Forces and the Security Sector: Norms and Reality/ies* (Belgrade, 2001).

7. See, for example, Article 42 of the Latvian Constitution; Article 100 of the Croatian

Constitution; Article 100 of the Bulgarian Constitution; Article 106 of the Ukrainian Constitution.

8. Slovenia: Law on Defense, 28 December 1994, Arts. 33–36; The Basics of National Security of Lithuania, 1996; Estonia: Security Authorities Act passed December 20, 2000; RSA, Intelligence Services Act, 1994 (as amended).

9. Law on the Intelligence and Security Agency of Bosnia and Herzegovina, passed in March 2004.

10. *Harman and Hewitt v. UK* (1992) 14 EHRR 657; *V and others v. Netherlands*, Commission report of 3 December 1991; *Rotaru v. Romania*, Appl. No. 8341/95, May 4, 2000.

11. Lawrence Freedman, ed., *Superterrorism: Policy Responses* (Oxford; Blackwell, 2002).

12. U.S. Homeland Security Act 2002.

13. Intelligence and Security Committee, *Annual Report for 2002–3*, Cm. 5837 (June 2003), para. 62.

14. "EU to appoint anti-terror 'tsar.'" Available at: http://news.bbc.co.uk/1/hi/world/europe/3524626.stm (searched on 25 March 2004).

15. See Harold Hongju Koh, "The Spirit of the Laws," *Harvard Journal of International Law* 43 (2002): 23.

16. *McDonald Report,* vol. 1, 513 ff.

2

The Politicization of Intelligence: Lessons from the Invasion of Iraq[1]

Peter Gill

The intelligence activities of states—whether democratic or not—are inescapably bound up with politics. This is true whether we adopt the broadest definition of intelligence as knowledge generated for the benefit of decision makers in such areas as the economy, education, and environment or a narrower definition that limits the field to knowledge generated specifically for national security purposes. When governments gather information they do so in order to inform and pursue policies, to cement their rule, and to further their interests and designs at home and abroad. All these are core political activities. Therefore, in this sense, all intelligence is "politicized,"[2] but, if it is, how can we explain the major controversies that have erupted in those countries that made up the "coalition" that invaded Iraq in March 2003? This chapter seeks to examine this question with particular reference to the UK and the United States.

This is not the first time that major powers have gone to war in controversial circumstances (for example, Vietnam, Grenada, Falklands, Kosovo) but there has never been such widespread debate with respect to two major issues: the quality of the intelligence with respect to the perceived threat—both the capabilities and intentions of Saddam Hussein—and the extent to which the intelligence process was driven by political imperatives. Certainly, what we are seeing is in part the consequence of the general democratization of intelligence that has occurred throughout the world since the 1970s. Two aspects of these changes are especially relevant: the removal of the blanket of total secrecy that had concealed intelligence matters[3] and the growth of external oversight committees (some parlia-

mentary, some not). Taken together, these have encouraged incre
attention to intelligence and have required of governments more com
gies for dealing with intelligence issues. Where once they would simply refuse
comment, now they have to engage in some explanation and debate.

Power and Professionalism

In order to embark on an analysis of the relation between politics and intelligence, we need some clear benchmarks. In the broadest terms, since the mid-
nineteenth century liberal democratic states have sought to organize themselves
on the basis of a division between periodically elected governments and officials
who are appointed and who serve regardless of the political complexion of the
government. Although intelligence agencies have often developed outside of the
"normal" channels, their personnel are part of the permanent bureaucracy. As
such, the ideal type of their behavior is the "rational" model of the disinterested
expert or administrator whose product is determined by "professional" rather
than "political" criteria. Thus, intelligence is a resource that can support the
making and implementation of policy.

"Rational" models of decision making and power in organizations are, however, too simplistic: they assume away many of the most central features of political life. Power operates in, broadly, two ways: in the first, "actors" seek to
influence, persuade, or coerce others into behaving in ways that they would not
otherwise. This power is "zero sum"—the gains of one actor are balanced by the
losses of the other. The problem for researchers is that such exercises of power
might be traceable via documentary trails but often take place in secret and may
be reconstructed, if ever, only with the greatest difficulty. For example, by the
"law of anticipated reactions" an official may behave in a particular way anticipating how superiors would react were s/he to behave otherwise; thus the
"power-holder" does not always have to act.[4] But, theoretically, these exercises
of power or influence are observable.[5]

A "second stream"[6] of power is less concerned with the power of one actor
"over" another, but with power as an ability to make things happen. This is a
"non zero sum" view of power; it focuses less on specific holders and more on
the strategies and techniques of power. Various theorists[7] have developed this
view of power in which cultural and ideological factors are central to the construction of consent around particular ways of thinking. Thus the expertise that
derives from a particular form of knowledge can provide the basis for empower-
ment (for some and disempowerment for others) and is an important adjunct to
the (mainstream) power that derives from occupying a position of command.
This view of power is difficult to deploy in research because of the subtlety with

which it is often manifest. For example, if different groups of ministers and officials share a common set of assumptions about the nature of threats and "acceptable" ways of responding to them, it is futile to examine precisely who "took" particular decisions.

Professional power is founded on exclusive knowledge claims and, where professionals work within some private or public bureaucracy, they can act as a counterweight to the power of "command" inherent in the senior positions of the hierarchy. To the extent that politicians have no basis on which to challenge the knowledge claims of the professionals, they have to trust them or, if they ignore them, take the risk of policy failure.[8] Intelligence is a profession in which specialist "knowledge"—for example, "tradecraft"—is jealously guarded. It incorporates varieties of technological expertise, for example, regarding the manufacture, storage, and deployment of nuclear, biological, and chemical weapons, which political superiors are no more likely to possess than other lay members of society. Central to this discussion is the tension between, on the one hand, the needs for policy making (decision) and implementation (command) or power and, on the other, the knowledge claims on which they may be based.

Thus, we can develop a number of hypothetical possibilities of the relationship between intelligence (knowledge) and policy (power) that, in turn, can guide us through the fog that has enveloped the controversies regarding the invasion of Iraq. At the "professional" end of the spectrum is the "purest" form of relation in which governments react to the intelligence that is presented to them; if this requires the government to change its domestic or foreign policy, then so be it. Along the spectrum is space for various relationships between knowledge and power, while at the "politicized" end, the knowledge-power connection may actually be reversed. Here the will to act pre-exists the search for information and the significance of what is collected will be judged in terms of its ability to support the chosen course of action rather than to inform it. Here, the relation between knowledge and power is like that of lamppost and drunk—to provide support, not illumination. Here, intelligence is not the reason for policy but provides a post hoc rationalization for it; it may temporarily empower governments but disempowers the public if they are misled.

Information Control

However, the complexities of intelligence and politics cannot be confined to a one-dimensional spectrum between the "politicized" and the "professional"— other factors are in play. A more inclusive model of "information control"[9] incorporates four discrete processes: gathering, evaluation, influence, and secrecy. (Clearly, these mirror the main activities of intelligence agencies themselves: surveillance, analysis, and dissemination of intelligence, all protected by secrecy.) Gathering information is the core business of intelligence agencies and, indeed, of any other organization that seeks to inform itself in order to further the organizational mission. Analysis or evaluation is the process by which sense is made of what is gathered. "Facts" do not "speak for themselves"—difficult judgments of validity and reliability have to be made and information placed in the broader context of the organizational "store" of knowledge.

Information can influence others only if it is disseminated. Even the simple decision whether or not to pass on "intelligence" to another person or organization will have consequences for power. There is an important distinction between intelligence disseminated that is believed to be true and thus amounts to a form of "education" and a situation in which the intelligence disseminated is believed to be misleading; in this case *deception* or *manipulation* are more appropriate terms.[10] "Secrecy" distinguishes the intelligence business from knowledge management elsewhere in government, but it is clear that "commercial confidentiality," "personal privacy," and group "loyalty" all establish similar processes of secretiveness around information control processes.

So far we have discussed the politics (power)–intelligence (knowledge) relationship primarily in terms of the interaction between intelligence agencies and government. Two other "institutions" are centrally involved in the politics–intelligence relationship: oversight bodies and the media. The former include both those permanent committees now established in most liberal democracies and ad hoc inquiries and commissions of which several have been instituted regarding the Iraq controversy. For present purposes the UK reports of the Intelligence and Security Committee,[11] the Commons' Foreign Affairs Committee,[12] the Hutton Inquiry,[13] the Butler Review,[14] and the work of the U.S. congressional intelligence committees are most relevant. The media is the primary mechanism by which governments, agencies (to a lesser extent), and oversight bodies seek to transmit information to the public. However, the media are much more than passive transmitters; because of their "gathering" and "evaluating" activities they are important "players." Therefore, there are potentially six sets of power/knowledge interaction to be studied within which each of these actors[15] will deploy the four methods of information control (see figure 2.1).

Of course, the relationships between these four different actors are different in many respects; some are formally subordinate to others and some seek the "public interest," while others seek profit; some are elected, and others are not; and the precise organizational architecture varies between countries. But, notwithstanding these differences, it is suggested that the relationships can be usefully generalized in terms of power/knowledge.

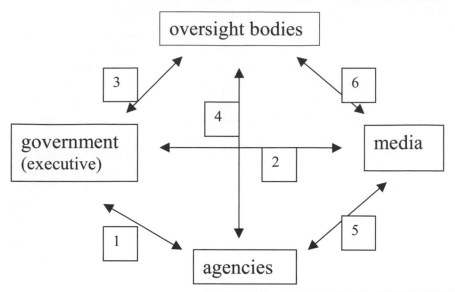

FIGURE 2.1   Model of Power/Knowledge Interaction

U.S. and UK Intelligence and the Invasion of Iraq

There is insufficient space to discuss the six dimensions in full; rather, the first three are examined in detail and some general observations are made on the position of the media. The main controversies boil down to this question: did the U.S. and UK governments develop intelligence that justified their public position that the regime of Saddam Hussein posed such a threat to regional and/ or international stability as to justify his immediate removal?

Government and the Agencies

The process by which intelligence reaches government is crucially different between the UK and the United States. Essentially, the Joint Intelligence Committee (JIC) in the UK carries out all source assessments based on what the separate agencies provide.[16] Consisting of the heads of agencies and senior officials, its object at its weekly meetings is to produce a consensus. This reflects rather well the "village" atmosphere pervading the upper echelons of Whitehall and is in stark contrast to that in Washington, D.C., where a larger number of agencies (reflecting the highly fragmented structure of U.S. government in general) generate a greater variety of opinions that may well be reflected in dissenting footnotes to National Intelligence Estimates (NIE), as in the central one relating to Iraq's weapons of mass destruction (WMD) in October 2002. The task of government may be simpler in the UK, whereas U.S. policy makers can cherry-pick their preferred interpretations; however, it cannot be concluded that the latter is politicized and the former not. If the ideal relationship is one in which intelligence professionals provide the best information to governments who then decide what to do with it, in the view of a former Chair of the UK JIC, this is not what happened with respect to Iraq:

> [JIC] stepped outside its traditional role. It entered the prime minister's magic circle. It was engulfed in the atmosphere of excitement that surrounds decision-making in a crisis. Whether they realized it or not, its members went beyond assessment to become part of the process of making and advocating policy. That inevitably undermined their objectivity.[17]

There has been similar controversy in the United States, for example, as to the extent to which analysis and assessment were influenced by the greater political pressure on Iraq emanating from the Bush administration, especially after 9/11. A recent Carnegie Foundation study provides a systematic review and identifies the strengthening of conclusions in the October 2002 NIE compared with its predecessors: the later NIE concluded that Iraq had restarted its nuclear program and had "high confidence" that it had stockpiles of chemical and biological weapons. Of course, this might have accurately reflected a flow of new intelligence to this effect but, given the decline in information once the UN inspectors withdrew from Iraq in 1998, the authors conclude, rather, that it suggests undue influence by policymakers' views.[18]

In January 2004 David Kay resigned as head of the Iraqi Survey Group—whose job it was to search for evidence of WMD in Iraq—and in subsequent congressional testimony[19] admitted that intelligence agencies had failed to recognize that Iraq had all but abandoned its efforts to produce large quantities of chemical and biological weapons after 1991. An institutional post mortem had actually already started: by August 2003 George Tenet, U.S. director of central intelligence, had commissioned internal reviews of tradecraft and the work leading up to the October 2002 NIE. Tenet acknowledged that close examination was needed of the extent to which factors such as the history of deception and denial by Saddam Hussein and the very absence of information in key areas, especially after 1998, contributed to a failure to test prevailing assumptions. "We did not have enough of our own human intelligence," said Tenet, commenting on the risks inherent in information from defectors and indirect information from partner agencies.[20]

Both Kay and Tenet denied that CIA analysts had been subjected to political pressure in the run-up to the October 2002 NIE, but others have argued otherwise. Kenneth Pollack, a CIA analyst for the Persian Gulf who later worked for the NSC under Clinton, disputes that the strength of the October 2002 NIE can be put down solely to political pressure because it reflected what the agencies had been saying for some years (contra the Carnegie investigation). However, Pollack does acknowledge that the Office of Special Plans (OSP)[21] set up in the Pentagon was an attempt to manipulate intelligence. Ironically, given the soul searching now underway in the CIA over its failure to test assumptions, it was the very fact that it did question the assumptions of the case for links between Iraq and al Qaeda that frustrated Defense Secretary Donald Rumsfeld, Under-Secretary Paul Wolfowitz, and other administration officials. So OSP was created to find evidence of what they believed to be true: that Saddam Hussein had close ties to al Qaeda and possessed WMD that threatened the region and potentially the United States. A particular aspect of OSP's search for new intelligence was its reliance on Ahmad Chalabi and the Iraqi National Congress, which subsequently became the core of the regime installed after the invasion.[22]

In the UK the general issue of the absence of WMD in Iraq in the wake of the invasion concentrated on the more specific information received by the Secret Intelligence Service (SIS, aka MI6) that biological and chemical weapons could be deployed in twenty to forty-five minutes. It reported on August 30, 2002, "that on average it took 20 minutes to move BCW [*sic*] munitions into place for attack. The maximum response time was 45 minutes."[23] The SIS told the ISC that the sourcing of this report was regarded as reliable[24] and Sir Richard Dearlove, head of SIS, subsequently confirmed that the report originated with "a senior Iraqi military officer who was certainly in a position to know this information."[25] This report was incorporated in the JIC Assessment of September 9: "Intelligence also indicates that chemical and biological munitions could be with military units and ready for firing within 20–45 minutes."[26]

The ISC questioned JIC Chairman, John Scarlett, and Assessments Staff about the preparation of the September 9 assessment:

> The Assessments Staff stated that they, and the people they had consulted, did not know what munitions the Iraqi officer was referring to or their status. Nor did they know from where and to where munitions might be moved. They assessed that the Iraqi officer was referring to the time needed to move the biological and chemical battlefield munitions from where they were held by Iraqi Security units in forward-deployed storage sites to pre-designated military units.[27]

There was dissent within the UK intelligence community as to the strength with which the forty-five-minute claim was made—these dissents were expressed in the process of compiling the September 24 dossier[28] but were "finessed" (in the words of the main dissenter) on the grounds that there was other "compartmented" intelligence that justified the certainty.[29] The ISC concluded "that the

JIC has not been subject to political pressures and that its independence and impartiality has not been compromised in any way."[30] Yet Hutton did comment on the possible impact of pressure from 10 Downing Street on John Scarlett's subconscious[31]—this is precisely the kind of pressure envisaged in the "second stream" of power.

Finally in this section, we need to consider the possibility that the accuracy or otherwise of western intelligence was actually unimportant. What rapidly became clear once the Bush administration took office was the preparedness for unilateral action in cases where multilateral action was seen as inadequate in the defense of U.S. interests.[32] With respect to Iraq in particular, then–Secretary of the Treasury Paul O'Neill reported that the discussion of Iraq at the first NSC meeting of the new administration—that is, before 9/11—was about finding a way to overthrow the regime, not about what the intelligence said;[33] former counterterrorism coordinator Richard Clarke has testified to the U.S. Commission regarding the White House attempt in the immediate aftermath of 9/11 to pin the blame on Iraq.[34] This is why OSP was established. If so, then why all the fuss about WMD? Well, Wolfowitz said that this was for bureaucratic reasons: it was the one reason over which the cabinet could present a united front.[35] Support for this thesis is provided by the fact that, if the removal of Saddam Hussein was to be a legitimate multilateral action, then it needed to be carried out under the auspices of the various UN resolutions passed since 1991. They did not refer to the awfulness of the regime, or to its alleged links with al Qaeda; the ultimately unsuccessful quest for a specific UN resolution authorizing the invasion could be made only if grounded on WMD. On this reading, the only role for intelligence was to provide support for a policy already determined—knowledge was simply to support power[36]—and intelligence was "perfectly" politicized.

Government and the Media

Conscious that their respective publics were not entirely convinced of the necessity for war against Iraq, the Bush and Blair governments coordinated their strategies. They attempted to justify invasion at two key points: in the autumn of 2002 and early in 2003 as they sought to obtain a second UN Security Council resolution. In September the UK government produced a dossier entitled "Iraq's Weapons of Mass Destruction,"[37] and Bush made a major speech in Cincinnati on October 7 as he tried to obtain a congressional resolution authorizing the use of force. On January 30 the UK government published a further dossier—"Iraq: Its Infrastructure of Concealment, Deception and Intimidation"—and on February 5 Secretary of State Colin Powell made a presentation to the Security Council in New York.

In the UK it was the September 2002 dossier that would eventually receive the closest attention because of the forty-five-minute claim and the establishment of the Hutton Inquiry, but the January dossier achieved even more rapid notoriety when it emerged that most of it had been plagiarized from academic sources.[38] Although it did contain some material from SIS, it had been compiled in Downing Street's communications department and was not cleared by the JIC.[39] It rapidly became known as the "dodgy dossier" and sank from public view. Government embarrassment was compounded by the fact that Powell had approvingly referred to the dossier in his UN presentation.

An examination of these public statements make it clear that, at the very least, the case for the continued and threatening existence of WMD in Iraq was presented at a level of certainty quite unheard of in intelligence assessments. For example, addressing the UN Security Council with audio and video extracts of intelligence, Powell said:

> My colleagues, every statement I make today is backed up by sources, solid sources. These are not assertions. What we are giving you are facts and conclusions based on solid intelligence.[40]

Initiating the House of Commons debate the previous September, Blair said:

> The intelligence picture that they (the intelligence services) paint is one accumulated over the last four years. It is extensive, detailed and authoritative.[41]

Equally, there is no doubt is that the government was highly selective in presenting the intelligence assessments that tended to support its determination to invade Iraq while not publicizing those that cautioned against. For example, in an assessment of February 2003 JIC reported that not only was there no evidence that Iraq had transferred WMD to al Qaeda or that it intended to use them for terrorist attacks itself but also that the risk of such a transfer would be increased in the event of regime collapse:

> The JIC assessed that al-Qaida and associated groups continued to represent by far the greatest terrorist threat to Western interests, and that threat would be heightened by military action against Iraq.[42]

Blair judged that this assessment should not be published in the build-up to the invasion.[43]

In the UK government's dossier published on September 24 there were four references to the forty-five-minute claim: for example, in the Executive Summary:

As a result of the intelligence we judge that Iraq has . . . military plans for the use of chemical and biological weapons, including against its own Shia population. Some of these weapons are deployable within 45 minutes of an order to use them.[44]

And, in chapter 3:

Intelligence indicates that the Iraqi military are able to deploy chemical and biological weapons within 45 minutes of an order to do so.[45]

Speaking to the Commons on the day of publication, Blair said:

[The intelligence picture] concludes that Iraq has chemical and biological weapons, that Saddam has continued to produce them, that he has existing and active military plans for the use of chemical and biological weapons, which could be activated within 45 minutes, including against his own Shia population, and that he is actively trying to acquire nuclear weapons capability.[46]

George W. Bush was equally uncompromising in a speech two weeks later:

The danger is already significant, and it only grows worse with time. . . . We know that the regime has produced thousands of tons of chemical agents, including mustard gas, sarin nerve gas, VX nerve gas. . . . We know that Iraq and al Qaeda have had high-level contacts that go back a decade. . . . Facing clear evidence of peril, we cannot wait for the final proof—the smoking gun—that could come in the form of a mushroom cloud.[47]

The last of these is an especially evocative image given that the NIE had just said:

Without [sufficient fissile] material from abroad, Iraq probably would not be able to make a weapon until 2007 to 2009, owing to inexperience in building and operating centrifuge facilities to produce highly enriched uranium and challenges in procuring the necessary equipment and expertise.[48]

The State Department's Bureau of Intelligence and Research (INR) entered a dissent to the NIE doubting that the evidence was adequate even then to support a judgment that the nuclear program had been restarted. As it turns out, INR has been proved right; even George Tenet has acknowledged:

Saddam did not have a nuclear weapon. He still wanted one and Iraq intended to reconstitute a nuclear program at some point. But we have not yet found clear evidence that the dual-use items Iraq sought were for nuclear reconstitution. We do not know if any reconstitution efforts had begun but we may have overestimated the progress Saddam was making.[49]

Blair made no explicit reference to the possibility of nuclear attack but the first draft of his foreword had included the sentence: "The case I make is not that Saddam could launch a nuclear attack on London or another part of the UK (he could not)." This was excluded from the published dossier.[50]

In seeking to "persuade" the public to support a controversial policy, governments have no use for the measured or conditional language of intelligence assessments. People must be reassured that the government knows precisely what they are doing and why; anything less is to invite opposition. Therefore, by a mixture of "creative omission"[51] and "cherry-picking," professional doubts are translated into political certainties.

Oversight and Government

Not surprisingly, as time has gone on since the overthrow of the former Iraq regime but without the discovery of any of the expected WMD and not much by way of evidence of redundant programs, the existing oversight committees in the coalition countries have taken steps to investigate. By early June 2003 the Senate Committees on Intelligence and Armed Services announced that they planned a joint inquiry into pre-war intelligence and the House Intelligence Committee announced its own.[52] In the UK the controversy grew throughout May and then erupted into the war between Downing Street and the BBC over Andrew Gilligan's May 29 broadcast that the government had included the forty-five-minute claim knowing it was probably wrong (see the following discussion). Within a few days, the Foreign Affairs Select Committee (FAC) had announced that it would examine whether the government had "presented accurate and complete information to Parliament in the period leading up to military action in Iraq, particularly in respect of weapons of mass destruction."[53]

One problem facing the FAC was that, as with other Commons select committees, it could gain access only to those people and papers that the government allowed and, although it did interview the foreign secretary in closed session, it was refused permission to speak with any agency heads or the chair of the JIC. Its report, completed and published in not much more than a month, concluded that ministers did not mislead Parliament (para. 188) but voiced a number of criticisms of the presentation of the case for war, including the certainty of the government's assertion that Iraq had sought uranium from Niger (para. 60); that the forty-five-minutes claim did not warrant the prominence given to it in the September dossier (para. 70); that the language used in the dossier was more assertive than traditionally used in intelligence documents (para. 100); and that it was wholly unacceptable for the government to have plagiarized work for the "dodgy dossier" (para. 140).

As the FAC started work the prime minister sought to deal with the growing furor by asking the ISC[54] to investigate. Just as with a select committee, ministers can act as gatekeepers of the ISC's access to intelligence papers, but in the ten years of its operation it has steadily increased its reputation and enjoyed more access to material than would have been envisaged when it was established in 1994.[55] However, some MPs remain skeptical because it is appointed by and reports to the PM. After the removal of sensitive material, reports are sent to Parliament. Given the temper of the times it is not surprising that the PM promised the ISC access to all the JIC assessments and the people who produced them and also that he would publish the report.[56] Accordingly the ISC sought

> to examine whether the available intelligence, which informed the decision to invade Iraq, was adequate and properly assessed and whether it was accurately reflected in Government publications.[57]

It reported that, based on the intelligence it had seen, "there was convincing intelligence that Iraq had active chemical, biological and nuclear programmes and the capability to produce chemical and biological weapons."[58] But it also noted that the JIC assessment of September 9, 2002, "did not highlight in the key judgments the uncertainties and gaps in the UK's knowledge about the Iraqi biological and chemical weapons."[59]

In its response to this point the government drew what might be described as a fine distinction: The "key judgments" section of a JIC assessment is to highlight the judgments to be drawn from the assessment; it "is not intended to be a summary of the main facts of the paper."[60] With respect to the September 24 dossier, ISC said that it was "founded on the assessments then available" and had not been "'sexed up' by Alistair Campbell or anyone else." It reported that the JIC had not been subjected to political pressures and that its independence and impartiality had not been compromised.[61]

ISC criticized the removal from the PM's foreword of the sentence regarding nuclear attack on London (para. 83 and see preceding discussion) and rebuked the government over the presentation of the forty-five-minutes claim in the dossier (e.g., paras. 83, 110–112). ISC concluded:

> The dossier was for public consumption and not for experienced readers of intelligence material. . . . The fact that it was assessed to refer to battlefield chemical and biological munitions and their movement on the battlefield, not to any other form of chemical or biological attack, should have been highlighted in the dossier. This was unhelpful to an understanding of the issue.[62]

In its response the government took no responsibility for the silences in the dossier. It was content that the ISC recognized that the dossier did not say that Iraq posed a "current and imminent" threat to the UK mainland[63] but made no response to the criticism of the exclusion of the UK attack caveat in the foreword (see preceding discussion). Similarly, regarding the ISC criticism that the forty-five-minute claim was "unhelpful," the government merely noted that the dossier did not say that Iraq could deliver chemical or biological weapons by ballistic missiles "within 45 minutes."[64] No, it did not, but it was precisely this failure to make clear just what the assessments were that amounted to serious misrepresentation of the nature of the threat from Iraq.

The stakes in the political contest in the UK over the adequacy of the government's case for the invasion were significantly increased on May 29, 2003, when a BBC radio journalist, Andrew Gilligan, broadcast to the effect that the government probably knew that the statement that the Iraqi regime could deploy WMD within forty-five minutes was wrong and that the prime minister's office had ordered the September 2002 dossier to be "sexed up." The government, mainly in the person of Alistair Campbell, the PM's press secretary, reacted furiously to the broadcast and demanded an apology from the BBC, which it declined to give. On July 8 the Ministry of Defence announced that a civil servant had come forward and admitted being the source for the May 29 story. The following day the MOD confirmed his name as Dr. David Kelly to those journalists who had successfully worked out who he was from the clues given. Both the FAC (that had just completed its enquiry—see preceding) and the ISC (just commencing its) requested to interview Kelly, and he appeared before the FAC in public on July 15 and the ISC in private on July 16. The following day he disappeared from his home and was later found dead, apparently having committed suicide. The government rapidly sought to quell the mounting media pressure by appointing Lord Hutton, a House of Lords judge "urgently to conduct an investigation into the circumstances surrounding the death of Dr. Kelly."[65]

The inquiry was conducted in two stages: the first was inquisitorial in order to obtain information from witnesses as to the course of events, and the second was adversarial when those who might be subject to criticism by the inquiry were recalled to be examined further and possibly cross-examined by counsel for other parties represented. Hutton interpreted his terms of reference as requiring him to examine five issues: first, the process of the preparation of the September dossier; second, Kelly's meeting with Gilligan on May 22, 2003; third, the BBC's handling of Gilligan's May 29 broadcast and its aftermath; fourth, how Kelly's name became public as the source for Gilligan's broadcast; and fifth, the specific causes of Kelly's death.[66]

On the first issue, Hutton exonerated the government of any wrongdoing: the report that it had inserted the "45 minute claim" knowing it was probably wrong was unfounded; the wording in the September 24 dossier had been modified by the chair of the JIC, John Scarlett, after suggestions from Downing Street but only when he was satisfied that the wording remained consistent with the intelligence.[67] The shift between the September 9 JIC assessment that WMD "could be" deployable to the September 24 dossier that they "are" deployable came under close scrutiny at the inquiry—clearly it was central to the issue of the "sexing up" or otherwise of the dossier. Under cross-examination, John Scarlett maintained that the former contained no indication of uncertainty[68] and that therefore, by implication, there had been no exaggeration in the dossier.

However, Hutton concluded that the dossier had not been "sexed up" only by interpreting the term narrowly to imply that people would have understood the phrase to mean that the dossier had been embellished with information known to be false or unreliable, not in the broader sense that the dossier was drafted so as to make as strong a case as the intelligence would permit.[69] Readers can make their own judgment by reference to the evidence given to Hutton, but the preceding analysis justifies a conclusion that the dossier was clearly misleading. On the other issues, Hutton concluded that Kelly had not provided the controversial claims on which Gilligan's May 29 broadcast was based, that BBC management was seriously at fault in handling the broadcast,[70] that the government had not improperly allowed Kelly's name into the public domain, and finally, he accepted medical evidence that Kelly had committed suicide.[71]

But if the government enjoyed some moments of triumph in what had been a long battle with the BBC—it started over its coverage of Iraq before Gilligan's fateful broadcast—they were short-lived. Two newspapers—the tabloid *Sun* and the *Times*—accepted Hutton's conclusions, but the rest of the papers expressed varying degrees of skepticism and a number made accusations of a "whitewash."[72] In an opinion poll after Hutton was published, 54 percent said they believed Blair had lied over the threat from Iraq, and 51 percent said he should resign.[73]

Thus it was quickly clear that Hutton had not had the desired effect: significant controversy continued regarding the pre-invasion intelligence. Arguably, indeed, the government's success in diverting the widespread public concern over the war by its attack on Gilligan and the BBC in June 2003 lasted just until Hutton reported on January 28, 2004. The very narrowness of his terms of reference meant that the more important issues had simply not been dealt with. So, on February 3, Blair announced that an inquiry would be conducted by five privy councilors, headed by Lord Butler, a former cabinet secretary, and including two members of the ISC. As ever, the terms of reference were crucial; in this case there was such an argument between the government and the opposition parties that one of them, the Liberal Democrats, refused to join the inquiry from the outset because it took the view that the terms of reference excluded the crucial question of the use that the government made of the intelligence,[74] and the Conservative Party withdrew its official support a few weeks later. Reflecting the cynicism of the public view of Hutton's report, a poll found that 23 percent believed the new inquiry would be a "genuine attempt to find the truth while 68 percent believed it would a 'whitewash.'"[75] When published in July 2004, the Butler report[76] provided a detailed examination of the collection, analysis, and dissemination of intelligence (especially the September 2002 dossier) regarding Iraqi WMD. Some of its criticisms were to be echoed by the Senate Intelligence Committee (see following discussion); for example, the unreliability of human intelligence (HUMINT) and the poor procedures for validation of sources (paras. 440–45) and tendency over time for caveats to get lost in the assessments process (paras. 458–59). Yet although the report shows clearly that the language of the dossier and the prime minister represented the intelligence as far more certain than it was, Butler and his colleagues would only conclude that this "may have left readers with the impression that there was fuller and firmer intelligence behind the judgments than was the case . . ."[77]

Throughout January 2004 political pressure had grown steadily in the United States also, and the president was obliged to institute an inquiry he did not want. Bush announced the establishment of a Commission on the Intelligence Capabilities of the United States Regarding Weapons of Mass Destruction[78] with broadly similar terms of reference to the Butler inquiry; that is, they were to compare the state of pre-invasion intelligence with the findings of the Iraqi Survey Group but were also to explore the more general problems involved in gathering intelligence with respect to WMD. The Commission was chaired jointly by Charles Robb, former Democratic senator and Laurence Silberman, a Republican appeals court judge. There was some criticism of the relative lack of experience and independence among the members and, importantly, the Commission was not to report until March 2005, safely after the presidential election.[79] After the announcement of this commission, an opinion poll found Bush suffering from a similar "credibility gap" to Blair: 54 percent thought Bush had exaggerated or lied about prewar intelligence.[80]

In July 2004 the Senate Intelligence Committee published the first report of its two-phase review of U.S. intelligence on Iraqi WMD, and its main conclusions[81] were that most of the major "key judgments" in the October 2002 NIE were not supported by the underlying intelligence reporting; that the uncertainties behind these judgments were explained to policymakers inaccurately or inadequately; that the collective presumption within the intelligence community that Iraq did have an active WMD program led it to ignore or misinterpret contrary evidence; and that failures of collection (especially HUMINT), sharing (especially by the CIA), and analysis stemmed from "broken corporate culture and poor management"[82] throughout the community. Although the Committee had begun its review in June 2003, it extended its coverage in February 2004 to include, for example, whether the government's statements were substantiated by the intelligence;[83] however, the Democrats on the Committee agreed that, as with Robb–Silverman, there would be no report on this until after the presidential election in November.[84]

Role of the Media

The UK government's attacks on the BBC and efforts to track and then expose Gilligan's source constituted the central part of Hutton's inquiry into the death of Dr. David Kelly and thus focused attention on relations between journalists and people within the intelligence community. These have always been a mixture of the formal and the informal. Both seek to guard their sources closely and, as in any other area of government, journalists will seek to cultivate their own sources within the intelligence community. Formally, press enquiries about MI5 and MI6 are handled by the Home Office and the Foreign Office respectively while GCHQ has its own press officer. The heads of agencies and other nominated senior staff are authorized to have contact with the media. JIC and Defence Intelligence Staff (DIS) media contacts are handled via the Cabinet Office and Ministry of Defence respectively.[85]

After his examination of the contacts between David Kelly and Andrew Gilligan, Hutton concluded that their meeting of May 22 (which was the basis for the May 29 broadcast) was unauthorized and that Kelly was in breach of the Civil Service code of procedure.[86] However, given the frequency of Kelly's contacts with the media and of his public presentations based on his expertise, this conclusion, though technically correct, is perhaps too legalistic to provide much help in understanding intelligence-media relations. May 22 was Kelly's second meeting with Gilligan—the first was when Gilligan had sought Kelly's advice on what to look out for on an upcoming trip to Iraq earlier in 2003. So, for Kelly, the object of the May 22 meeting was mainly to find out what Gilligan had seen.[87] This was, of course, true to longstanding practice in which intelligence agencies use journalists both as sources and as conduits for information at least as much as the journalists use them.

For example, giving evidence to the ISC, David Kelly explained in answer to a question from the chair, Ann Taylor, that within the DIS he liaised with the "Rockingham cell" that serviced the weapons inspectors in Iraq.[88] This DIS group had the role, according to Scott Ritter, the former weapons inspector, of using intelligence from the UNSCOM inspectors in order to sustain in public the claims that Iraq was not in compliance with UN resolutions while ignoring ambiguous or contrary findings.[89] That a similar (if not part of the same) operation had been run by SIS—Operation Mass Appeal—in the late 1990s was reportedly confirmed.[90]

The tragedy for David Kelly in this whole battle for the control of intelligence

information and public opinion was that Gilligan's broadcast led to a full government hue and cry for the source. There are always tensions in the routine
relations between journalists and intelligence officials because of the secrecy that
envelops the field,[91] but they cannot be regulated simply by the legalistic application of a code that seeks to protect governments from controversy and criticism
as much as national security (for example, see principles governing disclosure of
information[92]). Gilligan's May 29 broadcast clearly included specific errors, but
he was correct in reporting general unease within some official quarters at the
(ab)use of intelligence. Some now fear that Hutton's wholesale condemnation of
the BBC will "chill" investigative journalism into controversial policy areas.

Conclusions

Although we await further reports from the Senate Intelligence Committee and
Robb–Silberman, it is timely to take stock of the central question identified earlier: did the U.S. and UK governments receive intelligence that justified their
public position that the regime of Saddam Hussein posed such a threat to
regional and/or international stability as to justify his immediate removal? The
ambiguities of language and significance of official silences inherent in intelligence mean that generally accepted conclusions may never be reached. Only the
discovery of significant evidence of WMD in Iraq can resolve the question in
favor of the governments. Meanwhile, the detailed examination of controversies
such as this can serve useful purposes for oversight bodies and public education
more generally because they shine a torch into normally dark places of government and intelligence. But while the forensic examination of precisely "who said
what to whom and when" is useful in illustrating the interplay of information
control processes, it is important that we do not lose sight of the forest for the
trees. There can be few issues of greater significance for any state than the relationship between intelligence and decisions to go to war.

Such decisions will always be politically contested; they cannot be made on
some simple empirical test. Whatever the inquiries find, there will be those for
whom this episode represents neither intelligence nor political "failure." Gary
Schmitt, executive director of the Project for a New American Century, argued
recently that the intelligence assessment that Saddam Hussein had not given up
his desire to reconstitute WMD programs was right and therefore he asks, rhe-
torically: would continuing the policy of containment have been sufficient to
prevent him from becoming a dangerous threat to U.S. interests?[93] But beyond
this small but powerfully entrenched view, the controversy remains one in which
governments and intelligence agencies have keen interests. The inquiries concentrated on the issue of intelligence failure—how could such a consensus among

the best-endowed intelligence agencies in the world as to the existence of WMD be so wrong? Such inquiries are entirely appropriate and need to investigate the "usual suspects": group-think, over-reliance on TECHINT, the problems of defectors as human sources, the failure to question prior assumptions, and the search for evidence that supports rather than negates them.

However, the issue of political failure must not be ducked.[94] The evidence presented here is that the dossier in the UK and similar presentations in the United States did exaggerate the nature of the threat from Iraq's WMD, and continued government denials of that are dangerous. In general, the democratization of intelligence in the past thirty years has required some reduction in secrecy. Unable to rely on blanket refusals to comment, governments have sought to maintain their "information control" over security debates by compensatory measures of increasingly publicizing intelligence in order to influence the new oversight bodies and the media and thereby the public. So, intelligence has not been immune from the growing culture of "spin" in the presentation of government policies. Thus it has been harder for professionals to resist the "will" of politicians for "relevant" intelligence that will support policy. Yet, on the other hand, it becomes harder for governments to "control" the flow of information because other policy-actors—oversight committees, media, think tanks, whistleblowers[95]—"evaluate" what governments say and provide alternative analyses.

It is hoped that the analysis here has indicated the utility of examining the relation between intelligence and policy through the prism of processes of information control; however, there is much more to this than an academic debate. The fundamental danger for democratic polities is that these processes between government and other institutions can run out of control: that the interaction of attempts by governments, oversight committees, and media to gather information, maintain secrecy, evaluate information, and influence others leads to a spiral of uncertainty, mistrust, and paranoia. The poll figures presented in this chapter provide some evidence of that. All of these institutions have a crucial role to play in breaking this spiral by contributing to public education as to the real possibilities and limits of intelligence. Without that, the real danger is that public cynicism may, at some point in the future, refuse to accept the significance of a threat that is, really, "current and serious."

Notes

1. Thanks to Mike Mannin, Joe Sim, and the editors for their helpful suggestions on an earlier draft of this chapter.

2. For an earlier consideration of this issue see H.H. Ransom, "The Politicization of Intelligence," in *Intelligence and Intelligence Policy in a Democratic Society*, ed. S. J. Cimbala (Ardsley-in-Hudson: Transnational Publishers, 1987), 25–46.

3. Michael Howard, one of the official historians of wartime intelligence, observed nearly twenty years ago: "In Britain the activities of the intelligence and security services have always been regarded in much the same light as intra-marital sex. Everyone knows that it goes on and is quite content that it should, but to speak, write or ask questions about it is regarded as exceedingly bad form." (cited in C. Andrew, "The British View of Security Intelligence," in *Security and Intelligence in a Changing World*, eds. A.S. Farson, et al. [London: Cass, 1991], 11).

4. C. J. Friedrich, *Man and His Government* (New York: McGraw-Hill, 1963) 201–202.

5. In essence these are the first two "dimensions" of power discussed by S. Lukes, *Power* (Basingstoke: Macmillan, 1974). J. Scott, *Power* (Cambridge: Polity, 2001), 6–12, describes these approaches as "mainstream." See also S. Clegg, *Frameworks of Power* (London: Sage, 1989).

6. Scott, *Power*, 2001, 6–12.

7. Notably Foucault, Giddens, Gramsci, Habermas, Lukes.

8. Scott, *Power*, 2001, 99–109.

9. R. Wilsnack, "Information Control," *Urban Life* 8(4), 467–99; P. Gill, "Reasserting control: recent changes in the oversight of the UK intelligence community," *Intelligence and National Security* 11(2), 313–31.

10. Cf. Scott, *Power*, 16–25; Wilsnack, "Information Control."

11. ISC, *Iraqi Weapons of Mass Destruction*, 2003. Accessible at www.cabinetoffice.gov.uk/intelligence

12. FAC, *The Decision to go to War in Iraq*, 2003. Accessible at www.parliament.uk/parliamentary_committees/foreign affairs_committee

13. Hutton, *Report of the Inquiry into the Circumstances Surrounding the Death of David Kelly C.M.G.*, 2004. Accessible at www.the-hutton-inquiry.org.uk

14. Butler, *Review of Intelligence on Weapons of Mass Destruction*. Accessible at www.butlerreview.org.uk This was published after this chapter was written and only brief reference is made to its findings.

15. Also, it should be noted, contests of information control will take place *within* each of these "actors": turf wars between different agencies are a well-known phenomenon since different departments within the Executive pursue different interests; different branches of the media are highly competitive and, if there is more than one oversight body, they may also compete for information, prestige etc.

16. Two recent accounts of the JIC are P. Cradock, *Know Your Enemy: How the Joint Intelligence Committee Saw the World* (London: John Murray, 2002); and P. Hennessy, *The Secret State: Whitehall and the Cold War* (London: Allen Lane, Penguin Press, 2002).

17. Roderic Braithwaite, *The Hutton Inquiry*, Panorama, BBC1, January 21, 2004.

18. J. Cirincione, et al., *WMD in Iraq: Evidence and Implications* (Washington, D.C.: Carnegie Endowment for International Peace, January 2004), 50–51.

19. This can be accessed at www.nsarchive.org in the Saddam Hussein Sourcebook.

20. Remarks as prepared for delivery by DCI George Tenet at Georgetown University, Washington, D.C., February 5, 2004.

21. K. M. Pollack, "Spies, Lies and Weapons: What Went Wrong," *The Atlantic Monthly*, January/February 2004. See also Johnson, this volume, chapter 4.

22. S. M. Hersh, "Selective Intelligence," *The New Yorker*, May 12, 2003; K. Kwiatkowski, "The New Pentagon Papers," *Salon*, March 10, 2004.

23. ISC, *Iraqi Weapons of Mass Destruction—Intelligence and Assessments*, para. 49. Cm 5972, September 2003, (London: The Stationery Office).

24. ISC, *Iraqi Weapons*, para. 51.

25. Hutton, *Report*, para. 177. Subsequently the Butler Report revealed that postwar source validation by SIS had called into question the reliability of this report. Butler, *Review*, para. 512.

26. ISC, *Iraqi Weapons*, para. 50; Hutton, *Report*, para. 180.

27. ISC, *Iraqi Weapons*, para. 52.

28. For the progress of the forty-five-minute claim from its receipt by SIS through various drafts of the September 24 dossier, see Hutton, *Report*, 2004, paras. 198–209.

29. B. Jones, "There was a lack of substantive evidence . . ." *Independent*, February 4, 2004.

30. ISC, *Iraqi Weapons*, para. 108.

31. Hutton, *Report*, 2004, para. 228(7).

32. P. Rogers, *Losing Control* (London: Pluto Press, 2002), 132–50.

33. R. W. Stevenson, "Bush sought to oust Hussein from start, ex-official says," *New York Times*, January 12, 2004.

34. R. Clarke, *Against All Enemies* (New York: Free Press, 2004).

35. P. Waugh, "Government blames spies over war," *Independent*, May 30, 2003.

36. An especially powerful version of this thesis and critique of the UK being reduced to "abject thrall to Bush and his gang" is Hugo Young, "Under Blair, Britain has ceased to be a sovereign state," *The Guardian*, September 16, 2003. Why Blair was such a steadfast supporter of the United States is a question beyond the remit of this chapter.

37. The earlier drafts of the dossier were entitled *Iraq's Programme for WMD*. The various drafts are in the appendices to the Hutton Report and can be read at www.the-hutton-inquiry.org.uk/content/report/index.htm

38. Mainly from I. al-Marashi, "Iraq's Security and Intelligence Network," *Middle East Review of International Affairs*, 6(3).

39. ISC, *Iraqi Weapons*, paras. 129–35.

40. Presentation can be accessed at www.state.gov/secretary/rm/2003/17300pf.htm

41. House of Commons debates, Hansard, September 24, 2002, col. 3.

42. ISC, *Iraqi Weapons*, para. 126.

43. ISC, *Iraqi Weapons*, para. 128.

44. HMG, *Iraq's Weapons of Mass Destruction*, 5.

45. HMG, *Iraq's Weapons of Mass Destruction*, 19.

46. House of Commons debates, Hansard, September 24 2002, col. 3.

47. Remarks by the president on Iraq, Cincinnati, October 7, 2002. Accessible at www.whitehouse.gov/news/releases/2002/

48. *Key Judgements*, 2002. Accessible at www.fas.org—Saddeim Hussein Sourcebook.

49. Remarks as prepared for delivery by DCI George Tenet at Georgetown University, Washington, D.C., February 5, 2004.

50. Hutton, *Report*, para. 209. The existence of this sentence in the first draft makes even odder Blair's admission in the Commons debate on the Hutton Report that it was only after the war that he became aware that the forty-five-minute claim had referred only to battlefield weapons. See, for example, R. Norton-Taylor, "45 minutes from a major scandal," *The Guardian*, February 18, 2004.

51. Pollack, "Spies, Lies and Weapons."

52. J. Risen, "Iraq arms report now the subject of a CIA review," *New York Times*, June 4, 2003. The SSCI announced on February 12, 2004, that it was extending its terms of reference to include possible exaggeration of intelligence by officials.

53. FAC, *The Decision to Go to War in Iraq*, HC813-I, para. 4 (London: The Stationery Office, July, 2003).

54. For a discussion of recent developments in intelligence oversight arrangements in UK, see Leigh, this volume.

55. For example, see Gill, "Reasserting Control," 1996.

56. ISC, *Iraqi Weapons*, paras. 13–14.

57. ISC, *Iraqi Weapons*, para. 11.

58. ISC, *Iraqi Weapons*, para. 66.

59. ISC, *Iraqi Weapons*, para. 67.

60. Prime Minister, *Government Response to the ISC Report*, 2004, para. 7. Accessible at www.cabinetoffice.gov/uk/intelligence

61. ISC, *Iraqi Weapons*, paras. 107–108.

62. ISC, *Iraqi Weapons*, para. 86.

63. Prime Minister, *Government Response*, para. 14, but PM's foreword described it as "current and serious" (HMG, *Iraq's Weapons of Mass Destruction*, 3).

64. Prime Minister, *Government Response*, para. 15.

65. Hutton, *Report*, para. 1.

66. Hutton, *Report*, para. 160.

67. Hutton, *Report*, para. 467[1].

68. Hutton, *Report*, para. 214.

69. Hutton, *Report*, para. 467[1][viii].

70. No attempt is made to analyze Hutton's extensive critique of BBC management since it goes well beyond the core concerns of the chapter. After publication both the BBC chair of governors and the director-general resigned.

71. Hutton, *Report*, para. 467.

72. *Guardian Wrap*, January 29, 2004. Accessible at www.guardian.co.uk/

73. P. Waugh, "After Hutton, the verdict: 51 per cent say Blair should go," *Independent*, February 7, 2004.

74. P. Wintour and R. Norton-Taylor, "Swift and Secret, Blair's inquiry," *The Guardian*, February 4, 2004. The foreign secretary, Jack Straw, reportedly said the Butler inquiry had been modeled in part on the Franks Inquiry into the Falklands War in 1982. Given the context, this is somewhat ironic because after Franks published his Report, absolving the government of the day of any blame for the failure to prevent the Argentine invasion, the then leader of the Labour Party, James Callaghan, described Franks as chucking "a bucket of whitewash" over it (P. Hennessy, *Whitehall* [London: Secker and Warburg, 1989], 586).

75. P. Waugh, "After Hutton," *Independent*, February 7, 2004.

76. Butler, *Review*, 2004.

77. Butler, *Review*, 2004, para. 464. In a subsequent debate in the House of Lords, Butler said it was for the people, not his committee, to draw a conclusion as to how grave a fault this was in the run-up to war. (R. Norton-Taylor, "Butler criticises government over 'thin' evidence for WMD," *The Guardian*, September 8, 2004.) For a detailed analysis of the Butler Report see Gill P., "Keeping in touch with 'earthly awkwardnesses,'" in *Reforming Intelligence Across the World*, eds. T. Bruneau and K. Dombrowski (Austin: University of Texas Press, forthcoming).

78. Executive Order 13328, February 6, 2004.

79. D. Jehl, "Bush sets Panel on Intelligence before Iraq War," *New York Times*, February 7, 2004.

80. R. Morin and D. Milbank, "Most think truth was stretched to justify Iraq war," *Washington Post*, February 13, 2004.

81. Senate Select Committee on Intelligence, *Report*, July 7, 2004, 14–29. Accessible at http://intelligence.senate.gov/iraqreport2.pdf

82. Senate Select Committee on Intelligence, *Report*, July 7, 2004, 24.

83. Senate Select Committee on Intelligence, *Report*, July 7, 2004, 2.

84. W. Branigin and D. Priest, "Senate Report Blasts Intelligence Agencies' Flaws," *Washington Post*, July 9, 2004.

85. ISC, *Iraqi Weapons*, para. 138.

86. Hutton, *Report*, para. 259[2]; for extracts from code see paras. 23–25.

87. Hutton, *Report*, para. 255.

88. Hutton, *Report*, para.112.

89. TV interview with Amy Goodman, December 30, 2003, transcript in *Security and Intelligence Digest*, Intel Research, PO Box 550, London SW3 2YQ.

90. N. Rufford, "Revealed: how MI6 sold the Iraq war," *The Times*, December 28, 2003.

91. For a full discussion of these issues see M. Caparini, ed., *Media and Security Governance* (Münster: Nomos verlagsgesellschaft, 2004).

92. Hutton, *Report*, para. 23.

93. G. Schmitt, "Our basic instincts were sound," *Los Angeles Times*, February 1, 2004.

94. This is argued with respect to the Senate Intelligence Committee July 2004 report by Thomas Powers, "How Bush Got It Wrong," *New York Review of Books*, September 23, 2004.

95. Katherine Gun, a translator at GCHQ, leaked a request from the NSA for a "surge" of surveillance to be conducted on members of the UN Security Council as the UK and United States sought a second resolution in 2003. She was charged under the Official Secrets Act but charges were dropped in February 2004. It was reported that this was because her trial would have seen the airing of controversial arguments about the legality of the invasion of Iraq (R. Norton-Taylor, "Whitehall united in doubt on war," *The Guardian*, February 27, 2004). But this has been denied by the Intelligence and Security Committee, *Annual Report 2003–2004*, Cm 6240, para. 72. Accessible at www.cabinet-office.gov.uk/reports/intelligence/pdf/govres2004.pdf

3

Beyond the Nation State: The Influence of the European Court of Human Rights on Intelligence Accountability

Iain Cameron

This chapter examines the influence of the European Court of Human Rights (hereafter, "the Court" or the "ECtHR"), on the issue of intelligence accountability. In particular, it examines the case law of the Court insofar as it relates to intelligence surveillance and intelligence files/screening, in order to determine to what extent common European legal requirements could be said to exist in these fields. It concludes with a number of comments on the "added value" of the supervision the Court exercises over states' laws and practices in this field.

The Court and the Convention

The European Convention on Human Rights (ECHR),[1] is a treaty, the creation of an international organization, the Council of Europe.[2] The parties to the Convention—now forty-six European states—undertake to secure to everyone subject to their jurisdiction the fundamental rights set out in the Convention.[3] The Convention establishes a court in Strasbourg that is competent to hear complaints from individuals, after they have exhausted domestic remedies in the state against which they bring a case. The protection of the Convention covers some 800 million people and the ECtHR adopts around nine hundred judgments per year. It also takes about eight thousand "admissibility decisions" per year—that is, decisions to dismiss an application without an examination of the merits of the dispute (which occurs in approximately 90 percent of cases), or to take up a case on the merits (a function previously performed by the European Commission on Human Rights).[4]

The Convention has also been incorporated in the national law of all forty-six states, requiring national courts and administrative agencies to apply it and to take account of the case law of the ECtHR. The ECtHR thus develops pan-European legal principles by means of its case law.[5] It is also part of the "general principles" of European Community law, and as such binding on the EC. The importance of the Convention as a superior source of EC/EU law is increasing, as the EC/EU has begun legislating in the general field of security, and the principle of the supremacy of EC law means that one cannot challenge EC norms on the basis that these breach national constitutional rules.[6]

Certain of the rights provided for in the Convention contain an express clause permitting a state to limit the right in question on the basis of "national security." This clause can be found in the rights to a fair trial (article 6), to privacy, respect for family life and inviolability of correspondence (article 8), to freedom of expression (article 10), and to freedom of assembly and association (article 11). There are also national security limitations on the rights to liberty of movement and freedom to choose a residence within a state (article 2(3), protocol 4) and to review of a deportation decision (article 1(2), protocol 7). Under certain circumstances national security considerations can be taken into account in other articles where there is no such express limitation.[7]

Like domestic courts applying domestic human rights norms, the Court must strike a balance between the competing interests of individuals and the state. The Court nonetheless has less "legitimacy" compared to national constitutional courts when it comes to imposing its will on recalcitrant governments or legislatures. The Court does not, and should not, function as a final court of appeal from domestic courts, as a form of European *cour de cassation*. Nor does it have an explicit function to harmonize the parties' national laws. All the Court does is to test the compatibility of national law and practice against the standards of the Convention. All the members of the Council are sovereign states that are jealous of their sovereignty.

The Convention was designed to be, and clearly is, subsidiary to the domestic systems of protection of human rights.[8] The Convention organs are aware that there is a fine line between being perceived as brave defenders of basic human rights and being seen as a (more or less) self-appointed group of interfering foreigners in Strasbourg. This is particularly so as regards the extremely sensitive area of policy making covered by national security.

Thus, in this and other sensitive policy areas, the Court has permitted states a "margin of appreciation" as to how they perform their obligations under the Convention. The Court justifies this on the basis of the subsidiary nature of the protection afforded by the Convention[9] and the difficulty in identifying common European conceptions of the extent of the rights or restrictions in question. (With the great expansion of the Council of Europe in the late 1980s and 1990s to encompass the central and eastern European states, it can no longer be described as a homogenous organization.) The doctrine is in essence one of judicial restraint, inevitable in the circumstances if the Court is to avoid criticism from the contracting parties that it is pursuing too dynamic an approach to interpretation.

As with any system of law built upon the development of norms by means of adjudication, the "accident of litigation" is significant. The person complaining must show that he or she is a victim of an alleged violation of the Convention. This is no easy business as regards secret measures, so the test has been modified to allow a person to complain of a violation if it can be shown that there is a "reasonable likelihood" that he or she has been the victim of such practices.[10] Still, even with this relaxation of the requirements, some potential issues, for a variety of reasons (lack of awareness of one's legal rights, resignation on the part of the victim, cost of litigation, poor legal advice, etc.) never make their way through the mill of domestic courts and the admissibility procedures to a judgment on the merits.[11] These factors can explain the relative lack of cases (so far) from central and eastern European states, notwithstanding the major deficiencies that exist in security law and practices in many of these states.

The Convention system is best described as a semi-autonomous legal system. National law necessarily provides the framework within which Convention concepts operate. The normal material remedy the Court can require for breach of the Convention is the award of monetary compensation (article 41), but a negative judgment can also indirectly involve other obligations, in particular, law reform and/or the reopening of domestic proceedings.[12] A judgment against the state thus "returns" to the national legal system for implementation. There is thus a risk that the implications of a judgment will be misunderstood.

In the area of national security law and practice there is also the risk that a judgment will be interpreted in a minimalist fashion so that any resulting law reform may be cosmetic only. The impact of even national case law, indeed, even of statute law, on the arcane world of security should not be taken for granted. Reforms made in the field of policing or security can naturally be wholly or partially blocked by bureaucratic resistance. The more closed an area is to public scrutiny, the more chance there is of such resistance succeeding.[13] It is evident that in this area the law can serve, and has on occasion served, as a facade, concealing more or less serious divergences in practice. In particular, case law can be responsible for maintaining a gap between ideology and law/legal practice.[14]

Thus, one should not automatically assume that Court case law disapproving of a particular law or practice will be implemented wholeheartedly.

In any event, the Court's relative political weakness vis-à-vis respondent governments means that the Court has been reluctant to engage in any activity that can be attacked as "judicial legislation." This has meant, inter alia, that the steps to be taken to bring law and practice into line with the Convention have relatively rarely been explicitly spelt out in a judgment. Having said that, this restrained approach is now changing under the combined pressure of the vast, and growing, caseload of the Court and the need to be more pedagogical with legal systems that fall far short of the requirements of a Rechtstaat and which need clear, not cryptic, guidance on what legislative changes are necessary.[17]

The Court and Intelligence Accountability in General

In what way does the Court deal with intelligence accountability? To begin with, "accountability" is a broad concept. One leading constitutional lawyer has described it as "being liable to be required to give an account or explanation of actions and where appropriate, to suffer the consequences, take the blame or undertake to put matters right, if it should appear that errors have been made."[15]

"Intelligence" in the sense I am interested in can be defined as information gathered in such a way as to convey understanding for cause and effect (thereby creating conditions for acting). However, in the present context, it means such information gathered by the agencies responsible for the security of the state. So, intelligence accountability means executive (civil service) accountability to government and the accountability of executive and government to the legislature and the courts.

By contrast, under the Convention system, the "accountability" is at the state level: The contracting states are responsible at international (rather than constitutional) law to the Court, and each other, for how they comply with the Convention.[16] However, the constitutional aspect of accountability is also relevant indirectly, as a reason for finding, or not finding, a breach of the Convention. In other words, the failure to construct and implement satisfactory accountability mechanisms and institutions at the national level, thus allowing the exercise of unrestricted intelligence powers, will entail state responsibility.[18]

In another sense, the Court is a "fire brigade" system of intelligence accountability.[19] It starts working only when a problem seems to have emerged. Indeed, the requirement of exhaustion of domestic remedies, and the slowness of Strasbourg procedures, means that the Court starts working many years after the fire has started, and by the time a judgment is delivered, the fire may well have gone out.

Moreover, the Court cannot take a holistic approach to intelligence account-ability in the way a legislature can, laying down general rules as to the mandate of an organization, its powers, the necessary internal and external controls over these, and the available remedies against abuse of power. The particular facts of the case provide a strict procedural framework for the Court, a crucial difference between judicial and legislative power. An allegedly unsatisfactory intelligence law or practice must be "fitted in" to a Convention right. Thus, such vitally important aspects of control as training of intelligence staff (designed to foster democratic sensibilities and "rights awareness"), dividing responsibility between different agencies, and fiscal management can rarely, if ever, be the focus of Court scrutiny.

The procedural restraints on the Court mean that it is limited to examining systems of accountability as indirect components of the requirements that a limi-tation on a given human right be for the "protection of national security," "in accordance with the law," "necessary in a democratic society," and accompanied by "effective remedies" at the national level. What does each of these concepts mean?

The Court has been reluctant to give abstract definitions of Convention terms, and this has also been the case with national security.[20] The Court naturally refuses to accept that issues of security are "outside of the law," although it has also stressed that the Convention is not neutral as regards "enemies of democ-racy."[21] The Court is prepared to take a very wide view of national security, hold-ing, for example, that the German system of loyalty tests for teachers[22] and the Greek government's protection of "national cultural and historical symbols" fall within the concept.[23]

"Accordance with the law" means that the exercise of state power, in particu-lar coercive power, must have support in statute law, subordinate legislation, or case law. This in itself is hardly onerous; however, the Court has increasingly stressed the need for minimum standards of foreseeability and for discretionary powers to be drafted carefully, identifying the addressees, the objects of the exer-cise of power, and the limits, temporal and otherwise, on its exercise. The "neces-sity" requirement is essentially a test of the proportionality of an infringement, and involves looking at the control system for preventing abuse of discretionary powers. Where the Court finds that a measure complained of is not "in accor-dance with the law," then it does not proceed to examine whether the measure satisfies the requirements of "necessity in a democratic society." The majority of cases relating to intelligence accountability have dealt only with the "accordance with law" requirement, the Court, probably with some relief, confining its criti-cism to this issue.

The requirement of "effective remedies" in article 13 is a variable requirement. The more serious the alleged violation of a Convention right, and the more important the right is to the individual in question, the more remedies should be available. However, in the first significant intelligence case the Court dealt with, *Klass v. FRG*, the Court considered that article 13 had a subsidiary character to the substantive rights in the Convention. The Court stated that "an effective remedy . . . must mean a remedy which is as effective as can be having regard to the restricted scope for recourse inherent in any system of secret surveillance."[24] Thus, article 13 could not be interpreted so as to nullify the efficacy of the measures of secret surveillance already found to be compatible with the protection of privacy set out in article 8.

The main Convention article that has given rise to discussions regarding intelligence is, in fact, article 8, in relation to the specific issues of surveillance and records/screening. The ECtHR has also delivered important judgments relating to the provision of remedies for deportations on security grounds (articles 3 and 8, respectively, where the deportee risks torture or inhumane treatment or the deportation interferes with family life)[25] and as regards the availability of judicial remedies for security decisions affecting "civil rights" (article 6).[26] In these cases the Court has required the creation of special mechanisms, reconciling the use of intelligence material with the right of fair proceedings, and as such they are relevant to intelligence accountability in the wide sense.[27] However, for reasons of space I will concentrate in the next two sections on the issues of intelligence surveillance and records/screening.

Intelligence Surveillance

Although there are considerable, and growing, overlaps between intelligence surveillance and law enforcement surveillance, most states still subject these to different legal regimes. Law enforcement surveillance is still seen primarily as a mechanism for obtaining evidence of crime against identified suspects, whereas intelligence surveillance is still seen primarily as a mechanism for gathering intelligence on more nebulous threats to national security, not necessarily connected to crime, or at least, specific criminal offenses. Some countries have a "strategic surveillance" capacity, allowing them to monitor large sections of national, and even international, microwave and sea/land line telecommunications traffic in a proactive way, without any suspicion of ongoing offenses.

The mandate of the intelligence agencies to engage in surveillance is usually framed in a less, or much less, clear way, with more, or much more, room for speculative "fishing expeditions" and correspondingly less protection of the rights of the targets. The time limits are usually more lenient, most intelligence operations going on for much longer periods than law enforcement operations.[28]

The information obtained may be kept forever (an issue that goes more to files, considered in the following discussion). The authorizing body may differ from the usual, judicial, method in relation to law enforcement surveillance and be less objective. Even if the authorizing body is objective, as the surveillance will rarely, if ever, result in a prosecution, a definitive judicial assessment of whether the information available at the time really justified the surveillance may never be made. These are some of the special problems of intelligence surveillance.

As mentioned, most of the Court's cases have concerned the adequacy or inadequacy of the legal framework regulating the ordering of both law enforcement and intelligence surveillance. The first such case in which a violation was found was *Malone v. UK*. The Court found that the British administrative practice did not "indicate with reasonable clarity the scope and manner of exercise of the relevant discretion conferred on the public authorities."[29] The Malone case led to the enactment in the UK of the Interception of Communications (IOC) Act 1985, subsequently superseded by the Regulation of Investigative Powers Act (RIPA) 2000. In the later cases of *Kruslin v. France*[30] and *Huvig v. France*[31] the Court specified that the following matters in particular should be laid down in the law so as to minimize the potential for abuse of the law: the categories of people liable to have their telephones tapped by judicial order, the nature of the offenses that may give rise to such an order, the permitted duration of the telephone tapping, the procedure for transcribing the relevant parts of the intercepted material, the precautions to be taken to secure that the entire recordings are available for inspection by the judge and the defense, and the circumstances in which the recordings may or must be destroyed, particularly when the accused is acquitted.[32]

These cases concerned law enforcement surveillance. However, in *Amman v. Switzerland*[33] the Court extended these safeguards to intelligence surveillance. Under the applicable domestic law at the time (the Federal Council's Ordinance on Police Services of the Federal Attorney's Office 1958) the police were given competence to engage in the "surveillance and prevention of acts liable to endanger the internal or external security of the Confederation." The Court, however, found that these provisions were not sufficiently foreseeable to serve as a basis for telephone tapping. It stated that these provisions contain:

> no indication as to the persons concerned by such measures, the circumstances in which they may be ordered, the means to be employed or the procedures to be observed. [These rules] cannot therefore be considered to be sufficiently clear and detailed to afford appropriate protection against interference by the authorities with the applicant's right to respect for his private life and correspondence.[34]

The judgments of the Court have led to law reform in a number of states, providing for tightened mandates. However, while requiring more detailed legal authority for surveillance is undoubtedly a step forward, it is not so great a step if the Court allows "national security" to be undefined, and if it does not subject intelligence agencies' retention and use of material obtained as a result of surveillance to tight controls. The only Court[35] case to date concerning the controls on intelligence surveillance is *Klass v. FRG*. In this case, the applicants were German lawyers (one a judge) who were concerned with the lack of safeguards that applied to German intelligence telephone tapping, regulated by the "G10 legislation,"[36] as compared to law enforcement telephone tapping, regulated by the Code of Criminal Procedure.[37] Government ministers authorize intelligence tapping, but two supervisory bodies are established by the federal act: the independent G10 Commission and the parliamentary G10 Board. The Commission has the power, ex officio or on application by an individual who suspects that he or she is under surveillance, to rule on the legality or necessity of a particular interception and order its termination.[38] As regards strategic interception of communications, the G10 Commission supervises in particular the key words used and the guidelines on surplus information. The Court in *Klass v. FRG* took it for granted that internal controls and remedies were insufficient and stated that some, preferably judicial, monitoring mechanism must exist.[39] In the event, the Court concluded that the G10 Commission and the G10 Board "are independent of the authorities carrying out the surveillance and are vested with sufficient powers and competence to exercise an effective and continuing control."[40]

A number of points can be made in conclusion on this issue. The adequacy or otherwise of a legal mandate is an issue on which judges are eminently suitable to pronounce. However, the real challenge for the future relates to the adequacy of the control-and-remedies mechanisms. This is a more sensitive area for the Court to take on, as it will involve it in a more policy-oriented exercise of assessing whether a particular blend of controls contains adequate safeguards in practice for preventing abuse of power.

It is probably correct to say that a system of internal controls, in particular the maintenance of the democratic sensibilities of staff themselves, is the most important safeguard against abuse of power.[41] The extent of the necessary external controls will naturally vary depending upon the political context of the state, its history, the power and role of the press in the state, the size of the security agency and its relative importance vis-à-vis the bureaucracy and the police, the concrete national security threats the state is facing, and so on. But, it seems axiomatic that, in any country, internal controls cannot work properly without external controls to back them up. A properly functioning system of external control of surveillance authorization can provide a safeguard against political policing while at the same time encouraging the higher ranks of the security agency and the responsible civil servants to keep track of what their subordinates are up to, as well as encouraging the responsible politicians to keep an eye on their security chiefs.[42]

What is important is not so much the character of the review body (parliamentary, judicial, quasi-judicial, etc.) but its powers.[43] A review is of very limited use if it simply checks whether the formalities of an authorization are satisfied (Has an authorization been issued? Did it concern the right address? etc.) without going into the substance of why it was issued, and whether it should have been issued at all. Indeed, such a review is worse than useless as it gives the decision to authorize surveillance a legitimacy it may not deserve. Nor can such a limited review provide any assistance to the authorizing body, government minister, or court, in determining whether similar future operations are likely to produce enough information to justify their cost (both financial and in terms of damage to human rights). Where the review is a formality, the requesting agency and the authorizing body will be implicitly encouraged to err on the side of caution.

There are hopeful signs, in particular the judgment in *Amman v. Switzerland*, indicating that the Court is no longer willing to accept preferential treatment of intelligence matters without question. Certainly, such preferential treatment is becoming more difficult to justify the more the areas of policing and security overlap. For example, the Court accepted strategic surveillance in *Klass v. FRG* because it related to external armed threats to the security of the state. However, it is plain that this is by no means limited to such threats today.[44] Interestingly, a new application regarding the German system is currently pending before the Court.[45] However, the German system was reformed and subjected to tighter controls following a challenge to the German Federal Constitutional Court (BverfG) in 1999.[46] The Court is unlikely to feel the need to set higher standards than those laid down by the BverfG. Even so, this would call into question the present systems of strategic surveillance in a number of other European states that have, and use, this capacity.

Intelligence Files and Security Screening

Intelligence files and security screening are at the heart of the work of an intelligence agency. They can pose a number of threats to human rights, and some of these should be briefly mentioned here. Security intelligence is partly speculative in nature and it is collected for a preventative purpose. It is thus crucial that there exist clear and tightly drawn criteria for determining when sufficient suspicion exists against an individual to justify opening a file on him or her, and for what sort of information can be added to it.[47] It is also crucial that there exist even more stringent criteria for when and to whom information can be revealed from the file. Bearing in mind the fact that the intelligence agency is essentially engaged in risk assessment, there will be a natural tendency to collect more rather than less intelligence in case the security agency is found to be wanting in a crisis. And where "progress" for a security official is indicated by the growing thickness of the files for which he or she is responsible, then there is a strong personal motivation for more intelligence gathering. There is also a natural tendency to retain out-of-date information on the off chance that it may prove to be relevant in the future. But old information can give a misleading picture of an individual and the degree of risk, if any, which this person poses today.

As with secret surveillance, there are dangers involved in the mere fact of technical advances in this field, the lure of technology as it were. The potential for abuse also exists with manual records, but computerization adds a new dimension to this. The question is whether the technological advances have gone so far as to constitute qualitative rather than simply quantitative change.[48]

This intelligence is collected partly for the purpose of communication. It can thus obviously be used to the disadvantage of an individual in a variety of different ways. The interference may, like secret surveillance, occur in secret so that the person does not know why he or she has been disadvantaged, or even that he or she has been disadvantaged. The factual information communicated may be inaccurate. The person on whom the information is communicated may have been wrongly identified. A case of mistaken identity can have catastrophic consequences for the victim's career. The dangers of inaccurate information are multiplied when information is exchanged between states; at the same time it is increasingly being recognized that timely exchange of information is crucial in intelligence cooperation, particularly against international terrorism.

The information can obviously be misused in a number of ways. It can be used by the security agency itself or a faction of it to discredit someone for its own purposes. A security official can pass on the information to a politician, a businessman, or a journalist for personal gain. The security agency can be forced or persuaded by its political master to hand over intelligence to him or herself or to another agency, in order to discredit a political opponent, in or outside of the government. Finally, the mere collection of security intelligence can have a deterrent effect on political activity. One can take the view that only extremist political groups are likely to be deterred and that this is a small price to pay for improved security. But the political rights enjoyed by the fringe cannot be so easily separated from those enjoyed by the political mainstream. The rights of freedom of expression and association are protected by the Convention (articles 10 and 11), and the Court has made it plain that individuals should not be penalized for exercising their Convention rights.[49]

However, it is no simple matter to create an effective mechanism of control. Security information within the agency tends to be compartmentalized, that is, available only on a need to know basis.[50] This is to minimize the damage that would result from a penetration of the agency by a hostile service, but it means that the register is not, and cannot be, constructed wholly on the basis of the principle of ease of use. It can be very difficult for an "outsider" to obtain an overview of, for example, all the information held on a particular individual and to provide an effective level of supervision and control. Intelligence files are not simply personal files, but also organizational, event, and place files. There may be extensive cross-referencing between these different categories. Informants are not identified, but are given code names and numbers. The reliability of intelligence is graded, but the information on which this grading is based may in turn be in several, or even many, other files. And as security intelligence is based partly on more or less well-founded speculation, essentially, all that an independent monitor can offer is a second subjective opinion on whether a particular file or entry is justified, and why.

There are three Court judgments and a number of Commission decisions dealing with the issue of the adequacy of the legal mandate to collect and use intelligence. The case of *Leander v. Sweden* studied both the issue of the legal mandate and controls/remedies. I have commented on this case at length else-where.[51] Suffice to say that a government inquiry, long after the Court judgment, revealed that the legal authority for the collection of security data, accepted by the Court, was fatally flawed: it said one thing, but the practice was quite differ-ent. Notwithstanding the requirement that one was to individually assess the need for registration of people, there was more or less automatic registration of political parties that the Security Police regarded as potentially dangerous.

In the cases after *Leander*, the Commission set relatively minimal require-ments of foreseeability in relation to the mandate, but certain states nonetheless failed to satisfy these. In *V et al. v. Netherlands*, the applicants complained to the Commission that they had been subjected to surveillance by the Army Intelli-gence Service.[52] The Commission stated that the decree did not "in sufficiently clear terms indicate the circumstances in which and the conditions on which the authorities were empowered to carry out measures of secret surveillance."[53] In particular, there was no statement as to the limits to be respected, there was no definition of the categories of people to be subject to surveillance, the circum-stances in which this could occur, and the means to be used. Nor were the func-tions of the counterintelligence section within Army Intelligence set out. Finally, the safeguards to which the respondent government referred, the possibility of making a complaint to the ombudsman or a parliamentary committee consisting of the leaders of the political parties, were not contained in the Royal Decree.[54] For these reasons, the Commission considered that the interferences with the applicant's rights were not in accordance with the law.

A similar approach was taken in *Hewitt and Harman v. UK (No. 1)*, and *Nimmo v. UK*. At the time, the only legal basis for the Security Services activities was a set of administrative guidelines, which were, moreover, regarded by the Commission as unacceptably vague. The legislation introduced after the *Hewitt and Harman (No. 1)* and *Nimmo* cases, the Security Service Act 1989, was regarded by many as a minimalist interpretation of what the Convention required, and attempts were made to challenge it before the Convention organs. In the second *Hewitt and Harman* case,[55] the applicants, both involved with a civil liberties organization, argued that the term used in the act, "the interests of national security," was an unacceptably vague basis on which to collect and retain information, and that there should be a connection with violent activities before files could be opened on individuals.

The Commission considered that the breadth of the term "national security" was qualified by certain express limitations on the activities of the service and the existence of supervisory organs (the Security Service Commissioner and Tribunal) that were able to interpret it. The limitations were that arrangements must be in place to ensure that "no information by the Service except so far as necessary for the proper discharge of its functions or disclosed by it except so far as necessary for that purpose or for the purpose of preventing or detecting serious crime" and that "the Service does not take any action to further the interests of any political party."[56] The Commission took a similarly tolerant approach in *Esbester v. UK*, which concerned both the collection and the use of intelligence in vetting proceedings.

In *Tsavachidis v. Greece*,[57] the Commission found, over the denials of the Greek government, that the Greek intelligence service had collected information on a religious minority. Under Law 1654/1986 on the National Intelligence Service (NIS), the service is, first, to collect, process, and distribute information concerning national security; second, to deal with the activities of foreign intelligence services against Greece; third, to coordinate the activities of other services collecting relevant information; and fourth, to discharge any other relevant functions assigned to it by the Council of National Security or the prime minister. The government accepted that it is not within the competence of the NIS to subject persons to surveillance because of their religious beliefs. Thus, the conclusion was inevitable that the information had not been collected "in accordance with the law." If the respondent government had instead argued that the religious activities in question did pose some form of threat to national security, then there would have been a statutory basis for the NIS to collect the information. The emphasis would then have either shifted to the question of the quality of law or, more likely, the necessity for such collection.

In *Rotaru v. Romania*, what was at issue was the then existing law on filing of security information that provided simply that the security service may collect, by any necessary means, information on threats to the national security of Romania.[58] The Court found that the Romanian law on filing was not sufficiently clear as regards the grounds for filing (and the methods which might be used—something which relates to security surveillance). Moreover, there were insufficient safeguards against abuse of discretion. Accordingly it was not "in accordance with law." The Court also found a violation of article 13 because there were no remedies available.

In *Amman v. Switzerland*, the Court, as well as finding the surveillance unlawful, went on to examine whether the retention of the file on the applicant was "in accordance with the law." The Swiss law at the time provided that data that was not "necessary" or that had "no further purpose" should be destroyed, but there was no mechanism for checking that these rules were actually followed. The Court came to the conclusion that, when it became apparent that the applicant was not preparing a criminal offense, the retention of the file was not "in accordance with the law."[59]

The conclusions that can be drawn from this case law are that a general clause allowing collection of intelligence on grounds of "national security," for example, must be qualified by internal procedures for opening, adding to, and retaining files, as well as some form of external control mechanism. There must be legal authority for the use, that is, the revealing, of material from the files, although the exact conditions and limitations on this may be left to administrative practice. I would argue that it must be a minimum demand as far as use of the intelligence is concerned that the subject know, first, that the post he or she has applied to or is applying for is subject to vetting and second, that a vetting check that has been made has given a result which has influenced the employer or potential employer. Without knowledge of these two factors, whatever remedies might exist are illusory.

To turn now to the issue of the working of the external controls, the only Court case to date where controls have been studied is *Leander v. Sweden*. There are also four significant Commission admissibility decisions, *Sandberg v. Sweden*, *Hewitt and Harman v. UK (No. 2)*, *Esbester v. UK*, and *Volpi v. Switzerland*.[60] The Convention organs accepted the necessity for some form of collection of security data and some system of security screening more or less without question. The Court in *Leander* confirmed that it is the use to which information is put that is the most important. In doing so, it indirectly approved of the Swedish approach of placing the bulk of the safeguards at the stage when information is to be released. The Court granted a wide margin of appreciation to states in how they design control/remedies for systems.[61] This means, in effect, that the applicant must prove that the measures adopted by the government are not proportionate to the aim to be achieved.

However, the *Leander* case is most interesting because subsequent official inquiries have shown that the controls and remedies that the government argued existed—and the majority of the Court accepted at the time—did not work.

There was, in fact, no objective body exercising a degree of independent supervision of the filing procedures and close control over the release of intelligence from the files. Such a control now exists in the form of the Swedish Register Board.

That the Convention requires there to be a remedies/supervisory body, or bodies, is nonetheless clear. However, the question arises of how strong its powers must be. The Commission accepted that, where internal controls existed, and there existed no evidence that these were not working (although such evidence was almost impossible to come by) then a very limited degree of external control was sufficient to satisfy article 8. For example, the control exerted in the UK by the part-time Security Service Commissioner over filing is minimal. Bearing in mind this person's lack of time, staff assistance, and expertise, the only things the Commissioner is likely to find out about are blatant and widespread breaches of internal rules. The majority of the Commission nonetheless found in *Esbester v. UK* and *Hewitt and Harman v. UK (No. 2)* that the Commissioner "takes an active and authoritative approach to his role" and concluded that "the framework of safeguards was an acceptable compromise between the interests of state security and the rights of the individual."[62]

The Commission likewise set only minimal requirements as to remedies. The UK Security Service Tribunal can order deletion of files and compensation. However, where a complaint concerns alleged intelligence gathering by the Security Service, the Tribunal is to determine only whether there were "reasonable grounds" for initiating or continuing these inquiries.[63] In particular, as regards people subjected to scrutiny because they are members of an organization which is believed to be dangerous to national security, the Tribunal is limited to determining whether the Security Service had "reasonable grounds" for believing the person in question to be a member of the organization, even if it may refer the general policy issue to the Security Service Commissioner.[64] The narrow scope of the Tribunal's review, combined with the Swedish experience of the dangers of registering groups, means that the effectiveness of the remedies for individuals aggrieved at simple collection/collation of intelligence is highly doubtful.

What conclusions can be drawn on controls/remedies? Arguably the Court should be much more demanding in the future than the Commission has been in the past. Even though the *Amman* and *Rotaru* cases only concerned the issue of the legal mandate, these cases give good grounds for concluding that the Court is aware that the controls in many states are woefully inadequate—and not simply states in eastern and central Europe. But the remedies and safeguards that should operate in this area can rarely, if ever, be judicial in nature. The operation of the sort of quasi-judicial, political, or administrative remedies appropriate to this area can thus be assumed to be outside the experience of the majority of the judges on the Court. Moreover, the requirements of articles 8 and 13 in this respect are to ends (effective remedies and safeguards) rather than means. There is obviously room for different approaches in design of systems, particularly for vetting. For example, the supervisory body can be a preventive control, such as the Swedish Register Board, or a remedy, such as the UK Security Service Tribunal. But it is one thing for the Court to say that a particular judicial proceeding satisfies or does not satisfy the procedural requirements of a "fair trial" in article 6. It is quite another to lay down what type of remedies are necessary to comply with article 13. As noted before, the Court is not in the business of legislating for member states, especially in areas that can be assumed to be politically controversial.

Having said this, it is not the Court's job to balance the different factors and design the perfect system. The Court needs to say only that the system before it in a concrete case is imperfect. In reaching its conclusions in this regard, I would say that the Court should have as its point of departure the fact that it is very difficult to exercise effective supervision of intelligence files. What is needed is an external monitor with an independent staff and sufficient power and authority to compel the production of all information, and sufficient expertise to evaluate it critically.

Still, these are of little significance if there is no desire on the part of the monitor to use these powers, or no political support for him or her to do so. In practice, the value of an external monitor will depend mainly on the political climate in which he or she works, the dedication of the office holder, and the competence of his or her staff. These are fairly intangible things on which to form an opinion, far away in Strasbourg. The Court is relatively ill-equipped to judge whether formal safeguards are real safeguards, and it knows it.

Conclusions[65]

What is the "added value" of this supranational level of protection? The Convention is one of the few common standards applicable to all European states, and as such is invaluable as a platform on which to elaborate more detailed European principles of accountability. There is undoubtedly a great need for such principles, especially when, as mentioned, the EU has begun legislating in the field of internal security. The Convention case law shows that there can be situations when an international body places greater demands than those set by national courts and legislatures. The pan-European legal culture of the Court can give a different perspective on the need to reform an unsatisfactory system, and on the direction reform can take.

So far, the main value of the Convention in this area, aside from whatever preventive effect it might have had, has been in setting minimum levels of force-seeability regarding legal authority to engage in secret surveillance and security filing/screening. A negative judgment on formal grounds, requiring legislation to correct, can obviously give the legislature the opportunity to overhaul the whole area.

There is potential for further cases, even though the Court's present caseload means that it is unlikely to want to create other "growth areas." There are none-theless limits to what the Court can achieve as regards substantive matters. In order to be able to make real advances in this direction, the Court needs more comparative knowledge of how European states' national security laws and practices are constructed and applied. Projects such as this volume have a role to play in analyzing and systematizing national laws and practices as well as highlighting best practices. But having access to objective comparative material is not enough. Where a state's legislature has been given the opportunity to consider the issue of intelligence accountability, but has failed to do so, it is asking a lot of the Court to disapprove of the solution adopted democratically by the state, even if most impartial observers would regard the system adopted as gravely deficient. The attempts within the Council of Europe to adopt common rules in this area,[66] something that seemed possible following the end of the Cold War, have made no real progress. If even stable Western democracies block progress on this issue, the scope for the Court to make further meaningful advances in the field is limited.

Notes

1. 1950, European Treaty System (ETS) No. 5 (hereafter "the Convention").

2. The Council of Europe was established after the Second World War and is an organization for regional cooperation concerning all matters except security. It has adopted some 190 conventions on different matters. It consists of a secretariat, a committee of (foreign) ministers, and a parliamentary assembly, consisting of delegates from member states legislatures. It is not to be confused with the Council of the European Communities (EC).

3. It should be noted that there are fourteen protocols to the Convention. These are separate treaties under international law. Eight deal with procedural matters and the others with additional substantive rights. Not all the member states have ratified all the protocols providing for additional substantive rights.

4. The functions of the Court and the Commission were amalgamated by protocol 11, in 1998. *As shown below*, some of the old Commission case law, although having less "status," can still be important where the Court has not yet produced a judgment on the issue. *In the following discussion*, this is the case for several intelligence accountability issues.

5. The Court has spoken on several occasions of the Convention as a "common public order," e.g., *Ireland v. UK*, April 18, 1978, A/25 at para. 25. For discussions of the

constitutional nature of the Convention see, e.g., J. G. Merrills, *The Development of International Law by the European Court of Human Rights* (2nd ed.) (Manchester: Manchester UP, 1993), 9–62; and Iain Cameron, "Protocol 11 to the ECHR: the European Court of Human Rights as a Constitutional Court?" *Yearbook of European Law* 15 (1995), 219–62.

6. For discussion of the problems caused by EU antiterror blacklists (drafted partly on the basis of secret intelligence material) see Iain Cameron, "EU Antiterrorist Blacklisting," *Human Rights Law Review* 3 (2003): 225–56. However, the fact that the EU has not ratified the Convention as such (and cannot as of yet do so) means that there are awkward procedural gaps in rights protection. See *Segi and others* and *Gestoras Pro-Amnistia and others v. 15 States of the EU*, No. 6422/02 and 9916/02, May 23, 2002 (Applicants not "victims" of EU Common Position 2001/930/CFSP). This will change if the treaty establishing a constitution for Europe (OJC 310, Vol. 47, December 16, 2004), currently going through the ratification process in the member states, is accepted. The treaty provides, first, that the EU ratify the ECHR and, second, that the Charter on Rights and Fundamental Freedoms will become legally binding.

7. The Court has held that where there is an exceptional situation threatening public order, such as a wave of terrorist violence, then this background can be taken into account in determining the legitimacy of measures taken which allegedly infringe Convention rights. See, e.g., *Brogan and others v. UK*, November 29, 1988, A/145-B, para. 48.

8. This is expressly recognized in article 53.

9. See, e.g. *Handyside v. UK*, December 7, 1976, A/24, para. 48.

10. See, e.g. *Hilton v. UK*, 12015/86, 57 DR 108 (1988), *Nimmo v. UK*, 12327/86, 58 DR 85 (1989), *Hewitt and Harman v. UK*, No. 12175/86, 67 DR 88 (1989). Having said this, problems of proof can arise where it is, on the facts, equally likely that a private actor (e.g. a private security firm) has infringed an individual's rights. To ground state responsibility for active measures (as opposed to responsibility for a failure to stop interferences), an applicant must show "beyond a reasonable doubt" that state agents are responsible for the alleged violation. Thus, proving, for example, the existence of an illegal bugging device in one's home will not in itself suffice to create state responsibility for this surveillance.

11. Another important factor here is the requirement in article 35 that a case be brought before the Court within six months of the final domestic decision (in the case of secret measures, within six months of the decision becoming known to the applicant). It can be noted that some of the issues which do reach Strasbourg undergo a transformation and become something other than what they were in the national context. See, e.g., *Guardian and Observer v. UK*, November 26, 1991, A/216 and *Castells v. Spain*, April 23, 1992, A/236 para. 39.

12. See Council of Ministers recommendation No. R (2000) 2. The Court has recently begun explicitly stating, in exceptional cases, that the respondent state has a duty not simply to pay just satisfaction but also to take specific measures redressing the situation of the applicant. *Assanidzé v. Georgia*, No. 71503/01, April 8, 2004.

13. See, e.g., the unsuccessful attempt made by the Canadian parliament to restrict its security agency's collection of information on nonviolent subversives, discussed by Peter Gill, *Policing Politics: Security Intelligence and the Liberal Democratic State* (London: Frank Cass, 1994), 110–11.

14. David Dixon, *Law in Policing* (Oxford: Oxford University Press, 1997), 33.

15. Dawn Oliver, *Government in the United Kingdom: the search for accountability, effectiveness and citizenship* (Philadelphia: Open University Press, 1991), 22.

16. The "sanction" is, ultimately, expulsion from the Council of Europe. However, noncompliance will probably also lead to multilateral political and economic sanctions (in particular EU pressure exerted in various ways through association, trade, etc. agreements).

17. The Committee of Ministers has now adopted a resolution, Res (2004) 3 "on judgments revealing an underlying systemic problem," which encourages the Court to exercise a more forward-looking "quasi-legislative" competence where it has identified a structural rights problem. The Court invoked this competence for the first time in *Broniowski v. Poland*, No. 31443/96, June 22, 2004.

18. Responsibility under article 1 of the Convention can exist for extraterritorial action, by a state's foreign intelligence service. See, e.g., *Öcalan v. Turkey*, No. 46221/99, March 12, 2003. However, the subject is complicated. The extent of responsibility can vary depending upon the extent of actual control exercised, and difficulties of proof in this area are likely to be even greater than for alleged abuse of domestic power.

19. M. D. McCubbins and T. Schwartz, "Congressional Oversight Overlooked: Police Patrols vs. Fire Alarms," *American Journal of Political Science* 28 (1984), 165–79. See also chapter 4 by Loch K. Johnson and chapter 12 by Hans Born in this volume.

20. Indeed, the Commission expressed the view that national security cannot be defined exhaustively. *Esbester v. UK*, No. 18601/91, 18 EHRR CD 72 (1993) and that in the first place it is for member states to decide whether it is necessary to criminalize particular conduct deemed to be damaging to national security. *M. v. France*, No. 10078/82, 41 D.R. 103, 117 (1985). See also discussion of *Hewitt and Harman (No. 2)* below.

21. See *Refah Partisi (The Welfare Party) and others v. Turkey* Nos 41340/98, 41342/98, 41343/98, and 41344/98, February 13, 2003, where the Court stated that Convention freedoms "cannot deprive the authorities of a State in which an association, through its activities, jeopardizes that State's institutions, of the right to protect those institutions . . . some compromise between the requirements of defending democratic society and individual rights [is] inherent in the Convention system" (at para. 96).

22. See *Vogt v. FRG*, September 26, 1995, A/323, paras 49–51.

23. *Sidiropolous v. Greece*, July 10, 1998, para. 38.

24. Op. cit. para. 69.

25. See *Chahal v. UK*, No. 22414/93, November 15, 1996, and *Al-Nashif and others v. Bulgaria*, No. 50963/99, June 20, 2002.

26. *Tinnelly and McElduff v. UK*, July 10, 1998.

27. Intelligence material can naturally arise in other contexts, in particular as regards article 5 (arrest and detention), see Iain Cameron, *National Security and the European Convention on Human Rights* (Uppsala/Dordrecht: Iustus/Kluwer, 2000), 267–86, and in relation to fair trial in criminal proceedings. See, e.g., *Hulki Günes v. Turkey*, No. 28490/95, June 19, 2003, and the pending case of *Haas v. Germany*, No. 73047/01.

28. e.g., in Canada the period is one year (Security Intelligence Service Act 1984, section 21(5)). Anti-subversion warrants, i.e., not involving acts of violence, may be issued for only sixty days, but no such warrants have been issued for many years. In the United States, domestic security warrants can be issued for three months and "foreign intelligence" warrants for one year (50 USC section 1805(d)(l)). Normal law enforcement warrants in the United States are issued for thirty days (18 USC section 2518(5)).

29. *Malone v. UK*, August 2, 1984, A/82, para. 79.

30. April 24, 1990, A/176-A.

31. April 24, 1990, A/176-B.

32. *Kruslin v. France*, para. 35, *Huvig v. France*, para. 34.

33. No. 27798/95, February 16, 2000.

34. Ibid., para. 58.

35. The Court dealt indirectly with surveillance methods in the *Rotaru* case. The UK controls introduced by the IOC Act, now improved slightly by RIPA, were examined by the Commission in *Christie v. UK*, No. 21482/93, 78A DR 119 (1994). The Commission in effect said that the mere existence of a part-time Commissioner who subjects warrants issued to (superficial) spot-checks was enough to satisfy the quality of law and necessity in a democratic society's requirements. I am critical of the Commission decision. See Cameron, 2000, pp. 114–19, 132–37, 144–47.

36. Gesetz zur Beschränkung des Brief-, Post und Fernmeldegeheimnisses (Gesetz zu Artikel 10 Grundgesetz), hereafter "G10," August 13, 1968, BGBl. 1 S. 949. Each Land has its own G10 legislation (Ausführungsgesetze zum G10 Gesetz). The description of the federal control system is applicable mutatis mutandis to the Länder.

37. Strafprozessordnung (Code of Criminal Procedure) section 101.

38. For a discussion in English of the powers of the supervisory bodies see Cameron, 2000, pp. 127–31, and Shapiro, 2002.

39. Op. cit., para. 42.

40. The Court also noted the parliamentary character of the Board. The G10 had previously been the subject of litigation before the German Federal Constitutional Court (Bundesverfassungsgericht, BverfG). The BverfG considered that the G10 Commission could be relied upon to exercise the independence and discretion of judges. BverfGE (collected judgments) vol. 30, pp. 1–47 at pp. 30–31.

41. Cf. Commission of Inquiry into certain activities of the Royal Canadian Mounted Police, 2nd report, *Freedom and Security under the Law* (1981), 698; Lawrence Lustgarten and Ian Leigh, *In From the Cold: National Security and Parliamentary Democracy* (Oxford: Oxford University Press, 1994), 424–48.

42. Stansfield Turner, *Secrecy and Democracy* (London: Sidgwick and Jackson, 1985), 263

43. See, e.g., Jean Paul Brodeur, "Parliamentary vs. Civilian Oversight," in *National Security and the Rule of Law*, ed. Dennis Töllborg (Gothenburg: Gothenburg University, 1997).

44. For example, the German law was subsequently changed allowing for monitoring of both domestic and foreign telecommunications to prevent and detect less drastic threats. These are listed as a threat of serious terrorist violence, the smuggling of weapons of mass destruction or dual use technology, smuggling of narcotics into Germany (not of a minor nature), forgery of currency, and money laundering. See laws of October 28, 1994 (BGBl. I S.3186) and December 17, 1997 (BGBl. I S.3108). As regards foreign communications, only radio waves may be intercepted, although a fair amount of telecommunications traffic is, at some point in the course of transmission, in the form of microwaves.

45. *Weber and Saravia v. Germany*, No. 54934/00.

46. 1 BvR 2226/94, 2420/95 and 2437/95, 14 July 1999.

47. Publicly available information—open sources—can still create a privacy issue under article 8, when it is "individualized" and stored systematically. See the *Tsavachidis* case, below, and *Peck v. UK*, No. 44647/98, January 28, 2003.

48. David Lyon, *The Electronic Eye: The Rise of the Surveillance Society, Polity Press*, (Cambridge: Cambridge University Press, 1994) 42–56.

49. *Enzelin v. France*, April 26, 1991, A/202, para. 53. However, this does not mean that

an intelligence agency is forbidden from collecting information on individual's exercise of such freedoms (see *Kalaç v. Turkey*, July 1, 1997). It is rather that the goal of not disproportionably infringing upon these freedoms should be seen as part of the interpretative context of the justifiability for opening and adding to intelligence files under article 8.

50. I will not go into the issue of the extent to which the need for fast intelligence caused, and enabled, by the "information society" is influencing primarily the U.S. intelligence community away from strict compartmentalization, and toward providing online access on secured networks for a wide range of "finished" intelligence products. For a brief discussion see P. Sharfman, "Intelligence Analysis in the Age of Electronic Dissemination," in *Intelligence Analysis and Assessment*, eds. David A. Charters, Stuart Farson, and Glenn P. Hastedt (London/Portland: Frank Cass, 1996).

51. See Cameron, 2000, 196–211, 225–40, 246–51; and Iain Cameron and Dennis Töllborg, "Internal Security in Sweden," in *Democracy, Law and Security: Internal Security Services in Contemporary Europe*, eds. Jean Paul Brodeur, Peter Gill, and Dennis Töllborg (London: Ashgate, 2002); and Dennis Töllborg, Personalkontroll, Symposion (Stockholm: Lund, 1986).

52. *V. and others v. The Netherlands*, Nos. 14084–88/88, 14109/88, 14195–7/88, report of December 3, 1991.

53. Op. cit. para. 43.

54. Ibid., paras. 44–45.

55. *Hewitt and Harman v. UK (No. 2)*, No. 20317/92

56. Security Service Act, 1989, Section 2(2)(a) and (b).

57. No. 28802/95, October 28, 1997.

58. Law No. 14, February 24, 1992 on the Organization and Functioning of the Romanian Security Service.

59. Op. cit., para. 79.

60. *Sandberg v. Sweden*, No. 11287/84, decision December 9, 1988, *Volpi v. Switzerland*, No. 25147/94 84 DR 106 (1996). The other cases have been cited earlier.

61. Op. cit., para. 59.

62. *Esbester v. UK*, op. cit. at CD 76, *Hewitt and Harman v. UK (No. 2)*, op. cit. at pp. 15–16. This repeats a formulation used by the Court in *Klass v. FRG* (para. 59).

63. Security Service Act 1989, schedule 1, paras 2(2) and (3).

64. Ibid. para. 2(4).

65. For fuller analysis I refer the reader to my book *National Security and the ECHR*.

66. Parliamentary Assembly, Recommendation 1402 on Control of Internal Security Services in Council of Europe Member States, adopted April 26, 1999, European Commission for Democracy Through Law, Internal Security Services (CDL-INF (98) 6), Parliamentary Assembly, Committee on Legal Affairs and Human Rights, Control of Internal Security Services in Council of Europe Member States György Frunda, (rapporteur) Doc. 8301, January 21, 1999.

PART 2

The Revolution in Intelligence Accountability

4

Governing in the Absence of Angels: On the Practice of Intelligence Accountability in the United States

Loch K. Johnson

> We probably didn't shake the [intelligence] agencies hard enough after the end of the Berlin Wall, to say: "Hey, look, the world is changing and you need to change the ways in which you operate . . . new strategies, new personnel, new culture." We should have been more demanding of these intelligence agencies.[1]

This chapter examines the current state of oversight with respect to supervision of America's intelligence agencies. Employing the methodologies of interviews and archival research, the analysis explores the fit of prominent oversight theories to this hidden side of government. As well, it evaluates the major obstacles to effective oversight in dealing with secretive agencies.

The Meaning of Oversight

"If men were angels," wrote James Madison in Federalist Paper No. 51, "no government would be necessary." In the absence of angels, however, he advised that "ambition must be made to counteract ambition." The most important safeguard against abuse in a democratic society is elections: supervision by the people. But Madison stressed, too, the value of establishing "auxiliary precautions" within the government. In the United States, this phrase has come to encompass an array of checks and balances exercised by the three governing branches, from lofty impeachment proceedings against the president and judicial review through investigations, commissions, hearings, and budget examinations, down to day-to-day legislative casework. Madison foresaw the necessity for a steady scrutiny of government programs, a feature of governance known today as accountability or, in the inelegant term adopted by political scientists, "oversight."

Executive branch oversight of intelligence agencies in the United States has been anemic. None of the major intelligence abuses during the 1960s and 1970s were uncovered by institutions of accountability inside the executive branch, but rather by media and legislative investigators. In 1975, the Ford administration strengthened the President's Foreign Intelligence Advisory Board (PFIAB) and created an Intelligence Oversight Board (IOB), both arms of the Executive Office of the Presidency; yet, with an occasional exception, neither of these panels has been engaged in a continuous and robust review of intelligence operations. New offices of inspector-general in the leading intelligence agencies, established after the Iran-Contra scandal of 1987, have displayed greater investigative tenacity than their weak forerunners with the same titles; but they, too, have proved unable to supervise the vast domain of the intelligence community.

The boldest attempts at intelligence oversight by the executive branch have been in the form of special commissions, one in 1975 (the Rockefeller Commission), a second in 1995 (the Aspin-Brown Commission), and a third in 2004 (the Silberman-Robb Commission). The Rockefeller Commission produced evidence of illegal domestic spying, which fueled the intelligence reform movement of that year; and the Aspin-Brown Commission issued a thoughtful report on how the intelligence agencies should reorient themselves in the aftermath of the Cold War, although the recommendations were largely ignored.[2] The Silberman-Robb Commission is still conducting its probe into the flawed intelligence reporting that predicted the existence of significant stockpiles of weapons of mass destruction (WMD) in Iraq on the eve of the second Persian Gulf War.

The most consistent and serious manifestation of intelligence oversight has come not from presidential commissions, but from the media and the Congress. Media reporters face high walls, however, in their efforts to track intelligence activities; with their subpoena powers and other constitutionally based investigative tools, lawmakers are in the best position to supervise the hidden side of government—if they have the will.

Lee H. Hamilton, a former House member (D-Indiana) and director of the Woodrow Wilson Center in Washington, D.C., offers this case for legislative oversight: "Congress must do more than write the laws; it must make sure that the administration is carrying out those laws the way Congress intended."[3] By means of oversight, lawmakers "can help protect the country from the imperial presidency and from bureaucratic arrogance. . . . [and] help keep federal bureaucracies on their toes." Former intelligence overseer and U.S. senator, Wyche Fowler (D-Georgia) notes simply that "oversight keeps bureaucrats from doing something stupid."[4] More formally, political scientist Joel D. Aberbach defines legislative oversight as "review of the actions of federal departments, agencies, and commissions, and of the programs and policies they administer, including review that takes place during program and policy implementation as well as afterward." He views these activities as "a significant facet of congressional efforts to control administration and policy."[5]

Theories of Congressional Oversight

Two broad theories of oversight dominate the scholarly literature: the police-patrol and the fire-alarm models. As explained by McCubbins and Schwartz, with police-patrol oversight "at its own initiative, Congress examines a sample of executive agency activities, with the aim of detecting and remedying any violations of legislative goals and, by its surveillance, discouraging such violations."[6] In contrast, with fire-alarm oversight "Congress establishes a system of rules, procedures, and informal practices that enable individual citizens and organized interest groups to examine administrative decisions (sometimes in prospect), to charge executive agencies with violating congressional goals, and to seek remedies from agencies, courts, and Congress itself." As "firefighters," lawmakers react to such stimuli as media revelations about wrongdoing or grievances from interest groups.

When on police patrol, members of Congress aggressively search for information and indications of wrongdoing or inefficiency—"sniffing for fires," in the McCubbins and Schwartz metaphor. Alternatively, as a firefighter, Congress places "fire-alarm boxes on street corners, builds neighborhood fire houses, and sometimes dispatches its own hook-and-ladder in response to an alarm."[7] Police-patrol oversight is comparatively centralized, active, and direct; fire-alarm oversight is less centralized and involves less active and continuous intervention. McCubbins and Schwartz, as well as Ogul and Rockman, found the fire-alarm approach most prominent on Capitol Hill.[8] Aberbach's data suggest, though, that in more recent Congresses police-patrolling has surpassed the reliance of lawmakers on fire alarms, at least with respect to the domestic policy domains that he investigated.[9]

For Aberbach, the explanation for this change in the approach of representatives to oversight lay in a dramatic transformation in public opinion that occurred in the 1970s and 1980s. Displaying a growing disenchantment with government performance (with Watergate and Vietnam as a backdrop, along with popular president Ronald Reagan's anti-government rhetoric), the public has increasingly demanded that lawmakers pay less attention to the creation of new government programs and focus more on the improvement of programs dy exist. This change in the political environment has provided a strong incentive for members of Congress to initiate oversight themselves, anticipating fires and claiming credit for their vigilance as overseers rather than waiting passively for alarms to sound. "As a consequence," writes Aberbach, "formal oversight proceedings (such as oversight hearings) became common activities in the 1970s, and it seems that aggressive information search also became more common."[10]

Police Patrolling and Firefighting

With respect to the police officer and firefighter approaches to intelligence oversight, the norm on Capitol Hill from 1975 to 2003 has been sporadic policing with various degrees of enthusiasm. This is true in part because this secret world has few interest groups and is sufficiently veiled to make media reporting on its activities difficult; therefore, the external "fire alarm" stimuli have been infrequent—although important when they occurred. However infrequent, this period of what may be called the "New Oversight" (in contrast to the minimal intelligence review by lawmakers that existed in the United States prior to 1975) began with a fire alarm set off by the *New York Times* in 1974, leading to the most extensive investigation ever conducted into U.S. intelligence: the Church Committee in the Senate. Moreover, three other alarms have erupted: the Iran-Contra affair in 1987, based on another (foreign) newspaper exposé, which led to the establishment of the joint congressional Inouye-Hamilton Committee of inquiry; an intelligence failure in Somalia (1993), coupled with concern about the discovery of a Russian mole inside the CIA (Aldrich H. Ames in 1994), which led to the joint executive-legislative Aspin-Brown Commission investigation; and the 9/11 attacks, leading to the creation of another joint congressional Goss–Graham Committee of inquiry, as well as an ongoing congressionally appointed Kean Commission. The controversy in 2004 over flawed WMD intelligence in Iraq produced no new panels of inquiry in Congress, just the presidentially appointed Silberman-Robb Commission. These reactive inquiries involving lawmakers sum to roughly five years worth of intense investigating by congressional overseers qua firefighters during the era of New Oversight, in contrast to the twenty-five years of reliance on individually motivated members of the Senate Select Committee on Intelligence (SSCI) and the House Permanent Select Committee on Intelligence (HPSCI)—however few—engaged in earnest policing.

Prominent Issues of Oversight
Since the 9/11 Attacks

Beyond responding to such external stimuli as domestic spying and other scandals, along with incidents of moles and terrorist attacks, what have been the issues that have—or should have—preoccupied the two intelligence committees? Questionable activities have been plentiful, among them flaws in the mission of collection and analysis, the uses of covert action and counterintelligence, how best to organize and manage intelligence, and how to protect civil liberties. An essential oversight responsibility, further, is to assist the intelligence community in the establishment of priorities from among the many possible ways to spend the annual intelligence dollar.

The Intelligence Cycle

With respect to the collection-and-analysis mission, intelligence professionals think of a cycle with five stages: planning and direction, collection, processing, analysis, and dissemination.[11] This theoretical construct provides a useful way to think about the range of responsibilities for serious overseers, since each stage in the cycle warrants close legislative review.

Planning and Direction

In the first stage of the intelligence cycle, policymakers and intelligence managers must decide how to allocate resources (widely reported in the media as a growing $35 billion per year in the aftermath of the 9/11 attacks) toward targets considered dangerous to the United States, an exercise known as a threat assessment. On September 11, 2001, al Qaeda leapt to the top of the threat list. Afghanistan and Iraq soon followed. But what other perils around the globe should attract intelligence resources? How much of the annual intelligence budget should be spent on the gathering of information about al Qaeda, as opposed, say, to warlords in Afghanistan, the unpredictable nations of Iran and North Korea, or such topics as leadership succession in China, Japanese economic strategies, organized crime in Russia, Colombian drug trafficking, and ethnic strife in Africa?

Collection

Pointing to his choice as the major problem facing U.S. intelligence today, intelligence scholar Angelo Codevilla declares: "The CIA has not been gathering enough quality data."[12] Overseers have a responsibility to evaluate the proper mix of spending on technical versus human intelligence. "We simply didn't understand . . . the need for human intelligence . . . we simply did not provide the resources," Senator Mike DeWine (R-Ohio) conceded in public hearings after 9/11.[13] How much "HUMINT" is enough? How well are the agencies recruiting case officers and translators with skills in the languages and cultures of the Middle East and South Asia? How effectively are they keeping up with the forward rush of communications technologies used by adversaries of the United States, such as the exponential growth in telephone lines over the past decade?

The HPSCI minority staff director (Sheeley, 2002) views the study of "overhead architecture," that is, the proper constellation of U.S. satellites in space, as the most important oversight question facing Congress. He asks: "How many satellites are necessary? How big or small should they be? How much money should be spent?" His second highest priority is equipping the National Security Agency (NSA) to monitor the new forms of communications used around the world by America's adversaries.

Processing

Extraneous information ("noise") gathered by intelligence agencies is always greater in volume than valuable information, a core vexation for intelligence officials. Processing is the effort to sift through the flood tide of information coming into the United States from worldwide collectors (satellites, reconnaissance aircraft, spies) in search of useful findings. The "raw" intelligence, say, a Farsi telephone interception, must be readied for examination by expert analysts (in this example, translated into English). The job of processing can be overwhelming, since the incoming information is like a fire hose held to the mouth.

Skill at data mining is vital, and in this regard the U.S. government continues to lag behind the private sector. Hunting for specifically relevant information, rather than broad gathering, is the goal. Most of the data—upwards of 90 percent in the case of satellite photographs, for instance—remain unexamined, because of the limits of time and trained staff.[14] Moreover, even key messages may not be handled with dispatch, as was the case with the Arabic telephone intercept of September 10, 2001, that said "Tomorrow is zero hour"—translated too late, on September 12. Kessler claims that for some eight years, under Director Louis Freer's reign, the FBI drifted with respect to information technology.[15] If so, where were the legislative overseers to halt the drift and demand better IT competence in the intelligence community?

Analysis

"The biggest failure of the Senate Intelligence Committee in recent years," according to a senior staffer, "has been its lack of focus on the quality of intelligence analysis."[16] Providing timely, accurate, objective, actionable insights to policymakers, based on the data that flow back to the United States from assets abroad, is the essential duty of intelligence agencies, as performed by their analysts. By combing through the evidence, if analysts could have warned that in September 2001 al Qaeda operatives would attempt to fly hijacked airlines into the World Trade Center and government buildings in Washington, measures could have been carried out to thwart the attacks (tighter airport security for one); instead, some three thousand Americans lost their lives. Again, the intelligence community needs more experts with knowledge of neglected regions like South Asia. Intelligence will remain ambiguous in most instances, as DCI Tenet emphasized on February 5, 2004, in an unusual public post-mortem of intelligence failures in Iraq preceding the second Persian Gulf War; but intelligence officers and overseers must nonetheless push harder toward the goal of greater—and more timely—specificity.

Dissemination

Despite enormous expenditures on intelligence, policymakers often ignore the product delivered to them by the secret agencies. As early as 1995, for instance, the CIA's Counterterrorism Center warned that America could soon be the victim of "aerial terrorism," with terrorists piloting aircraft into buildings.[17] Twelve reports to this effect were sent by the CIA through the higher echelons of the government between 1995 and 2002, including SSCI and HPSCI overseers.[18] Yet, neither the White House nor any other entity took significant action to increase airport security. In this sense, the attacks of 9/11 were as much a policy failure as an intelligence failure—and, on both accounts, failures of legislative overseers, who should have prodded the government into responding to these startling warnings.

The most important criticism of intelligence to emerge from the hearings of the Joint Intelligence Committee in 2003 was the lack of cooperation among the secret agencies—the problem of information sharing that drove President Harry S Truman to create a modern central intelligence in the first place. Well before the events of 9/11, virtually every scholarly study of American intelligence called for greater "all-source fusion" of information and better "jointness" among the secret agencies.[19] Yet, the U.S. intelligence agencies have changed little from the damning description of them as a "tribal federation" made by a deputy director of the CIA some thirty years ago.[20] As a commentary on this lack of institutional cohesion, the DCI and the secretary of defense never met with one another a single time throughout 1999 and 2000.

An important concern for overseers, too, is the question of intelligence politicization: "cooking" information to suit the political needs and ideological inclinations of policymakers. The Church Committee recorded instances of politicization[21] and, from time to time, new charges arise.[22] In 2002, Department of Defense officials complained that CIA intelligence on Iraq failed to match their expectations, and they established a new intelligence unit of their own (the Office of Special Plans), perhaps to bypass the intelligence community and produce information that better reinforced the administration's plans to invade Iraq and the preconceived views on Iraq held by Pentagon officials. In 2003, a CIA estimate that rejected the White House hypothesis of ties between al Qaeda and the Iraqi regime was first withheld, briefly released, then quickly buried by the administration.[23] On another issue, according to reporter Seymour Hersh, "the Bush Administration at the highest levels is a cocoon, resistant to information on North Korea—until it became a crisis [in 2003]."[24] Have legislative overseers examined these apparent efforts to politicize intelligence? If so, their findings remain out of sight from the public, which relies on representatives to keep them informed. This reliance may be misplaced, however, for the two congressional oversight committees rarely report to the public, seldom hold open hearings, and maintain a website that makes Mother Hubbard's cupboard seem well-stocked.

Speaking truth to power is notoriously difficult; those in high office often refuse to listen. The classic case is President Lyndon B. Johnson's shunting aside of the CIA's warnings about the bleak chances for U.S. military success in Vietnam. Even when policymakers are willing to remove ideological and political blinkers, intelligence officers face an additional dissemination challenge: those in power are frequently too busy to read intelligence reports. Members of HSPCI and SSCI must spend time working on ways to heighten the appreciation of policy officials for intelligence products. What good is it for overseers to labor hard toward improving their intelligence if the product is ignored or distorted by policy officials?

Covert Action

Each of the major oversight laws—the Hughes-Ryan Act of 1974,[25] the Oversight Act of 1980,[26] and the Intelligence Authorization Act of 1991[27]—focused on how best to supervise covert actions. The most contentious legislation to confront members of the congressional oversight committees—the Boland Amendments, named after their sponsor, HPSCI Chair Edward P. Boland (D-Massachusetts)[28]—also dealt with covert action (in Nicaragua). Among the most embarrassing moments for overseers and for the intelligence agencies came about as a result of the Iran-Contra scandal, an instance of covert action run amuck.[29]

No wonder covert action has been a hot potato for overseers and intelligence officers alike. This mission can involve coups d'etat and assassination plots, the mining of harbors with explosives, and bribes to foreign politicians, along with fiascos like the Bay of Pigs.[30] Prolonged legislative battles have been waged over when the executive branch should report to Congress on its covert action proposals. The formula in the Hughes-Ryan Act, bold at the time, was "in a timely manner." The Oversight Act of 1980 went a significant step further, requiring prior notice, except in emergencies (when the president would still have to inform eight leaders of Congress—the so-called "gang of eight"). Following two years of haggling, President George H. W. Bush forced lawmakers (by threat of a veto) to back away from the stringent "prior notice" standard. In the Intelligence Authorization Act of 1991, the president promised to continue to report in advance in most instances, but he insisted on more flexibility in times of crisis (as defined by the White House). Contentious, too, has been the detail of reporting, which has come to depend on how sternly and insistently lawmakers demand to know chapter and verse when the DCI presents the required briefing on a presidential approval ("finding") for a covert action.

With the ensuing war against al Qaeda and the Taliban regime in Afghanistan following the 9/11 attacks, covert action came out of the slumber it had been in since the end of the Cold War and—working jointly with overt U.S. military intervention by the Army's Special Forces—assumed a major role again in American foreign policy (as it last had during another war in Afghanistan when the CIA helped indigenous mujahideen warriors drive out a Soviet invading force during the 1980s). In 2002, the combination of overt Special Forces and precision bombing, along with the use of covert CIA drones and paramilitary (PM) operatives, proved too much for al Qaeda members and Taliban fighters. Those who escaped being captured or killed vanished like ghosts into the wild reaches of mountainous terrain in Afghanistan and contiguous nations. Noting the effectiveness of CIA/PM operations in Afghanistan, the Department of Defense has reportedly grown enamored of the idea that the Pentagon should develop its own covert action capabilities.[31] If so, this ought to be a matter of major concern for legislative overseers because, in the past, covert action has been the special preserve of the CIA; bringing the Pentagon behemoth into the picture will significantly complicate the supervision of this controversial form of intelligence activity.

The newest wrinkle in covert action is use of the CIA's unmanned aerial vehicle (UAV) known as MQ-1, or the Predator, a drone initially used for spying but then adapted during the 2002 war in Afghanistan with Hellfire missiles capable of killing an adversary once the UAV's cameras have spotted him. The murder of suspected individual terrorists became a part of America's approach to counterterrorism—an "extraordinary change of threshold," according to a former intelligence operative.[32] In 2003, a Hellfire missile launched from a Predator hovering at 10,000 feet over the deserts of Yemen struck a vehicle thought to have six al Qaeda passengers, one of whom (it turned out) was an American citizen. All met a fiery death, raising troubling oversight questions about the rights of suspects and the use of drones and Hellfires as an instrument of assassination beyond the original Afghani battlefield. "Who sees that evidence [demonstrating warlike intentions against the United States by a Predator victim] before any action is taken?" asks Yale University law professor Harold Hongju Koh.[33]

As with so many other aspects of intelligence, the 9/11 terrorist attacks against the United States reprised a topic that had been at the center of the Church Committee investigation: Should America resort to assassinations? Senator Church argued no, except in the most dire circumstances.[34] Agreeing, President Gerald R. Ford signed an executive order in 1976 [No. 11,905, 41 Fed. Reg. 7703] to halt assassination plots, although with a waiver in time of war. The waiver provision leaves the door open for the assassination of contemporary terrorists, since Congress authorized war against them soon after the 9/11 attacks. A rising chorus of television pundits now argues, however, that even the waiver is insufficient, and they call for the outright revision of the executive order altogether in this time of danger—yet another vital issue for consideration on the crowded agenda of congressional overseers.

Counterintelligence

Counterterrorism, a subsidiary of counterintelligence (the thwarting of enemy attacks and penetrations), is currently Priority One for U.S. intelligence officers and overseers. Still, counterintelligence officers have other responsibilities as well, as suggested by this unholy trinity: Walker, Hanssen, and Ames. The Walker family stole secrets from U.S. Naval Intelligence and sold them to the Soviets from 1968 until 1984, when a disgruntled wife in the family finally tipped off the FBI. Robert P. Hanssen and Aldrich H. Ames also spied for the Soviets, Hanssen beginning in 1979 and Ames in 1985. Both carried on their espionage for Russia after the Cold War, until Ames was caught in 1994 and Hanssen in 2001. How did these traitors slip through America's security defenses? Were legislative overseers vigilant enough in stressing the importance of the counterintelligence mission?

With the current emphasis on jointness and computer connectivity, intelligence compartmentalization will be on the decline in order to improve the sharing of information across agency barriers. This jointness can increase the danger of a major counterintelligence failure: an Ames with access to information across all agencies. Adding to the challenge is the recruitment of non-traditional intelligence officers into the ranks of the secret agencies. Most Americans of Middle Eastern and South Asian heritage, for example, are doubtless loyal to the United States; but among them may hide an al Qaeda sleeper. For a wide span of time between 1975 and 1995, counterintelligence did not receive the attention it warranted from intelligence managers or overseers. The country can ill afford a comparable laxity now, as the intelligence agencies begin to integrate better their communications channels in the quest for interagency all-source fusion.

Organization and Management

The organizational structure of the U.S. intelligence community is a morass. It remains too fragmented ("stovepiped"); the DCI is by statute—the National Security Act of 1947 [Pub. L. No. 80–253, 61 Stat. 495]—a weak leader, lacking final budgetary and personnel authority over the agencies (with the exception of the CIA) that are supposed to be the director's responsibility. In addition, the management of satellite imagery remains in a muddle, with tangled lines of authority and responsibility among the NSA, the National Reconnaissance Office (NRO), and the new National Geo-Spatial Agency (NGA, formerly the National Imagery and Mapping Agency). Further, other structures that have arisen in the aftermath of 9/11, such as the Department of Homeland Security and the Terrorist Threat Integration Center, suggest even more fragmentation and ambiguity over mission and authority. Congressional overseers have much work to do in bringing greater cohesion to the intelligence community and its allied agencies, not least the improved sharing of information between the FBI and the CIA.

The intelligence jurisdictional lines on Capitol Hill itself are a jumble, with accountability spread over too many committees: Appropriations, Armed Services, Judiciary, and now Homeland Security, in addition to the two intelligence committees. "Oversight has become too complicated," deplores NIMA Director Lt. Gen. (ret.) James R. Clapper, Jr. (2003). "There are too many jurisdictions, too much paperwork." Clapper notes that the new Department of Homeland Security presently has to answer to forty-four congressional committees. The whole intelligence wiring diagram cries out for reform and consolidation, both within and among the agencies and on Capitol Hill. Will overseers confront this Gordian knot?

Civil Liberties

Above all, overseers have an obligation to guard the precious civil liberties of U.S. citizens. The destruction of terrorism would be a Pyrrhic victory if, in the process, what matters most about American society was destroyed. Too often in the past, government paranoia has led to the trampling of basic rights, as with the FBI Counterintelligence Program ("Cointelpro") abuses uncovered by the Church Committee in 1975.[35] In the wake of the 9/11 attacks, the nation again faces not only the danger of future terrorist attacks, perhaps with even more lethal weapons, but also the erosion of constitutional principles.

The signs of risk to civil liberties have been abundant: a dubious Information Awareness Office in the Defense Department with the self-professed goal of "total information awareness," led by former Iran-Contra conspirator John M.

Poindexter; reports that the CIA will place agents in nearly all of the FBI's fifty-six counterterrorism offices in U.S. cities;[36] resistance from the Justice Department toward congressional requests to review the use of new antiterrorism powers, like the U.S.A. Patriot Act, passed in such haste in 2002 that many lawmakers had not even read the proposal before casting their votes in favor;[37] a distinguished visiting scholar from South Asia on his way to a seminar at the Brookings Institution snatched off the streets of Washington, D.C., by immigration officials;[38] the arrest and indefinite detention of Americans without trial and without access to legal counsel.[39] Here is a rich oversight agenda in itself.

Chief Obstacles to Contemporary Intelligence Oversight

It is one thing to have a serious oversight agenda; it is quite another to be successful in carrying it out. Several obstacles stand in the way.

Motivation

Nothing is more important to effective oversight than the will of individual lawmakers or executive overseers to engage in a meaningful examination of intelligence programs. "Determination is the key. Members [of Congress] have to be willing to break arms and legs," emphasizes a staffer with three decades of experience on the Hill.[40] "Not too many are willing," he concludes. In 2003, a former special assistant to DCI William J. Casey urged former lawmakers and other officials on the Kean Commission (investigating the 9/11 attacks) to pursue their responsibilities with utmost seriousness, in a "helicopter-raids-at-dawn, break-down-the-doors, kick-their-rear-ends sort of operation"[41]—although, with their reputation of trying to elude overseers themselves, this is hardly the approach to oversight that he or his former boss encouraged in the 1980s.

While such exhortations make an important point, one would almost settle just for a more serious participation of lawmakers in oversight hearings. For the period from 1975 to 1990, a study on the quality of intelligence oversight in public hearings found that although members will show up (along with the network television crews) for "firefighting" sessions dealing with scandals, attendance at hearings of a more routine, police-patrolling nature was spotty—only approximately one-third of the total SSCI and HPSCI membership, on average, during these years. Citing Woodrow Wilson's adage that "Congress in committee-rooms is Congress at work," the study concluded that "a good many legislators failed to show up for work."[42] The current HPSCI staff director claims, however, that

70 percent of the lawmakers on that panel (the Goss Committee) have b attending hearings in recent years.[43]

Among those who did show up at hearings in the 1975–90 study, the quality of the questioning of CIA witnesses varied greatly. Senator Barry Goldwater (R-Arizona) turned the questioning away from intelligence and back toward the imperfections of Congress, declaring that "this place has more leaks than the men's room at Anheuser-Busch." Some other members, though, engaged in a thorough probing and even harsh criticism of Agency operations. Yet, by and large, congressional questioning has leaned more toward the advocacy side of the ledger, except when scandals have been the focus; then a majority of members escalate their degree of questioning to difficult ("hardball") interrogations.

Former HPSCI member Tim Roemer (D-Indiana) frets about the level of commitment to intelligence accountability in today's Congress. "We've gotten away from the Church Committee emphasis on oversight," he suggests.[44] "There aren't even oversight subcommittees on HPSCI or SSCI anymore." Another expert offered a similarly pessimistic evaluation. Since the 9/11 attacks, the leading intelligence agencies "have managed to fend off the most important reforms advocated by the House and Senate intelligence committees," concluded retired Army Lt. Gen. William E. Odum, a former NSA director.[45] A *Washington Post* editorial observed that the "Congress has stood by in an alarming silence."[46]

Even director(s) of central intelligence (DCI) have been critical of oversight flaccidity. "Congress is informed to the degree that Congress wants to be informed," testified former DCI William E. Colby, pointing out that several lawmakers had expressed little interest in being briefed by the CIA.[47] Recalled another DCI, Adm. Stansfield Turner: "I believe the committees of Congress could have been more rigorous with me [during the Carter Administration] . . . it would be more helpful if you are probing and rigorous."[48] Were he alive, no doubt DCI Casey would disagree—with scatological emphasis. Several lawmakers also have quite a different view from Colby and Turner, preferring the role of advocate over adversary. For them, the president and the DCI know best in this sensitive domain; better to follow their lead than to second-guess and perhaps harm America's efforts against terrorism and other threats. Efficiency trumps accountability.

Executive Branch Cooperation

Vital for effective accountability, too, is the cooperation of the White House, the Justice Department, and the intelligence agencies in working with Congress. Lawmakers know about intelligence activities only to the extent that the president and the DCI allow them to know.[49] As Currie puts it, oversight works "only if there is honesty and completeness in what the members of the intelligence community tell their congressional overseers."[50] Or as a former HPSCI staff director has stressed, a "spirit of comity" between the branches is essential.[51] Yet this sine qua non is often missing. The Church Committee ran into one roadblock after another erected by the Ford Administration to slow the panel's progress. At one point, a Defense Department truck dumped enough documents on the committee's doorstep at the Senate Dirksen Office Building to keep it busy for weeks—without a single significant paper in the whole lot.

More recently, the Congress's Joint Committee complained in 2002 about stonewalling by the second Bush Administration. During that probe, DCI Tenet tried to put the Committee on the defensive with aggressive responses in public hearings to questions about 9/11. Allotted ten minutes to speak, he went on in a "somewhat defiant tone"[52] for fifty minutes, despite co-chair Bob Graham's request that he abbreviate his remarks. Tenet also refused to declassify information the Committee asked to make public; and, just before a scheduled hearing, the DCI withdrew intelligence witnesses the Committee had called to testify. "Witnesses are requested, refused, requested again, granted, and then—at the last minute—refused again," groused Richard C. Shelby (R-Alabama), a member and former chair of SSCI, on the Senate floor.[53]

When word leaked that the Committee's staff had cautioned members about the likelihood of elusive responses from a scheduled CIA witness, Tenet blasted the panel for prejudging the veracity of CIA officers. The staff, though, could hardly be blamed for reminding members that, in past inquiries, intelligence witnesses had not always been forthcoming; indeed, some had misled Congress, even under oath during the Iran-Contra investigation. Moreover, officers from the CIA had "flat lied" to SSCI in 1995–96, according to a senior staffer, when the Committee attempted to investigate the Agency's ties with a controversial military officer in Guatemala.[54]

With a growing unhappiness over Tenet's belligerent posture before the Joint Committee, Graham "toughened his stance toward the intelligence agencies when the Administration began to stonewall," recalls a staff aide on the panel.[55] When the DCI refused to provide SSCI with CIA documents on Iraq and then failed to appear at a closed Joint Committee hearing, Graham accused the CIA of "obstructionism" and said that this behavior was "unacceptable."[56] A former Hill staffer who follows intelligence closely concluded that the CIA had "stuck its fingers in the eye of the oversight committee, which—under Graham—was waking up very late to the fact that it is being rolled."[57] Despite the agitation of Graham and Shelby, most of their colleagues on the Committee adopted a more benign view of the intelligence community's behavior and preferred to concentration on the terrorist threat.

Reporting Requirements

Related to secrecy is the issue of what the intelligence agencies should tell the Congress, and when. Lawmakers now have, in theory at least, access to all information that the secret agencies provide to the executive branch, with the exception of the President's Daily Brief. In reality, Congress frequently has to throw a fit to make the agencies responsive to the requests of lawmakers, although certainly the degree of access accorded SSCI and HPSCI far outshines what overseers on Capitol Hill received prior to 1975.

As a means for guaranteeing a more systematic flow of information to overseers about intelligence operations, Congress has established formal reporting requirements—some in statutory form, others written or oral agreements between SSCI and HPSCI leaders and the DCI. Lawmakers and intelligence officers cleave into two camps on this subject. Some believe that reporting requirements, such as the prior-notice stipulation for covert actions (except in times of emergency), are indispensable points of leverage for keeping Congress up-to-date. Others balk at what they see as excessive involvement in the fine workings of intelligence by members of Congress, leading to an unwarranted surcharge on the time of intelligence officials who could otherwise be dealing with terrorism and other threats—"micro-management," in the favorite slight used by critics of any form of oversight they oppose (often all forms).

For proponents of robust accountability, reporting requirements are a must for keeping the oversight committees informed. Otherwise, intelligence managers might brief lawmakers merely when they were so inclined, or when forced to by scandal. Better to have important operations automatically brought to the attention of overseers, who might otherwise never know about them. Obviously, reporting requirements should not be excessive in number and should focus on important activities. The eighty-seven reports that were due on May 1, 2002, to HPSCI from the intelligence community seem excessive; but at the same time, a 92 percent delinquency rate in providing those reports reflects poorly on the community's attitude and efforts to communicate well with lawmakers.[58]

The purpose of oversight is not to stifle the vital work of the intelligence agencies, but rather to preserve civil liberties, maintain budget discipline, and bring to bear—as former SSCI member (and defense secretary) William S. Cohen has put it—"the combined wisdom of both branches."[59] Reporting requirements help ensure the sharing of information with Congress to allow this pooling of wisdom. If one is dead set against a role for Congress in intelligence matters, though, one is likely to endorse national security adviser Poindexter's characterization of lawmakers and their reporting requirements as nothing but an "outside interference."[60]

Co-optation

The danger always exists that lawmakers will "go native." Like ambassadors abroad accused of taking on the coloration of the country where they are in residence ("localitis") rather than the country they represent, HPSCI and SSCI members and staff can come to identify more with the intelligence agencies than with their roles as detached and objective supervisors. "They are awful nice to [overseers]," recalls former HPSCI chair Hamilton, "invite them to the CIA, give them a nice dinner, court them, seduce them."[61] Congressional members and staff who come out of the intelligence community might be especially prone to favoring their old agencies. As in the case of HPSCI chair Goss, a majority of staff members on the two Intelligence Committees have had earlier careers in one or another of the secret agencies. A remarkable number of SSCI and HPSCI staffers also take up (or resume) positions in the intelligence community after a tour of duty on the Hill, DCI Tenet most conspicuously.

For the most part, though, co-optation seems less of a problem than the pervasive philosophy among lawmakers (especially in the Republican Party)[62]—that Congress should pay deference to the executive branch on matters of national security. Occasionally, some staffers do exhibit an inability to criticize their former agencies; but, just as often, the Committees have benefited from having staffers who can tell whether their former colleagues in the intelligence community are playing it straight with Congress or spinning. Still, it would be prudent for the committees to recruit a higher percentage of non-intelligence professionals to provide ballast on their staffs, even though this would involve some training costs.

When SSCI and HPSCI were created, co-optation was very much on the minds of congressional leaders. Senators included a special provision in SSCI's founding language [Senate Resolution 400, Sec. 3 (b), 94th Cong., 1976] that required a rotation of members off the panel after eight-year periods of service—a provision later adopted in the House. This rule, so the thinking went, would help eliminate the development of cozy ties between lawmakers and intelligence officers. The growing consensus, however, is that rotation has actually harmed oversight because, just as members are becoming experienced and expert in arcane intelligence matters, they must depart the Committee.

Further, since one can never count on serving as committee chair in a rotation system (one may have to rotate off before arriving at the top), the incentives for working hard to learn the subject matter are diminished. Even those who do rise to hold the chair generally occupy that position for only a couple of years, although GOP leaders waived the eight-year limit to allow Porter Goss (R-Florida) a fourth term of leadership on HPSCI. Other observers insist, nonetheless, that it is valuable to have a large percentage of representatives flowing through the two Intelligence Committees, not only to guard against co-optation but also to disseminate throughout the legislative chambers expertise about this important and poorly understood aspect of American government. "It's better to have people with fresh eyes [on the Committees]," reasoned former Senator Fowler in favor of rotation (2003). On balance, though, having continuity and experience on the Committees seem to overshadow the benefits of rotation. The eight-year ceiling should be razed, or at least raised.

Conclusion

Intelligence oversight is a subject that is richly textured. It encompasses the supervision of a vast range of secret activities and thirteen major agencies. Oversight since 1975 has been relatively robust compared to earlier years, yet it falls far short of goals espoused by the Church Committee and other panels that have promulgated intelligence reform. Officials in the executive branch have been desultory in their oversight duties. And while lawmakers have responded responsibly to fire alarms—carrying out probes into domestic spying, improper covert actions, counterintelligence vulnerabilities, and major intelligence failures—they have done less well in the day-to-day police work that might uncover weaknesses in the first place and eliminate the need for hurry-up ex post facto firefighting.

There have been admirable efforts at oversight by individual members of both branches; and now and then the supervisory committees have worked well as a whole, as when SSCI and HPSCI, under chairmen David L. Boren (D-Oklahoma) and Larry Combest (R-Texas) labored aggressively to improve the performance of the intelligence agencies; or, more recently, inside the executive branch, when Brent Scowcroft, chairman of the President's Foreign Intelligence Advisory Board (PFIAB), insisted in 2002 on a hard-hitting review of intelligence organization (though his report has never been released to the public). Mostly, however, intelligence oversight since 1975 has been a story of discontinuous motivation, ad hoc responses to scandals, and reliance on the initiative of just a few members of Congress—mainly the occasional dedicated chair—to carry the burden. Absent still, despite the recommendation of one study after another, is a comprehensive approach to intelligence review that mobilizes most (if not all) members of SSCI and HPSCI, an approach that includes a systematic plan of police-patrolling without waiting for fire alarms. Responding after the fact to intelligence failures in this dangerous world is not good enough; overseers must try harder to prevent surprises like the 9/11 attacks from occurring in the first place.

What are the ingredients for better intelligence oversight? Of foremost importance is greater devotion to police-patrolling instead of waiting for fire alarms, which in the closed world of intelligence are unlikely to sound anyway until a major scandal or disaster strikes. Further, lawmakers need to pay closer attention to an administration's threat-assessment decisions, its balance between human and technical collection, its data-mining capabilities, the perspicacity of its analytic reports (with more external critiques by academicians—so-called A-team, B-team drills), charges of politicization, and efforts to achieve institutional and computer jointness to enhance all-source fusion.

Truly meaningful oversight would also more closely scrutinize covert action, especially with respect to the beguiling assassination option and efforts by the Department of Defense to develop its own capabilities in this area. One would expect to see, too, a renewed focus on counterintelligence: appraising the merits of an MI5-like unit in the United States; reviewing barriers to another Ames, Hanssen, or Walker; and building protections against hostile electronic penetrations of the new computer integration. Among other issues lawmakers need to examine more closely are the merits of greater authority for the DCI, to overcome the powerful centrifugal forces in the community. On the civil liberties side, overseers must also revisit the deeply flawed Patriot Act, the procedures of the Foreign Intelligence Surveillance Act (FISA) Court, and the rights of Muslim Americans.

Effective oversight depends as well on the development of a more systematic, comprehensive five-year plan for oversight, to include the welding together of existing intelligence laws into an Intelligence Charter comparable to the National Security Act of 1947, along with clear annual statements about the expectations of lawmakers regarding each of the intelligence missions. Better incentives must be created to encourage the involvement of officials in oversight, such as public praise by the White House and congressional leaders, as well as the granting of key committee assignments on Capitol Hill for lawmakers who have demonstrated skill and devotion to oversight. It would be useful, further, to establish more regular meetings between rank-and-file overseers and the DCI.

Sensible oversight would rely on fewer reporting requirements, but serious penalties for bureaucrats who fail to honor reasonable deadlines. Moreover, congressional jurisdictional lines for oversight need to be restructured, so that SSCI and HPSCI are given more authority over the full intelligence community, in place of the tangled strands that currently exist with the Armed Services, Judiciary, and Homeland Security Committees. Vital, too, are measures to make the government less secretive, including more SSCI and HPSCI opening hearings, more online reports about the activities of the oversight committees, and fewer classification actions by the executive branch. The two oversight committees should return to the use of bipartisan staff in the Congress and pursue the recruitment of more legislative staffers with backgrounds outside the intelligence community. Finally, PFIAB and IOB should recruit individuals better prepared and motivated to engage in a meaningful and continuous review of intelligence programs.

Despite its flaws and a tendency toward too much advocacy and too little criticism, the American system of intelligence oversight is robust compared to other nations. It represents a dramatic improvement over the relative absence of meaningful accountability in the United States before the intelligence investigations of 1975 and the establishment of Senate and House Intelligence Committees. These committees are independent from the executive branch and have a capacity to actively probe intelligence programs, including the power to subpoena any information they seek (although from time to time the executive has fought this privilege and the committees have often opted to negotiate a compromise, rather than seek legal redress). A number of laws allow the committees access to information about intelligence activities before they are implemented, not just after something goes wrong. The committees also have sizable staffs with extensive intelligence expertise. The membership of the committees reflects the spectrum of Republican and Democratic party politics and, even though partisan squabbling has increased on Capitol Hill in recent years, the committees have proven themselves reliable keepers of the nation's highest secrets.

Nevertheless, further reforms are in order to improve intelligence supervision. The time has never been more propitious for reform. Enormous incentives exist: the prevention of another 9/11 attack and better monitoring of WMD proliferation. If Congress and the executive branch will take the time to address these oversight deficiencies, James Madison will have his three cheers.

Notes

1. Senator Bob Graham (D-Florida) in "The Lehrer News Hour," Public Broadcasting System (PBS) Television, USA, October 17, 2002.

2. Loch K. Johnson, "Inside the Aspin-Brown Commission on Intelligence," Paper, Annual Meeting, American Political Science Association, Boston (September 1, 2002).

3. Lee H. Hamilton and Jordan Tamam, *A Creative Tension: The Foreign Policy Roles of the President and Congress* (Washington, D.C.: Woodrow Wilson Center Press, 2002): 56.

4. Wyche Fowler, interview with author (Washington, D.C.: May 9, 2003).

5. Joel D. Aberbach, *Keeping a Watchful Eye: The Politics of Congressional Oversight* (Washington, D.C.: Brookings Institution): 2.

6. Mathew D. McCubbins and Thomas Schwartz, "Congressional Oversight Overlooked: Police Patrols and Fire Alarms," *American Journal of Political Science* 28 (February 1984): 166.

7. Ibid.

8. Morris S. Ogul and Bert A. Rockman, "Overseeing Oversight: New Departures and Old Problems," *Legislative Studies Quarterly* 15 (February 1990): 14.

9. Joel D. Aberbach, *Keeping a Watchful Eye: The Politics of Congressional Oversight* (Washington, D.C.: Brookings Institution, 1990), 98.

10. Ibid., 193.

11. Central Intelligence Agency, *Fact Book on Intelligence* (Office of Public Affairs, April 1983): 16.

12. Jeffrey Goldberg, "The Unknown," *The New Yorker* (February 10, 2003): 45.

13. U.S. Congress, *Hearings* (Joint Committee on Intelligence, 103d. Cong., 2d sess. 2002).

14. John Millis [HPSCI staff director]. Speech, Central Intelligence Retiree's Association, Langley, Virginia (October 5, 1998).

15. Ronald Kessler, *The Bureau: The Secret History of the FBI* (New York: St. Martin"s, 2002): 447.

16. Loch K. Johnson, author's interview with senior staffer (Washington, D.C., February 6, 2003).

17. Loch K. Johnson, "Inside the Aspin-Brown Commission on Intelligence," Paper, Annual Meeting, American Political Science Association, Boston (September 1, 2002).

18. George J. Tenet, Testimony, Joint Committee on Intelligence (October 16) and "Written Statement for the Record" (October 17, 2002): 10.

19. e.g., Loch K. Johnson, *Bombs, Bugs, Drugs, and Thugs: Intelligence and America's Quest for Security* (New York: New York University Press, 2000); "The CIA's Weakest Link," *Washington Monthly* 33 (July/August 2001): 9–14.

20. Victor Marchetti and John D. Marks, *The CIA and the Cult of Intelligence* (New York: Knopf, 1974), 96.

21. U.S. Senate. *Final Report.* Select Committee to Study Governmental Operations with Respect to Intelligence Activities (the Church Committee), 94th Cong., 2d Sess., Rept. 94–755 (May, 1976).

22. e.g., Harry Howe Ransom, "The Politicization of Intelligence," in *Intelligence and Intelligence Policy in a Democratic Society,* ed. Stephen J. Cimbala (Dobbs Ferry, New York: Transnational Press, 1987): 25–46; Thomas Powers, "The Trouble with the CIA," *The New York Review of Books,* January 17, 2002.

23. Paul, Lashmar and Raymond Whitaker, "MI6 and CIA: The New Enemy Within," *The Independent on Sunday* (U.K.), February 9, 2003, A1.

24. Seymour Hersh, interviewed by television host Bill Moyers, "NOW" (February 21, 2003).

25. Pub. L. No. 93–559; 32, 88 Stat. 1804.

26. Pub. L. No. 96–450; 407(b), 94 Stat. 1981.

27. Pub. L. No. 102–88, 105 Stat. 441.

28. e.g., Department of Defense Appropriations Act 1985, Pub. L. No. 98–473, 98 Stat. 1935 (1984).

29. Frederick M. Kaiser, "Impact and Implications of the Iran-Contra Affair on Congressional Oversight of Covert Action," *International Journal of Intelligence and Counterintelligence* 7 (Summer 1994): 205–34; James Currie, "Iran-Contra and Congressional Oversight of the CIA," *International Journal of Intelligence and Counterintelligence* 11 (Summer 1998): 185–210.

30. Loch K. Johnson, "On Drawing a Bright Line for Covert Operations," *American Journal of International Law* 86 (April 1992): 284–309; Gregory F. Treverton, *Covert Action: The Limits of Intervention in the Postwar World* (New York: Basic Books, 1987).

31. Patrick E. Tyler, "Spy Wars Begin at Home," *New York Times,* November 3, 2002,

E3; CNN.com, "Pentagon Takes Quiet Aim at Terror," AP Report, November 13, 2002; Priest, *The Mission* (New York: Norton, 2003).

32. Quoted by Dana Priest, "CIA Killed U.S. Citizen in Yemen Missile Strike," *Washington Post*, November 8, 2002b, 1A.

33. James Risen and David Johnston, "Bush Has Widened Authority of C.I.A. to Kill Terrorists," *New York Times*, December 15, 2002, 1A.

34. Frank Church, "Covert Action: Swampland of American Foreign Policy," *Bulletin of the Atomic Scientist* 32 (February 1976): 7–11; Frank Church, "Do We Still Plot Murders?" *Los Angeles Times*, June 14, 1983, 5.

35. Loch K. Johnson, "Congressional Supervision of America's Secret Agencies: The Experience and Legacy of the Church Committee," *Public Administration Review* 64 (January–February 2004): 3–26.

36. Dana Priest, "CIA Is Expanding Domestic Operations," *Washington Post*, October 22, 2002a, A1.

37. Patrick Cohen, "9/11 Law Means More Snooping?" *New York Times*, September 7, 2003, A15; Harry F. Tepker, "The USA PATRIOT Act," *Extensions*, A Journal of the Carl Albert Center, University of Oklahoma (Fall 2002): 13.

38. George Lardner Jr., "Brookings Scholar Is Detained by INS," *Washington Post*, January 30, 2003, A1.

39. Anthony Lewis, "Marbury v. Madison v. Ashcroft," *New York Times*, February 24, 2003, A21; Michael Ignatieff, "The Burden," *New York Times Magazine*, January 5, 2003, 24ff.

40. Loch K. Johnson, author's interview with senior staffer (Washington, D.C.: February 4, 2003).

41. Herbert E. Meyer, "A Memo to the 9/11 Commission," *National Review*, January 6, 2003, online edition at www.nationalreview.com.

42. Loch K. Johnson, "Playing Ball with the CIA: Congress Supervises Strategic Intelligence," in *Congress, the Executive, and the Making of American Foreign Policy*, ed. Paul E. Peterson (Norman: University of Oklahoma Press, 1994): 56.

43. Timothy R. Sample [HPSCI staff director], author's interview (Washington, D.C.: January 29, 2003).

44. Tim Roemer, author's interview (Washington, D.C.: February 5, 2003).

45. Jim McGee, "Spies," *CQ Homeland Security* (Washington, D.C.: Congressional Quarterly, 2003): 3

46. Cited by Steven Aftergood, "Silence on the Hill," *Secrecy News* (Federation of American Scientists Project on Government Secrecy 2004, January 5, 2004): 2.

47. U.S. House, *Hearings on Congressional Oversight of Covert Activities* (Permanent Select Committee on Intelligence, 98th Cong., 2d. sess., September 20, 1983): 29.

48. U.S. House, *Hearings on H.R. 1013, H.R. 1317, and Other Proposals Which Address the Issue of Affording Prior Notice of Covert Actions in the Congress* (Permanent Select Committee on Intelligence, April–June, 1987): 66.

49. William H. Jackson Jr., "Congressional Oversight of Intelligence: Search for a Framework," *Intelligence and National Security* 5 (July 1990): 115; L. Britt Snider, *Sharing Secrets with Lawmakers: Congress as a User of Intelligence* (Washington, D.C.: Center for the Study of Intelligence, Central Intelligence Agency, 1997).

50. James Currie, "Iran-Contra and Congressional Oversight of the CIA," *International Journal of Intelligence and Counterintelligence* 11 (Summer 1998): 203.

51. Thomas K. Latimer, "U.S. Intelligence and the Congress," *Strategic Review* (Summer 1979): 48.

52. Ken Guggenheim, "Tenet Defends CIA's Pre-9/11 Efforts," *Washington Post*, October 17, 2002, A1.

53. Senator Richard C. Shelby, "Remarks," *Congressional Record* (September 24, 2002).

54. Loch K. Johnson, author's interview with senior staffer (Washington, D.C.: February 6, 2003).

55. Loch K. Johnson, author's interview, SSCI senior staffer (Washington, D.C.: December 18, 2002).

56. Neil A. Lewis, "Senator Insists C.I.A. Is Harboring Iraq Reports," *New York Times*, October 4, 2002, A12.

57. Johnson, e-mail communication to the author (October 4, 2002).

58. Walter Pincus, "Overdue Intelligence Reports," *Washington Post*, December 1, 2002, A1.

59. William S. Cohen, "Congressional Oversight of Covert Actions," *International Journal of Intelligence and Counterintelligence* 2 (Summer 1988): 162.

60. U.S. Congress, Senate Select Committee on Secret Military Assistance to Iran and the Nicaraguan Opposition and House Select Committee to Investigate Covert Arms Transactions with Iran (the Inouye–Hamilton Committee), (*Hearings*, Vol. 8, 100 Cong., 1st Sess., 1987): 159.

61. Russ Baker, "Chill on the Hill," *Nation*, October 14, 2002, 13.

62. Loch K. Johnson, "Playing Ball with the CIA: Congress Supervises Strategic Intelligence," in *Congress, the Executive, and the Making of American Foreign Policy*, ed. Paul E. Peterson (Norman: University of Oklahoma Press, 1994), 49–73.

5

Accountability of Security and Intelligence in the United Kingdom

Ian Leigh

The United Kingdom (UK) lacks a written constitution; thus, there is no foundational document allocating responsibility for security and intelligence matters. Government is carried out in the name of "the Crown" (i.e., the Queen) although in practice nearly all legal powers conferred on the Crown, whether by legislation or by the prerogative, are exercised by government ministers. Responsibility for intelligence and security, together with the closely related areas of defense and foreign relations, has until recently rested upon the prerogative—that is, the residual powers of the Crown recognized at common law. These powers are broad in nature and have adapted continuously since the medieval period. The courts have traditionally been highly deferential to national security claims, whether founded on the prerogative or on statutory powers and exceptions.

Against this time scale and background the legislation for intelligence and security matters is very recent—the relevant statutes are the Security Service Act 1989 (covering the Security Service, MI5) and the Intelligence Services Act (ISA) 1994 (covering the Secret Intelligence Service [SIS, or MI6] and Government Communications Headquarters, GCHQ). Other parts of the intelligence machinery such as Defense Intelligence and the Joint Intelligence Committee remain based on the prerogative—they have been established and can be reformed without reference to Parliament.

Until 1989 the only officially published details of the work of the security and intelligence agencies was the administrative charter governing the Security Service's work,[1] the Maxwell-Fyfe Directive—named after the home secretary who issued it in 1952. This brief document emphasized the role of the Service in the "Defense of the Realm" and its duty to behave non-politically. The Service was, nevertheless, responsible to the home secretary, and its director-general had a right of access to the prime minister. The Security Service Act 1989 made no change to these constitutional arrangements—the Service was accountable only to ministers and not to Parliament. However, the Act did provide an explicit statutory basis for the Service's work. This satisfied the objection that it was unable to conduct surveillance or gather personal information without violating human rights.

It became apparent that the UK would be found to be in breach of the European Convention on Human Rights (ECHR) unless legislation was introduced. Although the ECHR permits restriction of rights such as respect for private life (Article 8 of the Convention) where necessary in a democratic society in the interests of (inter alia) national security, this is with the important precondition that the restrictions must be authorized by law.[2] The prerogative basis of the Maxwell-Fyfe Directive was insufficient for this purpose, because it could be changed without reference to Parliament and established no formal legal limits or controls. Moreover, the Convention system required there to be some legal mechanisms, even if these were not courts proper, for dealing with complaints about abuses and violation of rights. The 1989 Act introduced a tribunal and a commissioner, each with limited powers and jurisdiction—a model followed in the 1994 Act and later modifications under the Regulation of Investigatory Powers Act 2000. The government estimated—correctly as it turned out in later challenges—that these mechanisms would satisfy the Convention system. The mere passing of the 1989 Act, although it came after the events in question, was treated as sufficient reason by the Convention organs to take no further action in two cases brought involving alleged surveillance and recording of personal details by the Security Service.[3]

GCHQ—the signals intelligence agency—came to public attention in the mid-1980s, largely because of a protracted labor dispute[4] and disclosures about wartime code-breaking, but it lacked a statutory remit until 1994. The Secret Intelligence Service (SIS or MI6) was not even officially acknowledged to exist until 1992. Both these agencies were created[5] and operated under the royal prerogative. The Intelligence Services Act 1994 provided a statutory charter for them. Unlike the previous legislation, this act acknowledged the concerns over lack of parliamentary oversight by also creating for all three agencies a statutory committee of parliamentarians, drawn from both houses of Parliament (the Intelligence and Security Committee).

The Agencies' Work

The Security Service's statutory aims (section 1 of the 1989 act) are the protection of national security, including (but not limited to) protection against threats from espionage, terrorism, and sabotage, and from the activities of agents of foreign powers. There is also a reference to a controversial area of work, although one that is currently dormant—"counter-subversion," concerning "actions intended to overthrow or undermine parliamentary democracy by political, industrial or violent means." In addition, the Service has a function to safeguard the economic well-being of the UK from external threats and (under the Security Service Act 1996) to assist in the prevention or detection of serious crime—a matter for which the police are primarily responsible.

These provide a broad base for the collection, storing, analysis, and dissemination of information. Section 2(2) of the 1989 act requires the director-general to ensure that there are arrangements limiting the collection of information to that necessary for the proper discharge of the Service's role or for preventing or detecting serious crime. This may be some safeguard to the over-wide collection of personal information. Nevertheless, thousands of files are held on individuals.[6] Under s.2(3) (unpublished), arrangements are to ensure that such information is not disclosed by the Service for employment purposes except in accordance with ministerial provisions. The Service may also conduct surveillance within the limits imposed by the Regulation of Investigatory Powers Act 2000. Other executive functions, such as arrest, legally sanctioned detention and questioning of suspects (even in cases of terrorism or espionage), and prosecution are in the hands of the police and the Crown Prosecution Service.

The Security Service is responsible to the home secretary, although operational control is in the hands of the director-general. In view of the politically sensitive nature of its role in the domestic arena, there are two important statutory restrictions that limit its work.[7] The first limits collection of information to what is "necessary for the proper discharge of its functions" and likewise disclosure. The second requires that: "the Service does not take any action to further the interests of any political party."

According to an official publication the main task of the Secret Intelligence Service:

> is the production of secret intelligence on issues concerning Britain's vital interests in the fields of security, defense, foreign and economic policies in accordance with requirements established by the Joint Intelligence Committee and approved by Ministers. SIS uses human and technical sources to meet these requirements, as well as liaison with a wide range of foreign intelligence and security services.[8]

Under the Intelligence Services Act (ISA) 1994 s. 1(1) its functions are: "(a) to obtain and provide information relating to the actions or intentions of persons outside the British Islands; and (b) to perform other tasks relating to the actions or intentions of such persons." However, the ISA limits the functions of the SIS in a way that reinforces ministerial control of the Service:

The functions . . . shall be exercisable only—
  (a) in the interests of national security, with particular reference to the defense
       and foreign policies of Her Majesty's Government in the United Kingdom;
       or
  (b) in the interests of the economic well-being of the United Kingdom; or
  (c) in support of the prevention or detection of serious crime.[9]

GCHQ's function is described in somewhat opaque statutory language: "to monitor or interfere with electromagnetic, acoustic and other emissions and any equipment producing such emissions and to obtain and provide information derived from or related to such emissions or equipment and from encrypted material."[10]

This provision gives it a brief to conduct all types of signals interception (and disruption) and decryption. There is also a more defensive function of providing technical advice on communications and information technology security to government departments and the armed forces.[11] These functions are exercisable "in the interests of national security, with particular reference to the defense and foreign policies of Her Majesty's Government in the United Kingdom."[12] The wording is a reference to ministerial control: signals intelligence priorities are determined through a regular cycle of "tasking," related to the foreign policy and defense objectives of the government of the day, in the ministerial-approved annual submission "United Kingdom's National Requirements for Secret Intelligence." A significant omission is the failure of the 1994 legislation to detail the arrangements for international cooperation (especially with the United States' National Security Agency, the NSA) which is known to affect much of GCHQ's work.[13]

In each case SIS and GCHQ come under the authority of the secretary of state for foreign and commonwealth affairs. Operational control is in the hands of the chief and director, respectively, who are appointed by the minister.[14] Each is required to give an annual report to the prime minister and the secretary of state. There are provisions requiring political neutrality comparable to those applicable to the Security Service.

The agencies are also overseen by judicial commissioners, who were appointed initially under the 1989 and 1994 Acts but now work within the Regulation of Investigatory Powers Act 2000 (RIPA). The position of intelligence services commissioner is currently held by Lord Justice Simon Brown. He is responsible for reviewing and reporting upon the issue and authorization, by the relevant minister, of warrants for operations by the agencies.[15] The interception commissioner (s.57 RIPA), who is currently Sir Swinton Thomas, reviews the issue and authorization of warrants to intercept mail and telecommunications by the intelligence and security agencies and law enforcement organizations. There is also a tribunal, the Investigatory Powers Tribunal, established to investigate public complaints against the agencies or about interception.[16] The commissioners report annually to the prime minister on their work, and their reports are in turn laid before Parliament. It is likely, having regard to a Strasbourg decision under previous legislation, that these review and complaints procedures satisfy the European Convention on Human Rights.[17]

The funding for all three agencies falls under the Single Intelligence Account, by which Parliament approves their expenditure. In 2002–3 this was £893m. The security and intelligence coordinator is the relevant accounting officer. Audit is handled by a combination of the comptroller and auditor-general (who has a statutory right to disclosure of details from the agencies) and the Intelligence and Security Committee (the remit of which extends to expenditure).

Three parts of the intelligence structure are outside the statutory framework—the Defense Intelligence Staff (DIS), the Joint Intelligence Committee (JIC), and the Intelligence Assessments Staff.[18] The role of the first two especially has come under close scrutiny as a result of events surrounding the use of intelligence in the public justification of the UK's involvement in the war in Iraq.[19] The DIS is part of the Ministry of Defence and supports the armed forces by analyzing information, from open and covert sources, and providing assessments both for them and for the Joint Intelligence Committee. The head, the chief of defence intelligence (who reports to the minister of defence) is also responsible for coordination of intelligence throughout the armed forces. The Joint Intelligence Committee sits at the hub of the intelligence machine, in the Cabinet Office, formally connecting it with government. It is responsible for tasking the agencies (especially SIS and GCHQ) and for providing intelligence assessments, based on the agencies' output, which are circulated within government, including the relevant ministers.[20] The JIC membership meets weekly and includes not only the heads of the security and intelligence agencies, but also senior officials from the Cabinet Office (the JIC chairman, chief of the assessments staff, security and intelligence coordinator, and the head of the overseas and defense secretariat), the Foreign Office, the Ministry of Defence, the Home Office, the Department of Trade and Industry, and the Treasury.

The chairman of the JIC is a senior Cabinet Office official, who has direct access to the prime minister. This arrangement was introduced following the Falklands War, where intelligence assessment failures within the Foreign Office were credited with the failure to predict Argentinean intentions. There is also within the Cabinet Office a security and intelligence coordinator, whose job is to advise the secretary of the cabinet on the funding needs of the agencies and their effective functioning.

Ministerial Responsibility for Intelligence

The legislation governing the intelligence and security services deals with ministerial responsibility for the agencies. Broad responsibility for these matters remains with the prime minister as head of the government. This is reflected in provisions that are unique in UK legislation, giving the heads of the agencies a right of direct access to the prime minister.[21] This right reflects the fact that the agencies are not simply conventional departments of state responsible to a secretary of state (minister). Although the Acts also refer to responsibility to a departmental minister—in the case of the security service to the home secretary, and in the cases of the SIS and GCHQ to the foreign secretary—the prime minister has traditionally assumed overall control and acted as the government mouthpiece on intelligence matters.

Relations between the agencies and the responsible ministers are quite different from the conventional one between a minister and his or her department. The agency heads—the director-general of the Security Service, the chief of the SIS, and the director of GCHQ—are named in law as having day-to-day responsibility. This is contrary to the prevailing constitutional tradition in Britain whereby ministers are legally responsible and officials are anonymous and, legally speaking, invisible. The rationale is undoubtedly to provide a safeguard of the services' neutrality in party political terms. Indeed, political neutrality is explicitly addressed by provisions that require the heads of all three agencies to ensure that the services do not take any steps to further the interests of any UK political party.[22]

Moreover, there was formerly an important non-statutory convention that reinforced the principle: the secretary of state would receive advice from the head of the agency but would not see the intelligence on which it was based. As we shall see, there are good reasons, based on events surrounding the second Persian Gulf War, to question the extent to which these principles still hold true.

In its annual reports the Intelligence and Security Committee has expressed a concern that ministers should be collectively more directly involved in overseeing decisions of the agencies. In theory the Ministerial Committee on Intelligence Services looks at the policy of the agencies and approves the annual budgets and National Intelligence Requirements under the prime minister's chairmanship.[23] In practice, the Ministerial Committee seems to be if not moribund at least in hibernation (it did not meet between 1995 and 2000), although the same group of ministers did meet regularly with security officials post–September 11.[24] Although the inactivity of the Ministerial Committee may give the picture of agencies responsible to the relevant departmental minister but otherwise left largely to their own devices, this would be misleading in view of the heightened importance of intelligence post–9/11. It may be a case, rather, that the formal structure has been overtaken by events. Nevertheless, the Committee's report for 2002–3 expressed concern that the relevant ministers did not see all JIC assessments as a matter of routine.

Some actions involving the services require explicit ministerial approval by the responsible secretary of state. Traditionally, telephone tapping or mail opening (which may also be undertaken by the police) has fallen into this category: the secretary of state is responsible for authorizing it under warrant.[25]

These are instances in which ministers are personally involved in authorizing day-to-day operations by the agencies and, if they are diligent, will require that they be shown convincing and detailed supporting evidence before they do so. Apart from that, the practice of the Security Service is to show to an incoming home secretary, for approval, a number of the non-statutory policy documents that the Service has adopted to govern its work; for example, concerning use of legally privileged information. Another instance where ministers are given specific powers concerning individuals is the field of detention of terrorist suspects and the deportation of foreign nationals on grounds of national security.[26] Here too, since the minister is legally responsible for signing the relevant order, a detailed case will be made by the Security Service to justify using the powers.

The circumstances surrounding the use of these powers, and, indeed, current events, necessarily mean that there is a continuing dialogue between officials and the home secretary over policy matters. To take a contemporary example, it is unthinkable that the Security Service would have involved itself in surveillance of Islamic mosques known to be recruiting grounds for al Qaeda without discussing the potential implications for community relations with the home secretary.

The changed climate after September 11, 2001, may also have affected the way that the agencies relate to other ministers and government departments. There is evidence that intelligence has become more visibly important to the work of other departments concerned, for instance, with protection from attacks to transport and other vital infrastructure. Consequently, direct briefing from the Security Service to these ministers has become commonplace—a recent development and a tangible effect of the "war on terror" on the government machine.

A similar effect is the growing politicization of intelligence material.[27] We are moving here into the controversial and difficult territory of the events surrounding the 2003 war with Iraq. The government chose, in the attempt to enlist public and political support for its policy, to release, in September 2002 and February 2003, two dossiers of intelligence-related material concerning the attempts of the Iraqi regime to acquire and develop "weapons of mass destruction" (WMD). Allegations that intelligence was fabricated or knowingly misstated for political ends in the build-up to the war have been refuted following official reports by the Intelligence and Security Committee (ISC) and by Lord Hutton. They have, however, found other unsatisfactory features concerning the process.

First, large parts of the February 2003 "dossier" (the so-called dodgy dossier) were found to have been plagiarized from a Ph.D. thesis written eleven years earlier. The ISC commented that it supported "the responsible use of intelligence and material collected by the Agencies to inform the public on matters such as these" but that it was "imperative that the Agencies are consulted before any of their material is published" and that this process was not fully followed with the February 2003 dossier.[28] A second concern was the misleading emphasis placed upon the claim contained in the September 2002 dossier that weapons of mass destruction could be deployed by Iraq within forty-five minutes. The ISC found this should have been explained in more qualified terms.[29] Most telling of all, however, was Lord Hutton's conclusion that the JIC chairman and staff may have been indirectly (or, as he put it, "subconsciously") influenced to make statements that were more definitive than was usual in intelligence assessments in compiling the dossiers with a view to publication.[30] While acquitting ministers of duplicity, or officials of malpractice, this nevertheless clearly highlights the dangers of politicization.

A further report by a Committee of Privy Counsellors chaired by the former cabinet secretary, Lord Butler, largely affirmed these points about the public use of intelligence. Controversially the use by ministers of intelligence was omitted from the committee's terms of reference, leading to a boycott by the main opposition parties. Nevertheless, the report emphasized the need for the chairman of the JIC to be above ministerial pressure and criticized the informal style of policy making on Iraq by the ministers in the Blair government.[31]

Parliamentary Accountability

Britain was relatively late in moving to a system including parliamentary oversight, largely because of government objections about the nature of ministerial responsibility at Westminster. According to the official argument at the time of the 1989 Act, insuperable difficulties lay in the way of true answerability of ministers to Parliament for how they exercised their control over the agencies: the detail of how accountability worked could not (it was said) be revealed without compromising necessary secrets. Parliament and the public therefore lay outside the ring of secrecy and had no alternative but to put their trust in ministers, who were within it.

Scrutiny within existing parliamentary mechanisms had long been thwarted: a convention had grown up of refusing to answer parliamentary questions from MPs on matters concerned with the agencies or touching on national security;[32] nondisclosure of the money spent by the services had been condoned through the "secret vote," where a global figure, without explanation or breakdown of the details, was approved annually;[33] and, despite occasional protests,[34] the work of the agencies had received no attention from parliamentary select committees.

It was notable, however, that Westminster-style ministerial responsibility had not prevented reform in Canada and Australia. In Canada's case the Canadian Security Intelligence Service Act of 1984 created a non–parliamentary committee (the Security Intelligence Review Committee) with a range of oversight and complaints functions, alongside an inspector-general who reported to ministers on the performance of CSIS.[35] In Australia a statutory parliamentary committee was established with oversight of ASIO (the security service),[36] although other agencies (ASIS, the intelligence agency, and DSD, the signals intelligence agency) remained outside this scheme until recent reforms.[37]

Eventually the obstacles were overcome in the UK also. In 1994 the Major government acceded to the call for scrutiny by a committee representing a cross-section of parliamentary opinion. The Intelligence and Security Committee, established under the 1994 Act, comprises nine members drawn from both the House of Commons and the House of Lords, whose task is to examine the expenditure, policy, and administration of all three security and intelligence services.

The Constitutional and Legal Basis of the Committee

The Intelligence and Security Committee is constitutionally unique. Parliamentary select committees are invariably established on a non-statutory basis (under the Standing Orders of Parliament), with a membership approved by Parliament itself, and report to Parliament. On all three points this committee is different. The Intelligence and Security Committee is a statutory committee. Its members are appointed from both houses of Parliament (the House of Commons and the House of Lords) by the prime minister after consultation with the Leader of the Opposition.[38] The Committee also reports to the prime minister, although, subject to editing,[39] its reports are subsequently laid in Parliament.

In all these respects the Committee is designedly not a parliamentary select committee. These differences may amount to little in practice, but they are intended to underline and reinforce the longstanding argument by governments of all political persuasions that the security and intelligence agencies are accountable to ministers and not to Parliament directly.

However, in some other practical respects the Committee does function like a select committee: members are nominated by the party whips, despite the formal legal requirement, and membership is in practice in proportion to the strength of the three main political parties in the House of Commons, although this is not a legal requirement.

The committee's role is "to examine the expenditure, administration and policy" of the three services.[40] These terms have been carefully chosen to echo the terms of reference of a departmental select committee, but they also preserve an exclusion zone around security and intelligence operations.

The agency heads may refuse to disclose what is described as "sensitive information."[41] This is defined in the Act to include information that might lead to the identification of sources, other forms of assistance given to the agencies, or operational methods. A second category of "sensitive information" concerns past, present, or future specific operations. A third category is information provided by a foreign government that does not consent to its disclosure. Within these categories refusal is discretionary. The head of one of the three agencies may disclose the information if satisfied that is safe to do so.[42] Moreover, the responsible minister may order disclosure to the Committee in the public interest notwithstanding,[43] thus overruling the agency head concerned. From a certain point of view, however, the status of the committee's requests for information is enhanced, since the demands that it makes have statutory backing, unlike those of a conventional parliamentary select committee.

Some shortcomings in the Committee's brief can be noted. Unlike the United States, there is no tradition in the United Kingdom of confirmation by the legislature of the appointment of key officials. The executive alone is responsible. Consequently, the appointments of heads of the agencies are made by ministers (presumably advised by the head of the civil service, the cabinet secretary) but without reference to the Committee's members. There are limits also to the committee's information-gathering powers that are not obvious at a first glance at the Act. It may request "information." It does not, however, have power to demand particular documents, even those referring to the policy, administration, or expenditure of the agencies. In practice, though, the committee normally works by receiving briefing documents from the agencies, setting out policy. There is no statutory right to see officials at a level lower than the director or director-general (in practice, however, members routinely meet officers at all levels during site inspections). Members of the Committee are not security vetted, but then neither are MPs or ministers within the UK constitutional arrangements.

The Committee is required by law to produce at minimum an annual report. This is delivered to the prime minister and thereafter published, with any deletions agreed upon on security grounds.[44] The prime minister has several levers in this process—the timing of publication is effectively with him rather than the Committee. Consequently, the impact can be diluted by publishing the government's response at the same time or by publishing a report when public attention is distracted elsewhere. Significantly, the Committee has complained of unnecessary delay in publishing some of its findings.[45] In the event of unresolved disagreement between the Committee and the prime minister over material to be deleted from the report, the latter can insist, although to do so would probably be counterproductive if it led to public dissent from the members of the Committee. In practice the Committee's annual published reports contain many deleted passages (indicated by stars) where excisions have been made.

One area in which the Committee and the government have had a long-running disagreement concerns publication of the budgets for the individual agencies, rather that a total "single intelligence vote." The Committee has consistently argued that publication of the information is not sensitive, at least provided it is not done every year. The Committee has gone so far as to record in its report the agreement of the agency heads to publication.[46] It is plain, however, that the government chose to remove the relevant figures from the published report. After protest at the government's continued intransigence,[47] the Committee seems to have given up on the issue.

Overall, compared to the published reports of the Security Intelligence Review Committee in Canada, the ISC's reports are much less informative. Readers are sometimes left with a reassuring feeling that the Committee has been active but without its full findings being published. This, however, is the recurrent difficulty of oversight—how to reconcile effectiveness with giving a public account.

The Committee in Operation

Although the legislation was passed in 1994 the Committee did not come into operation until the following year, and it had little opportunity to embark on a major substantive program of work before the 1997 election.[48] The bulk of the committee's work to date took place during the 1997–2001 Parliament. This period also represented an important change since, unlike the previous administration, from the start of the new Blair government ministers were accustomed to sharing oversight of the services with the newly established Committee.

The membership of the Committee remained nearly constant for the duration of the 1997–2001 Parliament and was an intriguing mixture of parliamentarians. Eight of the nine members were from the House of Commons—the sole peer was a former labor law officer, Lord Archer. The Committee was chaired by an experienced Conservative member of Parliament, Tom King, who had substantial security and defense experience from spells spent as secretary of state for Northern Ireland and secretary of state for defence. Another member of the Committee, also Conservative, Michael Mates, MP, had a military background and had been a junior defense minister. Equally, though, the Committee included one Labour MP, Dale Campbell-Savours, who had taken a close interest in security matters as an outsider and had been a prominent critic of the lack of accountability of the services (and of the new legislative arrangements). Also highly experienced was Alan Beith, MP, the former deputy leader of the Liberal Democrats—the political party that had championed parliamentary accountability for security and intelligence agencies earlier than any other. At the other end of the experience range was Yvette Cooper, a new Labour MP with no previous experience of government or parliamentary committees, and one of the youngest parliamentarians from the 1997 intake. She left the Committee during 1999–2000 on being promoted to ministerial office (ministers are debarred from membership of the Committee[49]). To all appearances the Committee had been constructed to work in a bipartisan fashion, in view of the fact that the previous chairman continued in office although he was a member of the parliamentary opposition following the May 1997 election. It was also representative of a range of different parliamentary interests, including those highly skeptical of the entire process.

The Committee was reconstituted after the 2001 election, due largely to individuals leaving Parliament, although four of the nine members from the previous Parliament remain. Tom King had retired and was replaced in the chair by Ann Taylor, a Labour MP who was a former chief whip (a senior government business manager in the House of Commons). Her nearest security-related experience was chairing a cabinet committee on drugs policy.

The Committee's working method was to begin by familiarizing itself with the agencies by meeting heads of the services and by reviewing agencies' premises. Officials seem to have been, if anything, keen to establish a new source of legitimacy for their work with a committee representative of Parliament, rather than just the government. The services themselves were in a transitional period following both the ending of the Cold War and also the transition to peace in Northern Ireland. In this context no doubt the Committee could be seen as a useful ally in battles within government over budget priorities. In any event good working relationships seem to have been established quickly.

From the start the Committee has been proactive. In an early report it warned that it expected to be "properly and promptly informed" by the agencies of their activities, rather than merely responding to requests for information.[50] (Recent evidence of this practice emerged when the Committee indicated that it had received regular briefings on WMD in Iraq before and during the 2003 war.[51]) It follows a published annual program of work, as well as considering topics that may emerge on ad hoc basis. It has tended to meet frequently (often weekly during the parliamentary session). Typically it interviews several dozen witnesses each year, and takes part in international liaison and exchanges, both by visiting oversight agencies abroad and receiving such visits (these have included many European and former Eastern bloc countries, the United States, and the other Commonwealth states). It also conducts about ten visits to agencies' premises each year (these have included periodically visiting the controversial NSA facility at Menwith Hill).

The Committee is supported by a clerk (whom it interviewed and appointed) and clerical assistance; neither was provided for in the 1994 Act but the government has recognized the need to make available the necessary funding. The Committee's staff are vetted and security cleared.

A key issue has been the acquisition by the Committee of an investigative capacity. It might be argued that, in view of the Committee's limited remit, investigation as such was unnecessary, since this would venture into operational matters. Nevertheless, the Committee argued that, compared to the oversight arrangement in other countries, it lacked direct ability to investigate the agencies' activities and that a power of independent verification would give added authority to its findings and so strengthen public confidence in the oversight system.[52] The government conceded the issue without making a formal change to the powers of the Committee.[53] The result was a compromise in that the Committee stopped short of calling for the creation of an independent statutory investigator, such as an inspector-general, but the government has agreed that the agencies would cooperate with an investigator who works for the Committee. The appointment is a part-time one. The incumbent is a retired deputy chief of defence intelligence.[54] Defense intelligence is not within the Committee's statutory remit and, thus, the Committee was able to appoint someone with intelligence expertise but without loyalty to one of the agencies overseen under the Act.

The investigator is "tasked" by the Committee as part of its annual program of work to investigate and report to it on certain topics. It is important to stress, however, that the investigator is not a substitute for an inspector-general. He or she has no statutory powers. The investigator allows the Committee to conduct the same type of investigation as previously, but without the members needing to immerse themselves in detail to an unnecessary degree. Material may also be excluded at the agencies' request from the investigator's report to the Committee. The Committee has argued that this facility encourages frankness on the part of the agencies.[55] However, it is curious in view of the fact that the Committee itself works within the ring of secrecy. In essence the arrangement allows the Committee to be satisfied that someone responsible to it can confirm the accuracy of information it has received without members seeing for themselves all the details. What is not provided for in this scheme, but is a feature of inspector-generals' powers elsewhere, is the ability to initiate audits to sample an agency's operational work.

It is clear that the Committee is also working well beyond its strict legal remit in terms of agencies overseen. The Committee has encountered no apparent opposition in investigating the work of the Joint Intelligence Committee and the Security and Intelligence Co-coordinator, parts of the intelligence machinery which, although closely linked to the agencies, are outside the statutory framework.[56] Similarly, it has taken evidence from a number of government departments that are in effect the security and intelligence agencies' "customers," that is, the users of intelligence produced by them.

A recent instructive example that shows the ability of the Committee to conduct an in-depth and independent investigation is the report on intelligence and threat warnings preceding the Bali bombing of October 12, 2002.[57] On the face of it the report went considerably beyond the statutory remit of the Committee, since it concerned specific intelligence available in relation to a specific event. Moreover, in the conduct of its inquiry the Committee examined all the relevant intelligence, intelligence assessments, and travel advice available before the attack—that is, it was given access to intelligence files as well as interviewing witnesses. The explanation is that the initiative for the inquiry seems to have come either wholly or in part from the government itself, which wanted to be able to substantiate the claim that no specific warning of a threat had been received that should have been made public. To make this claim credible it was necessary for it to be investigated by an independent body. Hence, it was the foreign secretary who announced to the House of Commons that the Committee was conducting an inquiry and that all material would be made available to it.[58]

The most controversial investigation by far that the ISC has conducted was into intelligence and intelligence assessments before the Iraq war. Although the initial impetus came from the ISC itself, the investigation was subsequently endorsed by a parliamentary resolution, and the prime minister promised full government cooperation. The report, published in September 2003,[59] is discussed in greater depth in chapter 2. In summary, however, it concluded that the government had not put political pressure on the JIC. The ISC's conclusion, based on interviews with all senior ministers and officials (including the prime minister and the foreign secretary) and on detailed analysis of the various intelligence assessments and the successive drafts of the dossiers, was that the published material had not been politically tampered with. Nevertheless, in some important respects the Committee was critical. It warned that "It is vital that the JIC's and the Agencies' credibility and effectiveness are not degraded or diminished by the publication of their product in an inappropriate manner."[60]

What does this show about the Committee? First, it demonstrates that it has an impressive ability to operate in a bipartisan fashion even in dealing with issues that have momentous political consequences. This may be due in part to its operating in private—had public hearings been held they would inevitably have invited "grandstanding" as undoubtedly occurred in both the Foreign Affairs Select Committee investigation and in the later Hutton Inquiry. However, precisely because the Committee worked in private and did not fully publish its evidence (although much more was passed to and later published by Hutton), this inevitably contributed to a perceived lack of legitimacy. This point was ironically underscored by evidence to the Hutton Inquiry that Geoff Hoon (the defence secretary) had insisted that Dr. David Kelly (the scientist from his department who subsequently committed suicide) should undergo public examination before the Foreign Affairs Committee because his earlier, private, appearance before the ISC lacked legitimacy.[61]

Second, the ISC's investigation shows that despite its limited formal powers the Committee can be successful in winning the cooperation of the agencies and getting to the facts. Of course, the government's own interests were served by cooperating fully, as it hoped that an independent report would deflect criticism. It is a testament to the Committee, however, that although the Hutton inquiry later picked over substantially the same ground with copious disclosure of documents and high profile public cross-examination of the witnesses (including live remote testimony from the chief of SIS), it reached essentially similar conclusions. In the politically charged atmosphere of claim and counter-claim surrounding the war it is not surprising, though, that the ISC inquiry failed to achieve public acceptance as a definitive account. Where a public inquiry by a Law Lord could not do so a committee of parliamentarians was hardly likely to succeed.

Despite these prominent investigations, there are also some glaring omissions from the published work of the Committee. Foremost among these is its silence on the allegations of the former Security Service officer David Shayler, finally convicted in 2001 under the Official Secrets Act of 1989 for his revelations concerning the agency, and his counterpart from MI6, Richard Tomlinson.[62] The allegations of incompetence and abuse made by these two insiders have received no public investigation. The reason is apparently that the Committee did not wish to encourage "whistle-blowers" who break the law. Instead, it has taken a close interest in the personnel policies of the agencies. The unstated implication is that the Shayler and Tomlinson cases are instructive only because of the failure to handle them in-house, rather than because of the substance of the allegations. And yet if the Committee is prepared to listen only to officially sanctioned evidence, it is arguably depriving itself of a valuable source of information.

The Intelligence and Security Committee can be counted a success on several levels. First, at a presentational level, the existence of the Committee has largely assuaged calls for more public accountability of the security and intelligence agencies. It is true that there remains the constitutional objection that the Committee is not responsible to Parliament as such. For this reason the Home Affairs Committee has continued to call for the Intelligence and Security Committee to be replaced with a parliamentary select committee.[63] However, even it has conceded that the existing Committee is a significant improvement on the previous arrangements and has paid tribute to its work.

Second, the Committee has plainly succeeded in establishing generally good working relations with the security and intelligence agencies. Only three examples stand out of friction or conflict, or of any attempt by the agencies to frustrate or obstruct any line of investigation. The retiring chairman noted (in a letter to the prime minister) that SIS apparently found it "more difficult" to be frank with the Committee than did the other services.[64] The Committee has failed in its repeated attempts to gain access to the full, unpublished reports of the judicial commissioners. The government has opposed this in principle, although, as a compromise, the Committee has met the commissioners.[65] Finally, in its Iraq investigation, the Committee criticized the lack of candor of the secretary of state for defence (which it called "potentially misleading") in initially failing to disclose the misgivings of some officials within DIS about material included in the September 2002 dossier.[66] These are the only disputes that have surfaced publicly over access to information.

It is significant, perhaps, that the government evidently trusted the Committee sufficiently to ask it to investigate matters that involved access to considerable operational detail (and which were therefore well outside the Committee's statutory entitlements)—the handling of the Mitrokhin Archive and of intelligence prior to the Bali bombing—and to cooperate in its inquiry into intelligence before the Iraq war. Moreover, the Committee has succeeded in behaving in a nonpolitical fashion so that its criticisms of the agencies have generally been responded to in a constructive fashion. Equally, it has proved a safe environment. There have been no leaks of information from the Committee to the press—something that would have severely damaged working relations with the agencies.

The Committee has worked well despite its relatively weak powers. This may be in part because the agencies were aware that withholding information in accordance with the strict terms of the Act would inevitably have produced public and parliamentary calls for increased investigative powers. Nevertheless, in view of the current controversy about intelligence analysis and reporting, this may be an opportune moment at which to extend the statutory framework to all parts of the intelligence establishment and to bring defense intelligence, the JIC, the intelligence assessments staff, and the security and intelligence co-coordinator formally under the wing of the Committee.

Conclusion

So far as the legislative oversight scheme as a whole is concerned, there are a number of broader defects, which can be briefly mentioned.

In the UK tradition the legislative framework is very permissive toward the executive. The only points at which there is relative precision concern the need to provide legal "cover" for potential violations of individuals' legal rights (mainly relating to personal privacy and property). Elsewhere the legislation lacks detail. It is startling to find, for example, that the key term "national security" is not defined with any precision. The legal implication is that the agencies are able to move flexibly into new areas of work without seeking explicit parliamentary approval.

Although there is complex scheme of statutory commissioners and a tribunal to deal with complaints, the absence of successful complaints over more than a decade in which variations on this scheme have been in operation is telling. Common experience of large public organizations in other spheres of life is that they simply do not achieve this degree of perfection in their relations with members of the public. It suggests here that the statutory balance may be excessively protective of state security as opposed to individual rights.

A clear gap within the UK scheme is the absence of an independent inspector-general with powers to initiate audits of the agencies' work. An office of this kind could be designed to provide reassurance of legality, propriety, and effectiveness that a haphazard complaints system and part-time judicial commissioners do not. It would benefit both ministers and Parliament.

Although much has changed since the 1980s, it remains the case that Parliament as such exercises little direct scrutiny of the agencies or their budgets. This may change. Experience of the Intelligence and Security Committee suggests that it could move to become a select committee in the proper sense with relatively little disruption.[67] The pressing need after September 11 and the Iraq war to enlist political and public support for the agencies and to strengthen the legitimacy of their work may make such a move attractive to the government, also, in due course.

On paper the UK scheme appears to be one of weak oversight because of considerable influence of the executive and the lack of parliamentary ownership of oversight arrangements. The government holds the reins in appointing members of the ISC, and in controlling their access to information and over the published form of their reports. As with so many things in Britain's unwritten constitution, however, appearances can be deceptive. No independent person would recommend these arrangements as a model to other countries, and the legal framework could certainly be improved, but in a stable democratic system they work tolerably well.

Notes

1. See *Lord Denning's Report*, Cmnd. 2152 (1963).
2. See chapter 3 in this volume.
3. Resolution DH(90) 36 of December 13, 1990. Ironically, the two complainants, Harriet Harman and Patricia Hewitt, are now both ministers in the Blair government.

4. The decision to prevent officers there from belonging to a trades union was unsuccessfully challenged in the courts: *Council of Civil Service Unions v. Minister for the Civil Service* [1985] AC 374. The ban was lifted by the Labour government in 1997.

5. The Secret Service Bureau, the forerunner of both MI5 and the Secret Intelligence Service (MI6), dated from 1909: C. Andrew, *Secret Service* (London: Sceptre, 1986), 121 ff.

6. In 1998 the Security Service had 290,000 personal files, of which 20,000 were active; 13,000 of these related to UK citizens (divided approximately equally between terrorism and the service's other current interests, espionage weapons-proliferation and serious crime): H.C. Debs, vol. 317, cols. 251–4, 29 July 1998. The Secret Intelligence Service (MI6) held 86,000 files (75 percent closed) of which approximately half related to UK citizens, although they were not files whose subject matter was individuals: *Annual Report of the Intelligence and Security Committee for 1997–98*, Cm. 4073 (1998), para. 52.

7. Security Service Act 1989, s. 2(2).

8. *National Intelligence Machinery*, 6.

9. ISA 1994, s. 1(2).

10. ISA 1994, s. 3(1)(a).

11. s. 3(1)(b).

12. s. 3(2)(a). GCHQ's functions can also be exercised under s. 3(2) "in the interests of the economic well-being of the United Kingdom in relation to the actions or intentions of persons outside the British Islands"; and "in support of the prevention or detection of serious crime."

13. See Jeffrey Richelson and Desomond Ball, *The Ties That Bind*, 2nd ed. (Sydney: Allen and Unwin, 1990).

14. ISA, ss. 2 and 4.

15. RIPA, s. 59

16. RIPA, s. 65

17. *Esbester v. UK*, App. No. 18601/91, April 2, 1993

18. For details see: *National Intelligence Machinery* (2nd ed., 2001).

19. See chapter 2 in this volume.

20. The standing terms of reference of the JIC are published in *National Intelligence Machinery* (2nd ed., 2001), 19.

21. SSA, s. 2(4) and ISA, ss. 2(4) and 4(4).

22. SSA 1989, s. 2; ISA 1994, ss. 2 and 4.

23. Intelligence and Security Committee, *Annual Report for 1999–2000*, Cm. 4897 (November 2000): para. 19.

24. Intelligence and Security Committee, *Annual Report for 2001–2*, Cm. 5542 (June 2002): para. 10.

25. RIPA 2000, Part 1. In practice, the home secretary, foreign secretary, Northern Ireland secretary, the secretary of state for defence, and the second minister in Scotland.

26. Under the *Anti-Terrorism Crime and Security Act 2001* and the *Immigration Act 1971*.

27. See chapter 2 in this volume.

28. Intelligence and Security Committee, *Annual Report 2002–2003*, Cm. 5837 (June 2003): para. 82.

29. Intelligence and Security Committee, *Iraqi Weapons of Mass Destruction—Intelligence and Assessments*, Cm. 5972 (2003): paras. 86, 112.

30. *Report of the Inquiry into the Circumstances Surrounding the Death of Dr. David Kelly C.M.G.*, H.C. 247 (2003–4): para. 467. www.the-hutton-inquiry.org.uk

31. *Review of Intelligence on Weapons of Mass Destruction, Report of a Committee of Privy Counsellors,* HC898 (2004–5).

32. Laurence Lustgarten and Ian Leigh, *In From the Cold: National Security and Parliamentary Democracy,* (Oxford: Oxford University Press, 1994): 441–42.

33. Lustgarten and Leigh, 447–450.

34. First Report from the Home Affairs Select Committee for 1992–3, *Accountability of the Security Service,* HC 265; and see the Government response Cm. 2197 (1993).

35. See chapter 6 in this volume.

36. Australian Security Intelligence Organization Act 1979; Australian Security Intelligence Organization Amendment Act 1986.

37. Intelligence Services Act 2001 (hereafter, "ISA").

38. ISA 1994, s. 10.

39. ISA, s. 10(7): "if the publication of any matter in a report would be prejudicial to the continued discharge of the functions of either of the Services or, as the case may be, GCHQ, the Prime Minister may exclude that matter."

40. ISA 1994 s. 10(1).

41. ISA, schedule 3, para. 4. In addition, ministers have power to withhold "non-sensitive" materials on grounds similar to those that apply to select committees: ISA, schedule 3, para. 3(4).

42. ISA, schedule 3, para. 3(2).

43. ISA, schedule 3, para. 3(3).

44. ISA, s. 10(6) and (7).

45. Intelligence and Security Committee, *Annual Report for 1999–2000,* Cm. 4897, para. 103.

46. Intelligence and Security Committee, *Annual Report for 1999–2000,* Cm. 4897 (November 2000): paras. 43 ff.

47. Intelligence and Security Committee, Interim *Report for 2000–01* Cm. 5126 (March 2001): para. 26.

48. It produced a brief report calling for examination of the implications of the government's proposal (subsequently implemented in the Security Service Act 1996) to add to the powers of the Security Service a power to assist in the investigation of serious crime: *Report on the Security Service's Work Against Organized Crime,* Cm. 3065 (Dec. 1995).

49. ISA, s. 10(2) (b).

50. Intelligence and Security Committee, *Annual Report for 1995,* Cm. 3198 (1996): para. 37.

51. Intelligence and Security Committee, *Iraqi Weapons of Mass Destruction—Intelligence and Assessments,* Cm. 5972 (2003): para. 17.

52. Intelligence and Security Committee, *Annual Report for 1997–98,* Cm. 4073, paras. 67–69

53. *Government Response to the Intelligence and Security Committee's Annual Report 1997–98,* Cm., 4089, para 21.

54. Intelligence and Security Committee, *Annual Report for 1998–9,* Cm. 4532, para. 84.

55. *Annual Report for 2001–2,* para. 17.

56. Ibid., paras. 8 ff.

57. Intelligence and Security Committee, *Inquiry into Intelligence, Assessments and Advice prior to the Terrorist Bombings on Bali 12 October 2002,* Cm. 5724 (2002).

58. H.C. Debs., October 21, 2002, cols. 21–24.

59. Intelligence and Security Committee, *Iraqi Weapons of Mass Destruction—Intelligence and Assessments*, Cm. 5972 (2003).

60. Ibid., para. 142.

61. Evidence to Hutton Inquiry, September 22, 2003.

62. Convicted under the Official Secrets Act 1989 in 1997 for publication of his disclosures.

63. Home Affairs Select Committee, *Accountability of the Security Service*, June 1999, HC291.

64. *Annual Report for 1999–2000*, Cm. 4897, v.

65. Intelligence and Security Committee, *Annual Report for 2001–2*, Cm. 5542 (June 2002), paras. 29 ff.

66. Intelligence and Security Committee, *Iraqi Weapons of Mass Destruction—Intelligence and Assessments*, Cm. 5972 (2003): paras. 104 and 115.

67. Also proposed by the Foreign Affairs Select Committee: see its *Ninth Report for 2002–3, Reasons for Going to War against Iraq* HC813–1, para. 167.

6

Canada's Long Road from Model Law to Effective Political Oversight of Security and Intelligence

Stuart Farson

During his 1976 trial for attempting to bomb the home of a Montreal supermarket executive, Robert Samson acknowledged he had done worse as a member of the Royal Canadian Mounted Police (RCMP) Security Service.[1] Given immunity from prosecution, Samson revealed details of a break-in at the offices of the L'Agence-Presse Libre du Québec. This set in train events that led the Canadian government to establish a public inquiry under Justice David McDonald into the federal police force. Five years later the Commission produced a comprehensive report that recommended severing the Security Service from the RCMP and establishing a new civilian security intelligence service in its stead.[2]

In many respects, the Canadian Security Intelligence Service Act that established the new agency in 1984 constituted a blueprint for change and a model law for establishing agencies with coercive or intrusive capacities. It largely followed McDonald's blueprint with one critical exception. It did not establish a permanent joint standing committee on security and intelligence with full purview over all of Canada's security and intelligence organizations and functions.[3] Some twenty years later, the neophyte Liberal government of Paul Martin has, in attempting to address the "democratic deficit," acknowledged the need for such a committee.[4]

This chapter examines the formulation of the model law initiated by the McDonald Commission and how Canada's security and intelligence community has subsequently developed and been scrutinized by internal and external review bodies and legislative committees. The discussion has two starting points. A central focus of the conference on which this book is based concerned an attempt to compare and contrast parliamentary oversight models with the congressional form. Though Canada is a constitutional monarchy with a parliamentary system of government, it has developed as a hybrid system, relying heavily on both British and American constitutional and institutional ideas. These have both had important implications for Canada's oversight systems. Second, the way Canada's security and intelligence community has developed is the result of several factors. These include its experiences in wartime; its geopolitical position and the threats it perceives; its close ties with Britain, other dominions, and the United States; and its own value system.

It is not possible to examine here all aspects of how Canada scrutinized its security and intelligence community during the last quarter century. Instead, the chapter focuses on certain key events. It examines the lessons that can be drawn both from Parliament's five-year review of the CSIS Act and the Security Offences Act, and also its recent adoption of the Anti-terrorism Act. While the latter was ostensibly in response to the terrorist attacks on the United States on September 11, 2001, this chapter argues that other rationales were afoot. It also provides an assessment of the measures taken by the new Liberal government to restructure Canada's security and intelligence community and the new forms of oversight now in the offing. By way of a conclusion, it reflects upon the capacity of Canadian oversight and the likelihood of weaknesses being overcome.

Canada's Security and Intelligence Community

Canada's security and intelligence community had its origins before Confederation but developed in an extensive way following the formation of the RCMP in the early 1920s. As Steve Hewitt has shown in his longitudinal study, *Spying 101*, the focus of the RCMP Security Service's work was in keeping elements of Canadian society under surveillance and in thwarting security threats, primarily from the political left.[5] In 1984, the role of security intelligence gathering was turned over to a new civilian organization, the Canadian Security Intelligence Service (CSIS). Whereas the RCMP Security Service had powers to deter and prevent activities that constituted a threat to the security of Canada, the new civilian organization had no police powers and a mandate only to warn the Canadian government of threats the country faced.

It would be wrong to think that the RCMP was removed from the world of national security intelligence or that CSIS and the RCMP were the only agencies involved in domestic intelligence gathering. The adoption of the CSIS Act was accompanied by the Security Offences Act. This legislation gave the RCMP the primary role in investigating an undefined number of security offenses. In the case of politically motivated violence, the CSIS Act did nothing to remove the forces' obligation to prevent such violence.[6] In fact, it is difficult to envisage how this duty could be implemented without specific intelligence gathering.

The Canadian Armed Forces are primarily concerned with the collection of defense intelligence about the military capabilities and intentions of foreign states and other entities. The auditor-general, however, has recently identified three units within the Department of National Defence involved in domestic intelligence gathering.[7] The National Counter-Intelligence Unit uses such investigative techniques as communication intercepts, physical surveillance, and search warrants. The Canadian Forces Information Operations Groups conduct signals intercepts to support the Canadian Armed Forces or the Communications Security Establishment (CSE). Finally, the Canadian Forces Joint Imagery Centre coordinates the collection of images in the support of domestic or international operations of the Canadian Armed Forces.[8] Also operating in the domestic sphere is the Financial Transactions and Reports Analysis Centre. This agency was involved in countering money laundering, primarily by organized crime, prior to September 11, 2001, but was given a new mandate to prevent and deter terrorist financing under the Anti-terrorism Act.

Unlike its G8 partners, Canada has never had an intelligence agency dedicated solely to gathering intelligence abroad using human sources or providing an external covert action capacity,[9] though there have been repeated calls for Canada to develop a foreign intelligence service.[10] Its ability to gather intelligence abroad still rests on CSIS's limited but expanding capacity to collect security intelligence outside Canada,[11] its signals intelligence agency, diplomatic and military personnel abroad, open sources, and the sharing of intelligence by foreign agencies.

The CSE's forerunner originated during the Second World War and quickly became a valued member of the UK/USA signals intelligence partnership. Established through secret executive orders, it has remained Canada's most secretive organization ever since.[12] Not until the mid-1970s was the organization even acknowledged by government. Only within the last ten years has it been independently reviewed and placed under a legislative mandate. Like the agency itself, the position of commissioner for the CSE was initially established by executive order. To date the commissioner has never been called before Parliament to discuss the office's annual report. Nor has Parliament considered in any depth the legislation subsequently adopted to establish the agency, the review body, and their respective mandates. Canada's capacity to analyze all-source foreign intelligence has traditionally rested on organizations within the Privy Council Office (PCO) and the Department of Foreign Affairs.[13] These intelligence analysis centers have only recently received adequate resources and their work has never been reviewed by any independent body.

Traditionally, the responsibility for providing the country with security and protecting it against the range of threats—both man-made and natural—has been spread across a wide range of agencies and departments. The new government under Paul Martin has undertaken a major reorganization of the sector. A central feature of this reorganization is the elimination of the Ministry of Solicitor-General and its replacement by the Ministry of Public Safety and Emergency Preparedness Canada headed by the deputy prime minister. In addition, the minister has been given responsibility for leading the cabinet's planning and policy making for the entire security and intelligence sector. Of critical importance is a shift in attitude towards the perception of threats. Previously, traditional national security threats were viewed separately. Now man-made threats are perceived under the same rubric as those stemming from natural sources. This realization is particularly apparent in the public health sphere where both forms of threats readily elide. Significantly, there has never been a body independent of the Executive that has had purview over the entire security and intelligence sector.

McDonald's Blueprint for Change, 1977–1981

The McDonald Commission represented the first detailed investigation into Canada's security intelligence apparatus.[14] Its numerous staff and consultant papers, many analyzing foreign intelligence structures and functions, coupled with its own comprehensive reports, provided a needed window on an area of government few in Canada then understood. Well covered by the media, it encouraged debate in Parliament and across the country. With adequate resources, it was able to ascertain that the RCMP Security Service had acted in ways neither authorized nor provided for by law while trying to counter and deter separatist elements in the Province of Quebec. Significantly, the commissioners did not perceive these unlawful actions as isolated incidents but as ones institutionalized within the organization.[15]

While the Commission recognized the state's obligation to ensure that national security threats are thwarted, it opined that this had to be done without destroying the democratic fabric in the process or unduly harming individual freedoms. Thus, it based its recommendations on the idea of a balance between these two dimensions. In this regard, it held that "security must not be regarded as more important than democracy, for the fundamental purpose of security is the preservation of our democratic system."[16] On the one hand, it favored providing the security forces with such powers as were necessary to accomplish the job. Thus, it would recommend additional powers the RCMP Security Service never possessed. On the other hand, it believed that when organizations had coercive or intrusive powers, there should be commensurate checks and balances. Of critical importance here was the notion that intelligence organizations should have enabling legislation explicitly defining their mandates and limiting their activities. Only in this way could the principle of everyone being accountable to law be maintained. Further, the Commission believed such legislation should clearly provide a system of accountability, control, and review that would ensure particular ministers were responsible to Parliament for the coercive and intrusive actions provided by such organizations.

To achieve these objectives, the Commission believed it was necessary to remove responsibility for gathering security intelligence from the RCMP. Several factors underpinned this premise. First, the commissioners held that the RCMP was not suited to providing this function because of the education and modes of recruitment and training individual officers received. Second, they considered that wrongdoing in the security sphere had brought not only the Security Service into disrepute but also the entire national police force. Finally, and most importantly, they held that in fulfilling their normal duties, police forces in a democratic state needed to have independence of action from political masters and discretion about when to invoke the criminal sanction. Thus, the Commission's approach was to have a separate civilian security intelligence service with no coercive powers, only those needed to investigate and analyze threats to Canada's security. Its responsibilities would end with reporting about the nature and implications of threats to other arms of the Canadian government. The RCMP was not to be removed from the national security arena altogether. Rather its responsibility was to be limited to post-intelligence activities where intelligence officials and political masters wanted the criminal sanction invoked or persons detained pending removal from the country.

The Commission also believed the new security intelligence service should be placed in a comprehensive system of accountability, control, and review. Accountability was to be achieved by making a specific minister responsible to Parliament for the new organization. There would no longer be a case for "plausible deniability" of domestic intelligence functions. Furthermore, the head of the new service, who had responsibility for managing day-to-day operations, was to report directly to the minister. Significantly, the head's tenure was to be limited so that the government could avoid falling vulnerable to J. Edgar Hoover–like characters. Executive control was to be exercised by providing the minister with clear authority to give the head instructions. While a lower threshold than that employed in criminal investigations would be used, the most intrusive investigative techniques were to fall under judicial controls by requiring the service to obtain warrants. Two review mechanisms that were external to, and independent of, government were envisaged. An Advisory Council on Security and Intelligence consisting of three part-time members appointed by the cabinet after approval by Parliament was to be established with a permanent full-time staff. The Council was to have a wide remit to investigate public complaints and illegal activities. In both instances the purview reached across the entire security and intelligence community and included an obligation to report both to Parliament and the relevant responsible ministers. No involvement in legal challenges was envisaged where individuals had been denied security clearances. Instead, a special quasi-judicial body called the Security Appeals Tribunal would fulfill that function.

There was also to be a permanent joint committee of Parliament on security and intelligence. This was to consist of not more than ten members representing all political parties and be chaired by an opposition member. Again, this body was to have authority to consider organizations other than the new security intelligence agency. But while the Advisory Council was to be concerned only with matters of propriety, the permanent committee was also to consider organizational efficacy. With the exception of in-camera hearings and security clearances for parliamentarians, the Commission made no recommendation about how this committee might use and protect classified information. Nor did it discuss how well-suited traditional parliamentary committee approaches might be for fulfilling the role.

The Adoption of the CSIS Act and Security Offences Act, 1983–1984

After tabling draft legislation to establish CSIS in 1983 the government immediately sent the bill for "pre-study" in the Senate, an infrequently used device. There it was reviewed by a special committee chaired by Michael Pitfield, until recently Prime Minister Pierre Trudeau's cabinet secretary. The bill created much public interest and criticism. The Committee's eventual report focused on the delicate balance between the state's right to protect itself and its obligation to preserve the freedoms of individual Canadians.[17] It made numerous recommendations to improve democratic protections. But in one important respect it diverged from the McDonald Commission's blueprint. It did not support a permanent role for Parliament. Without regard for the principle of ministerial responsibility or any discussion on how information might be secured, it said:

> We agree that, ideally such a committee could be of benefit. But there are many practical difficulties involved. A parliamentary committee would likely duplicate much of the efforts of the Security Intelligence Review Committee (SIRC). Further,

Parliamentary Committees are notoriously subject to the vagaries of time, changes in membership and over work. There is also the problem of maintaining the security of information. This has reference in part to the possibility of partisan motivations in some members; but it also refers to the general question of whether that type of committee can maintain the requisite confidentiality by reason of the nature of its proceedings. In view of these considerations, the Committee believes that it would not be advisable to establish a parliamentary committee with special access to CSIS operations and information.[18]

Criticism was such that the government decided to start afresh. The new bill followed most of the Pitfield Committee's recommendations and was finally adopted by Parliament in August 1984. It reflected the McDonald Commission's blueprint in many respects. It established a new civilian agency headed by a director who could only serve two five-year terms. The Service's mandate and functions were carefully spelled out and limited to collecting intelligence about particular threats and warning the federal government of their implications. It had no powers to thwart the threats it investigated or to force anyone it interviewed to answer questions. A broader investigatory mandate than the RCMP Security Service's authorized it to see personal health records and to intercept mail. While its primary role was to collect security intelligence—defined in terms of threats to the security of Canada and Canadian interests—it also had a limited role in collecting foreign intelligence. While it was not restricted as to where it could collect security intelligence, it was forbidden to collect foreign intelligence outside Canada.

The agency was also placed within the recommended framework of accountability, controls, and review mechanisms. The solicitor-general was specifically given responsibility for the Service and authorized to provide the Service with directions. While the director had day-to-day responsibility for control and management, the incumbent was made accountable to the minister for the Service's actions and obliged to consult with the deputy solicitor-general on its policies and operations.

The legislation also established two review bodies, one within the executive branch of government, the other independent of it. The role of the internal body was primarily one of compliance. In this regard, the inspector-general of CSIS was charged with certifying that the Service had operated within the law and according to policy directives. The annual certificate the office produced is submitted to the deputy solicitor-general but not made public. By contrast the external body, the Security Intelligence Review Committee (SIRC), has a wider remit to check for compliance and to consider efficacy issues. In addition to these reviews, which may be initiated on its own volition or at the request of the minister, SIRC investigates complaints against the Service and instances where security clearances are denied. The Act did not make, as the McDonald Commission had recommended, this body directly accountable to both the responsible minister and to Parliament. Consequently, SIRC reports on various matters to the minister in a confidential and frequently classified manner. Such reports are transmitted as soon as they are completed. By contrast, the annual report SIRC must submit to the minister each year, and which the minister is obliged to table in Parliament, is transmitted at the end of the reporting cycle. By this time many of the issues raised have lost their political urgency. The federal court also exercises another form of control and review. Whenever the Service wishes to intercept communications or to enter and search premises, it must first obtain a warrant from a specially designated judge.[19] Here the standard is less cumbersome than for criminal investigations conducted by the police. Instead of requiring reasonable and probable grounds to believe that a criminal act has taken place, CSIS is only required to show it has reasonable grounds to suspect that a threat to Canada or Canadian interests exists. Significantly, there is no obligation to obtain a warrant where the Service uses human sources, arguably the most invasive of techniques.

While the adopted version of the CSIS Act largely followed McDonald's blueprint, key elements were omitted. Two would have an important impact on the effectiveness of parliamentary oversight for years to come. There was to be no permanent standing committee of Parliament with a purview over the entire security and intelligence community. This had ramifications from two important perspectives. First, as none of the other members of the security and intelligence community had dedicated independent review bodies, it was unlikely they would receive more than a cursory parliamentary glance. Second, because Parliament has traditionally organized its committees along departmental lines, matters running across ministerial portfolios seldom receive the attention they deserve. This is particularly important when security and intelligence matters are considered because nearly every government department is either an intelligence producer or consumer.

The other missing element concerned SIRC. It was to focus only on CSIS. This meant it could review only other members of the community when they had specific dealings with the Service. Also, SIRC was to have no direct linkage to Parliament. Consequently, it could not alert parliamentarians to important issues until the minister had tabled its annual report in Parliament. This frequently meant there were delays between the timing of a particular incident and when MPs heard about it. Matters would be even worse with the inspector general's annual certificates. SIRC often did not receive these in time to consider them in its annual report. This meant Parliament was further removed from hearing about problems that inspectors-general uncovered or the difficulties incumbents had in fulfilling their duties.[20]

One important element, not envisaged by the McDonald Commission, was a complete review of the legislation after it had been in operation for five years. On its face, its inclusion in such a highly controversial act was sensible and necessary. However, it appears that no one in 1984, not even the Pitfield Committee that recommended it, had reflected on the implications it would have for Parliament and the difficulties that body might have in fulfilling its mandate.[21]

Five-year Review of the CSIS and Security Offences Acts

Both the CSIS Act and the Security Offences Act specifically required Parliament to conduct a comprehensive review of the provisions and operation of legislation. Important lessons can be drawn from the experiences of the Special Committee of the House of Commons that conducted this obligatory statutory review.[22] The parliamentarians chosen by their respective parties to review the two acts were, with the exception of the Committee's chair, all first-term MPs. Initially, they were not very knowledgeable about intelligence matters, the legislation before them, or the parliamentary powers they had at hand. Perhaps because of these common deficiencies, members proceeded in a more collegial and non-partisan manner than others had.[23]

Arguably, the most important issue for the Committee to review concerned whether the various requirements of the legislation, especially those concerning accountability, control, and review, were being met. While the Committee was obliged by law to review the legislation and had been delegated all the powers of Parliament for that purpose, it soon found itself confronting roadblocks that proved insurmountable within the review's time frame. In addition to being denied access to officials who had held senior positions in security and intelligence, the Special Committee was refused access to documents that would have shown whether the various actors identified in the legislation were operating as Parliament had intended. The government also denied the Committee access to the annual reports that the various CSIS directors had made to the solicitor-general along with all the Service's policy and budgetary documents. In the case of ministerial directives, the minister would only provide members of the Committee with an oral briefing without their advisory staff. Similarly, the Committee was denied access to the inspector-general's certificates and other reports as well as all of SIRC's reports, excepting its public annual reports. Though SIRC members wanted to help Parliament, they refused to discuss key issues or to allow members of the Special Committee or its staff to view its classified reports, thus putting an end to the myth that they were Parliament's "surrogate." In fact, the only documents seen by the Committee were the censored versions released under the Access to Information Act. Consequently, Parliament could not confirm that the complex system of accountability, control, and review was working as the Parliament had intended. Nor could it ascertain the degree to which SIRC functions overlapped with those of the inspector-general. Despite these difficulties, the staff of the Special Committee was able to demonstrate that SIRC had not followed basic social science research techniques in one particular report. Though SIRC admitted it was not one of their better reports,[24] the analysis left an uncomfortable question mark hanging over the Special Committee because it could not confirm whether the techniques used by SIRC were atypical or commonplace. Another roadblock affected the Committee's work but was of its own making. The Committee shied away from directly asking federal court judges questions about their role for fear of establishing undesirable precedents concerning the separation of powers. Consequently, it relied on staff interviews with the federal court's administrative staff.

The Special Committee used a variety of techniques for obtaining needed information. Such traditional methods as holding public hearings and questioning witnesses formed the Committee's public face. However, because only a limited number of issues could be raised during such procedures, these were augmented with staff interviews and requests for written government responses to additional questions. Even so, many requests were denied on "national security grounds."

Not surprisingly, one of the central recommendations of the Special Committee was for the government to treat security and intelligence as a special case.[25] In order to ensure appropriate access to classified information, it recommended that Parliament establish a small permanent standing committee. This committee would have its members work under an oath of secrecy, have security-cleared staff, and meet in secure premises, sometimes in camera.

The Special Committee also recommended that the government draft a national security act covering the various components of Canada's security and intelligence community. Three objectives underpinned this recommendation. One was to spur government to respond to earlier recommendations to revise such legislation as the Official Secrets Act and to provide elements of the community with enabling legislation that had hitherto relied on executive orders. Another was to focus Parliament's attention on the functions, capacities, and performance of the entire security and intelligence community. Finally, it was designed to provide all the various components of that community with some modicum of oversight.

Lessons from the Adoption of the Anti-terrorism Act

The tragic events of September 11, 2001, are probably forever etched into the memories of most North Americans and need no replaying here. However, the reactions of governments to those events do raise questions about the provision of national security, the way it is scrutinized, as well as new concerns over the freedoms of citizens, especially where new powers are enacted in times of "war." In Canada, reaction was immediate and from one perspective comprehensive. From another, the government, the media, and the public alike ignored the need for effective ongoing oversight of their security and intelligence apparatus and the mechanisms for maintaining the delicate balance.

In under five weeks, the government's legal drafters pasted a vast omnibus bill together. Ostensibly, Bill C-36 provided an array of antiterrorism measures. In truth, it served additional agendas. One concerned the need to convince the U.S. government that Canada was taking immediate steps to protect U.S. interests. This was essential if the border between the two countries was to remain open for trade. The other was less evident. The draft legislation consisted not only of a range of new antiterrorism powers but included several measures long on the intelligence bureaucracy's "to-do list." Thus, in some respects, it looked like the national security act that the five-year review process had advocated but without the very oversight components that underpinned its rationale.

The issue of content and questioning needs to be addressed. For many who had followed the McDonald Commission's investigations and had engaged themselves in the debates over whether the draft versions of the CSIS Act adequately preserved the delicate balance, Bill C-36 sounded a warning shot not heard in a generation. The provisions specifically geared to make investigating terrorist activities easier were immediately controversial. Two in particular— preventive arrest and investigative hearings—directly challenged long-standing notions of acceptable police practice and principles of criminal law. Thus, they created intense public disquiet, particularly among the criminal bar.[26] That these new powers became the central focus of the debate over the bill is both difficult to counter and countenance, given that they are yet to be used other than in relation to the investigation of the 1985 downing of an Air India jet. Certainly, important aspects of the bill received short shrift, particularly those on the intelligence bureaucracy's "to-do list," such as revising the Official Secrets Act and providing enabling legislation for both the CSE and its review body.[27] Given the many hours of scrutiny that the CSIS Act received, it is hard to believe that an agency with greater potential capacity to intrude on more people could have received such paltry attention. One could be excused for believing it was planned.

The bill increased the powers of many of the agencies named in the legislation. By making terrorism a crime under the Criminal Code, all police forces were now obliged to play a much greater role in national security. To this end, the RCMP is to receive $576 million over six years to enhance public safety and counter terrorism (RCMP 2002). A very significant portion of these funds is to go to new multi-force national security and border enforcement teams. Though the RCMP argues that their involvement in national security is for "criminal law enforcement purposes," it openly admits these units are intelligence led (RCMP 2003). The CSE also received new powers. Before its adoption the CSE had no authority to intercept communications entering or leaving Canada. The agency may now do so under certain conditions. The role of the Financial Transactions and Reports Analysis Centre of Canada was also expanded and enabled by the legislation. Prior to the act's adoption its focus was on money laundering. It now has the authority to detect and deter terrorist financing. None of these new intrusive and coercive powers received any concomitant increase in review and oversight. The lessons of the McDonald Commission appeared to have been forgotten. So too did warnings of emergency legislation overstaying its welcome.

Recent Structural Changes to the Intelligence Community and Oversight

In December 2003, Jean Chrétien resigned after ten years as prime minister. The new prime minister immediately announced significant structural changes to the way Canadian security would be provided. Of critical importance were changes to the way political control of policy would be exercised and how Parliament's capacity to oversee the entire intelligence community would be achieved. Hitherto security and intelligence policy making and coordination had been fairly decentralized and inconsistently applied in terms of cabinet control. As well, responsibility for much of its provision had fallen to junior ministers.

The new administration dramatically changed this by making the deputy prime minister responsible not only for a new cabinet committee dealing with all matters of national security and the PCO's supporting role, but also for a new and expanded security and intelligence portfolio. The security and intelligence role of the PCO has been raised both in terms of stature and direct access to the prime minister. Whereas the security and intelligence coordinator in the PCO had previously raised security and intelligence matters through the head of foreign and defense policy, the current incumbent has been given both deputy head status and new responsibilities as the country's first national security adviser. As a deputy head the coordinator will report directly to the deputy prime minister on all matters of security and intelligence policy and coordination. As national security adviser, he or she will report directly to the prime minister. Presumably, this will include ensuring that future prime ministers are regularly briefed on all intelligence issues.

The deputy prime minister now also has ministerial responsibility for a new and expanded security and intelligence portfolio. All of the functions of the old Ministry of the Solicitor-General have been retained. These include the agencies now principally responsible for intelligence work: CSIS, the RCMP, and the Criminal Intelligence Service of Canada. In addition, the new Ministry of Public Safety and Emergency Preparedness Canada has responsibility for the Office of Critical Infrastructure and Emergency Preparedness, formerly in the Department of National Defence, and a new Border Services Agency. This agency has brought together the intelligence and investigative arms previously with Citizenship and Immigration Canada and the Customs Service. In all the deputy prime minister will now have seven deputy heads reporting directly to him or her.

Ostensibly, the minister of national defence has always been accountable to Parliament for Canada's signals intelligence and communications security programs provided by the CSE and other elements of National Defence. However, the traditional system of accountability is unusually convoluted. Because chiefs of the CSE have not—like directors of CSIS—been deputy heads, incumbents have reported to the minister of national defence via two separate channels: through the deputy head of the Department of National Defence on administrative matters; and through the security and intelligence coordinator in the PCO for policy and operational concerns. Because of the cabinet responsibilities and the fact that the security and intelligence coordinator is now specifically the deputy prime minister's deputy, it appears that this position will also acquire some responsibilities for aspects of these programs.

As part of its structural and policy changes, the government has publicly encouraged Parliament to establish a Permanent Standing Committee on National Security with its membership drawn from the various parliamentary parties.[28] To this end it has committed to providing parliamentarians with a consultation paper. However, when it subsequently announced measures to attend to the "democratic deficit," it referred to a "committee of parliamentarians."[29] To date no one appears to have noticed either the impact of this subtle but significant difference or its implications for future ongoing parliamentary responsibilities.

By implicitly recognizing that it was Parliament's right to decide which committees to establish and that it could only propose a particular course of action, the Martin government clearly recognized that a Permanent Standing Committee on National Security would be a parliamentary body with all the rights and privileges resting with Parliament under the constitution. Significantly, Parliament delegates to all standing committees the right to call for "people, papers and records." Authority to do this in the case of the House of Commons rests on Standing Order 108. The powers contained therein are considerable. They permit committees to subpoena witnesses, to place them under oath, and to hold them in contempt for failing to answer questions or to produce records. In theory, the powers also include the right to arrest and incarcerate those held in contempt. Parliament, in conducting business within its own precincts, is not limited by either the laws of Canada or conventions unless it has specifically bound itself in statute law. Thus, it is not restricted in the documents it may see, as ordinary citizens are, by what might be released under the Access to Information Act or which might be constrained by the Privacy Act. Similarly, it is not bound by the Security of Information Act. Nor is it restrained from talking about matters that fall under the sub judice convention. In this regard, it should be noted that Parliament's choosing not to insist on the release of documents, or not discussing a particular matter before the courts, is quite different from being bound not to do so.

There are good examples in comparable jurisdictions of parliamentary committees scrutinizing security and intelligence activities. In both New Zealand and Australia such committees have a statutory basis. New Zealand specifically established a parliamentary committee under the Intelligence and Security Committee Act 1996 to examine the policy, administration, and expenditure of each security and intelligence agency. Both the prime minister and the leader of the official opposition are members along with three other persons. The Act specifically confirms their role as members of Parliament and requires procedures to follow the Standing Orders of the House of Representatives. Individual membership rests on the endorsement of the House but may be terminated by the prime minister, who chairs the Committee. The Act also requires security procedures to be followed by the Committee with the prime minister's department providing security-cleared staff to the Committee.

Australia recently established the Joint Parliamentary Committee on ASIO, ASIS, and DSB under its Intelligence Services Act 2001. This legislation replaced the Permanent Joint Committee on ASIO. The new committee has broader purview and can scrutinize the effectiveness and propriety of the key Australian intelligence organizations. It is obliged to submit an annual review of administration and expenditure to Parliament but may instigate other investigations to be reported on separately. The Act specifically confirms the right of the Committee to call the agency heads before it and obliges the inspector-general of intelligence to appear when summoned.

A "committee of parliamentarians" signals quite different arrangements from these parliamentary committees. It may suggest that the government envisages a model similar to the Intelligence and Security Committee, established under the UK Intelligence Services Act 1994. This is not a parliamentary body but an offspring of the executive branch drawing on parliamentarians for membership. If a British model were to be followed, committee members would be appointed by (and removed by) the prime minister, would be subject to the Security of Information Act, would have only limited powers to obtain information, and would report to the prime minister, rather than to Parliament.[30]

In addressing the "democratic deficit," Prime Minister Martin has committed his government to improve both the effectiveness of Parliament and the research capacities of both political parties and their individual members. There is to be greater funding for parliamentary committees and more resources for the Library of Parliament, the body providing nonpartisan research and advice to committees and individual MPs. These are all very positive and much needed initiatives. With regard to the Standing Committee on National Security the government has promised to make its members privy councillors. This has important implications as privy councillors must swear an oath of office requiring them to keep secret what they encounter as the result of their office. This should be sufficient to ensure that members do not leak classified information to other MPs or journalists. If a member of the Committee were to leak classified information, he or she could be held in contempt of Parliament. This might result in losing the rights and privileges of parliamentary membership. As this would prevent MPs from doing an effective job, it should prove to have a more cautionary effect on behavior than the mere threat of criminal sanctions under the Security of Information Act, which would likely be the case with a mere committee of parliamentarians.

Since the Anti-terrorism Act adoption, the RCMP has become more involved in antiterrorism efforts, requiring the Force again to be broadly engaged in intelligence gathering and analysis. Several events that have occurred since the September 11, 2001, attacks have given cause for public concern and have raised again the need for greater oversight of the Force's national security activities. The Mahar Arar case is of particular importance. During a stopover in New York when returning from Tunisia to Canada, Arar was arrested and deported by U.S. authorities. Though traveling on a Canadian passport and wanting to return to Montreal, he was sent via Jordan to Syria, his birthplace. There he was incarcerated and tortured. Though he was forced to make a false confession, the Syrian authorities could find no connection of Arar to terrorism and eventually released him some 375 days after his original detention. It appears that a Canadian intelligence organization provided U.S. authorities with information alleging his connection to al Qaeda. The former government tried to limit political damage by restricting inquiries to SIRC and the commissioner for complaints against the RCMP. An RCMP raid on the home and offices of an *Ottawa Citizen* reporter who had written a story on Arar based partly on a leaked document (O'Neill, 2003) led to her being charged under the Security of Information Act and to considerable media attention. As a result, the current government has since been forced to undertake two initiatives. The first is the establishment of a public inquiry into the Arar case under Justice Dennis O'Connor. Its terms of reference include the requirement to make recommendations concerning how best to provide an independent review mechanism for the RCMP's national security activities. The other initiative is to commit Section 4 of the Security of Information

Act to a parliamentary review. It is to be recalled that the Official Secrets Act was revised and renamed under the Anti-terrorism Act. Hence, it was already due for parliamentary consideration when the three-year review of that Act commenced in December 2004.

An unrelated matter has had important consequences for national security oversight. During the previous administration, substantial advertising contracts were awarded to Quebec organizations with close ties to the Liberal party, apparently for little return. These events have since been reported on by the auditor-general in scathing terms and have raised again the need for whistle-blower protection.[31] The new government has not only acceded to another public inquiry but has tabled the Public Servants Disclosure Protection Bill. It is important to recall that Jane Shorten claimed the CSE had breached its mandate in the 1990s when it spied on trading partners and intercepted and retained the transcripts of conversations between a foreign embassy receptionist, who was Canadian, and her gynecologist. Then her only recourse was to reveal what she perceived as wrongdoing to the media. Though the new legislation would exclude intelligence agencies from the provisions of the Act, it would still require agency heads to establish similar procedures for their organizations.

Conclusions

It is perhaps useful to recall what a former U.S. director of central intelligence told the CSIS Act Review Committee during its visit to Washington in 1990. When asked for his views on congressional oversight, he said:

> When it was first introduced, we fought it all the way. But now we wouldn't do without it. When the Agency is falsely maligned by the media there's someone to call who can put the record straight. And when the Administration doesn't respond to budgetary requests, there are other folks on the Hill who understand our needs and can go to bat for us.[32]

Unfortunately, Canada's intelligence bureaucracy has never seen oversight or review as having a beneficial side. But sentiments may be changing under the new administration.

The new government has already taken needed steps to improve how security and intelligence is structured and controlled by the executive branch, mainly through executive orders. Some, such as those dealing with the new Department of Public Safety and Emergency Preparedness, will still require legislation to amend existing statutes. In addition, the current government has committed to developing a new national security strategy, the first in the country's history.

Together these innovations will elevate the status of security and intelligence on the national political agenda and may tweak Parliament's interest.

Arguably, to be beneficial to both intelligence bureaucrats and those charged with preserving the democratic fabric, oversight must depend on two variables: the types of organizations involved and how they go about their business; and their legal remits and reporting relationships. In an insightful article on the congressional system, Mathew McCubbins and Thomas Schwartz posited that effective oversight is best performed through a combination of two organizational forms.[33] These they call respectively "fire alarms" and "police patrols." They argue that the former are more likely to be conducted by inherently political bodies such as legislative committees because they need to be seen to resolve issues that alarm the media and public. By contrast, they posit that "police patrols," the everyday sort of scrutiny needed to ensure that organizations operate effectively and efficiently, are less likely to attract legislative bodies because there is little political currency to be garnered. Furthermore, they seldom have the time, resources, and in-house expertise to provide such necessary but mundane functions.

Canada has historically relied on review bodies working in secure environments with security-cleared staff to perform the "police patrol" forms of scrutiny that routinely check for organizational efficacy and propriety. Some like SIRC are independent of the executive branch; others such as the inspector-general of CSIS are within it. But in every instance their purview is limited to a single intelligence organization, a significant weakness given the cross-departmental nature of security and intelligence. SIRC, for example, has a proactive capacity to conduct routine checks on the efficacy and propriety of CSIS, but no mandate to go further afield. Though these bodies have full access to the agencies they monitor, they sometimes are thwarted in using their powers, as inspectors-general of CSIS have found. Similarly, because they are limited in how they report, their capacity to draw public or media attention to an issue—and hence to call responsible ministers fully to account—is limited.

A further weakness in the system is that there are few real opportunities to evaluate how well these bodies perform and whether they have adequate support staff with institutional expertise. While the special committee that reviewed the CSIS Act found SIRC's research capacity to be wanting in one case, it could not tell whether this was atypical. Similarly, the review body dealing with the RCMP has found itself ill-equipped in the national security sphere. Since 1990, there has been but one independent study to evaluate the capacity of review bodies in the security and intelligence sector; significantly, this did not consider matters of organizational capacity, performance, or due economy. Initiated by the auditor-general after the post–September 11, 2001, budget increases, this concluded that the monitoring of compliance with law and ministerial direction varied widely.[34]

Only with CSIS was there any independent capacity to review the compliance of the Service. It also observed that there was no independent review capacity covering the various National Defence units involved in domestic intelligence collection. The same was true for the Customs and Revenue Agency and the Financial Transactions and Report Analysis Centre of Canada.[35]

Though the Senate has performed useful investigations into Canada's counterterrorism capabilities and the capacity of its national security sectors, these have been of an ad hoc nature.[36] There has been no effective legislative committee that could deal either with the "fire alarms" that have arisen or check whether those performing "police patrols" were acting effectively.[37] Such committees as have existed—even when performing a statutory duty—have often been thwarted from fulfilling their mandate by an executive branch intent on restricting necessary access to documents and people. Admittedly, this inadequacy rests partly with Parliament in not ensuring that committees work under oath, in a secure environment with adequate security-cleared staff.

A new effective oversight system encompassing fire alarm scrutiny with that of police patrols is now in the offing. Some form of permanent parliamentary oversight mechanism with real access to classified information will soon be put in place. It is far from clear, however, whether this will be a truly independent parliamentary body or merely a committee of parliamentarians working for the executive branch. If it is to attend to the democratic deficit, only a parliamentary body can effect true ministerial accountability. Also unclear is the breadth of the remit it will have. If it is to scrutinize Canada's security and intelligence community effectively, it will need a broader purview than the British Intelligence and Security Committee possesses. As recent events there reveal, important areas lie outside its purview—the Joint Intelligence Committee and the Defence Intelligence Staff, to name but two bodies not covered by British legislation. As well, it will need to consider not just whether organizations comply with Canadian laws and policy directives but whether they have the capacity to fulfill their mandates, whether they have performed as expected, and whether they are operating with due economy as Paul Light has advocated.[38] To do this it will have to work closely with the review bodies now in place doing the police patrol work. Today, Juvenal's question—Who will watch the watchers?—is as pertinent as when first posed.

Notes

1. Jeff Sallot, *Nobody Said No* (Toronto: James Lorimer & Company, 1979), 94–95.
2. McDonald Commission, 1981, Second Report, Volume 2: 754–76.
3. McDonald Commission, 1981, Second Report, Volume 2: 896–905.

4. Prime minister of Canada, *Changes to Government* (Ottawa, Government of Canada, 2003)

5. Steve Hewitt, *Spying 101: The RCMP's Secret Activities at Canadian Universities, 1917–1997* (Toronto: University of Toronto Press, 2002).

6. Stuart Farson, "Security Intelligence Versus Criminal Intelligence: Lines of Demarcation, Areas of Obfuscation and the Need to Re-evaluate Organizational Roles in Responding to Terrorism," *Policing and Society* 1 (1991a): 65–87.

7. Office of the Auditor-General of Canada, *Report* [Online], (2003): Chapter 10 section 10.132. Available at: www.oag-bvg.gc.ca/domino/reports.nsf/html/20031110ce.html. Accessed January 12, 2004.

8. The role of the private sector in providing intelligence is not considered here but may be significant. See: James Keeley, Rob Hubert, and Robert N. Huebert (eds.), *Commercial Satellite Imagery, United Nations Peacekeeping and Canadian Security: A View from Above* (Aldershot: Ashgate, 2004).

9. The current role of the highly secretive JTF2 is unclear.

10. Alistair S. Hensler, "Creating a Foreign Intelligence Service," *Canadian Foreign Policy* 3(3), (1995): 15–35.

11. Brian Laghi, "War on Terror: Inside Ottawa: CSIS admits to spying abroad, *Globe and Mail,* October 19, 2001; Steward Bell, "CSIS admits to spying abroad," *National Post* (October 20, 2003); Bruce Campion-Smith, "Global spy role grows: CSIS head Canadian agency operating 'sans frontiers.' Policy-maker wonders if new agency needed," *Toronto Star,* October 27, 2003.

12. Stuart Farson, "So you don't like our Cover Story—Well we have Others: The Development of Canada's Signals Intelligence Capacity through Administrative Sleight of Hand," in *(Ab)Using Power: The Canadian Experience,* eds. Robert Menzies, Dorothy Chunn, and Susan C. Boyd (Halifax, Fernwood Press, 2001), 78–94.

13. Privy Council Office, *The Canadian Security and Intelligence Community* (Ottawa: Government of Canada, 2001), 14.

14. Stuart Farson, "Restructuring Control in Canada: The McDonald Commission of Inquiry and its Legacy," in *Controlling Intelligence,* ed. Glen Hastedt (London: Frank Cass, 1991): 155–85.

15. McDonald Commission, 1981, Volume 1 Part III.

16. McDonald Commission, Second Report, Volume 2: 901.

17. Senate of Canada, *Delicate Balance: A Security Intelligence Service in a Democratic Society* (Special Committee on the Canadian Security Intelligence Service, Ottawa: Ministry of Supply and Services, 1983).

18. Ibid, 32.

19. *CSIS Act* Section 21.

20. Jim Bronskill, "The spy who snubbed me: Watchdog says CSIS boss refused meetings for years," *Montreal Gazette,* June 3, 1999.

21. Senate, 1983: 35.

22. Stuart Farson, "The Noble Lie Revisited: Parliament's Five-Year Review of the CSIS Act: Instrument of Change or Weak Link in the Chain of Accountability?" in *Accountability for Criminal Justice,* ed. Philip C. Stenning (Toronto: University of Toronto Press, 1995), 185–212.

23. Sharon L. Sutherland, "The Al-Mashat Affair: Administrative Accountability in Parliamentary Institutions," *Canadian Public Administration* 34(4) (1991): 573–603; Reg Whitaker, "The 'Bristow Affair': A Crisis of Accountability in Canadian Security Intelli-

gence," *Intelligence and National Security* 11(2) (1996): 279–305; Stuart Farson, "In Crisis and in Flux? Politics, Parliament and Canada's Intelligence Policy," *Journal of Conflict Studies* 16 (1) (1996): 30–56.

24. Stuart Farson, "The Noble Lie Revisited," 203.90

25. House Of Commons, Special Committee on the Review of the CSIS Act and the Security Offences Act, *In Flux but not in Crisis* (Ottawa: House of Commons, 1990): 203–215.

26. Ronald J. Daniels, Patrick Macklem, and Kent Roach, *The Security of Freedom: Essays on Canada's Anti-Terrorism Bill* (Toronto: University of Toronto Press, 2001); David Daubney, Wade Deisman, David Jutras, Errol Mendes, and Patrick Molinari, *Terrorism Law and Democracy, How is Canada Changing following September 11?* (Montréal: Les Édition Thémis, 2002); K. Roach, *September 11: Consequences for Canada* (McGill Queens University Press, 2003).

27. Jim Bronskill, "Government ignores calls to amend 'seriously flawed' Official Secrets Act," *Ottawa Citizen*, December 18, 2000.

28. Prime Minister of Canada, *Changes to Government* [Online] (Ottawa, Government of Canada, 2003).

29. Privy Council Office *Ethics, Responsibility, Accountability: An Action Plan for Democratic Reform–February 4 2004.*

30. See chapter 5 by Ian Leigh in this volume.

31. Office of the Auditor-General of Canada, *Report* [Online], (2003): Chapters 3–5).

32. Parliament does not record hearings held outside Canada. The quotation is from the author's personal notes.

33. Mathew McCubbins and Thomas Schwartz "Congressional Oversight Overlooked: Police Patrols versus Fire Alarms," *American Journal of Political Science* 28(1) (1984): 165–79.

34. Office of the Auditor-General of Canada, *Report* (2003).

35. Though the Auditor-General's Report mentions the Department of Foreign Affairs and International Trade, and Citizenship and Immigration Canada, it does not consider how these are reviewed. The role of the Privy Council is not considered by the report.

36. Senate of Canada, Special Committee of the Senate on Terrorism and Public Safety, *Terrorism* (Ottawa: Ministry of Supply and Services Canada, 1987); Second Special Committee of the Senate on Terrorism and the Public Safety, *Terrorism* (Ottawa: Ministry of Supply and Services Canada, 1989); Special Committee on Security and Intelligence, *Report* (Ottawa: Senate of Canada, 1999); Senate of Canada, Standing Senate Committee on National Security and Defence, *Canadian Security and Military Preparedness* (Ottawa: Senate of Canada, 2002); Senate of Canada, Standing Senate Committee on National Security and Defence, *Defence of North America: A Canadian Responsibility* (Ottawa: Senate of Canada, 2002); Senate of Canada, Standing Senate Committee on National Security and Defence, *For an Extra $130 Buck . . . Update on Canada's Military Financial Crisis: A View from the Bottom Up* (Ottawa: Senate of Canada, 2002); Senate of Canada, Standing Senate Committee on National Security and Defence, *The Myth of Security at Canada's Airports* (Ottawa: Senate of Canada, 2003); Senate of Canada, Standing Senate Committee on National Security and Defence, *Canada's Coastlines: The Longest Under-defended Borders in the World*, 2 Volumes (Ottawa, Senate of Canada, 2003).

37. Stuart Farson, "Parliament and its Servants: Their Role in Scrutinizing Canadian Intelligence," *Intelligence and National Security* 15(2) (2000): 225–56.

38. Paul Light, *Monitoring Government: Inspectors General and the Search for Accountability* (Washington D.C.: Brookings Institute, 1993).

7

Intelligence and Accountability in a State without Enemies: The Case of Norway

Fredrik Sejersted

The basic challenge of making intelligence and counterintelligence accountable is common to all democratic systems of governance. On the one hand, efficient intelligence services are vital for national security and stability, and they necessarily have to conduct most of their activities in deep secrecy. This limits the possibilities for democratic oversight and accountability. On the other hand, the need for such oversight and accountability is particularly acute with regard to secret agencies, which often will have the capability not only of endangering the basic rights and liberties of citizens, but also of covertly interfering in the processes of democratic governance. Intelligence oversight is a field riddled with inherent problems and paradoxes.[1]

Though the basic challenges are the same, the ways in which liberal democracies have responded to them differs widely. One reason for this is that the structural problems are too complicated for political and constitutional theory to construe one, or even a few, general models. There can be many solutions, some good, some not so good, but none of them ideal. And any model attempting to establish efficient intelligence oversight must be specifically tailored to national needs and characteristics—to the constitutional structure, the political and historical traditions, the perceived external and internal threats, the size and capabilities of the secret services, the democratic maturity and stability of the system, and a number of other factors.

From this perspective, Norway enjoys the privilege of being small, peaceful, and dull. There are no serious external or internal threats to national security, the secret agencies are well-behaved, and the political system is stable and mature. The preconditions for making intelligence accountable are among the most favorable in the world. If democratic oversight is not possible here, it is not possible anywhere.

So it should come as no surprise that Norway does have a model for intelligence oversight. The main characteristic of this model is a strong emphasis on legislative (as opposed to executive) oversight, or rather on oversight conducted on behalf of the legislature, by the Committee for Oversight of the Intelligence, Surveillance and Security Services (*Utvalget for kontroll med etterretnings-, overvåknings- og sikkerhetstjeneste*). This Committee is appointed by and reports directly to Parliament, but the seven members are not members of Parliament. The oversight they conduct is of a legalistic and professional rather than a political nature, and their mandate, as laid down by parliamentary statute, focuses on the observance of the rule of law.

Within this mandate, the Committee has extensive investigative powers. Its oversight covers the whole of the Norwegian intelligence machinery, which consists of the Intelligence Service, the Police Security Service, and the National Security Authority, but the extent and intensity of the oversight varies as regards the three agencies. Oversight of the Police Security Service is strict, while that of the Intelligence Service is more marginal. The oversight is primarily of an ex-post-facto nature, and the agencies are forbidden from consulting with the Committee about future operations.[2] The major part of the Committee's work takes place through regular inspections, during which the agencies are required to present documents, answer questions, and give briefings. The Committee can initiate inquiries, and it also deals with complaints from individuals and organizations.

This model of oversight has now been in operation for some nine years, and on the whole it seems to be working well. In its early days, the Committee uncovered one major "scandal," which resulted in the forced resignation of the head of the Police Security Service as well as the minister responsible (see the following discussion). Since then, there has been less controversy, but rather a steady and continuous oversight that seems to have gained the acceptance of the agencies, as well as the approval of Parliament and the press. In a small country, with a moderate-sized intelligence community, this has created the preconditions for an acceptable degree of political and administrative accountability. Indeed, within the limits set by the Committee's statutory mandate, it is difficult to envisage a stricter oversight regime, without at the same time seriously endangering the effectiveness and efficiency of the secret agencies.

The legislative oversight of the Norwegian intelligence machinery is supplemented by executive control and oversight of a more traditional administrative nature, less visible to the public and more concerned with the effectiveness, efficiency, and quality of the agencies. There is little coordination between the executive and the legislative oversight procedures, and results from the former are seldom channeled into the latter.

Background

The Norwegian Secret Services

The Norwegian secret services consist of three agencies, the Intelligence Service, the Police Security Service, and the National Security Authority. The organizational structure reflects the traditional distinctions between intelligence, counterintelligence, and other security tasks, as well as between "military" and "civilian" agencies.

The Norwegian secret services were formed by Norway's position during the Cold War, as a NATO member on the strategically sensitive northern flank, bordering upon the former Soviet Union, and with close military ties to the United States. The services are from a comparative perspective naturally quite small, but in relationship to the size and apparent stability of the country they are still rather large and well developed. As in other Western democracies, the challenges facing the services have been profoundly influenced by the breakup of the Iron Curtain and the new threats to national security and stability arising over the last decade.

The Intelligence Service (*Etterretningstjenesten*) is formally a military agency, though most of the staff is civilian. It is organized as part of the Armed Forces, and reports to the chief of defence and the minister of defence. Its mandate is to gather and analyze intelligence from abroad, and the main task has traditionally been that of electronic signal intelligence. It operates a number of listening stations and vessels for electronic naval monitoring of the Russian Northern Fleet, including the nuclear deterrence force based on submarines stationed on the Kola Peninsula, just across the border. Unknown to Parliament and the public, the financing of this quite large organization was, up until the early 1990s, for the most part (more than 90 percent) covered by the United States and NATO. Today, it is financed nationally. During the last decade, the tasks of the Intelligence Service have both grown and to some extent changed, reflecting new requirements for a broader range of intelligence information.

The existence and activities of the Intelligence Service have traditionally been shrouded in deep secrecy, and while this has changed somewhat recently, it is still by far the most secretive of the services. A statutory basis for the Intelligence Service was established for the first time by parliamentary legislation as late as 1998.[3] The Act states that the mandate of the Service is to gather intelligence on, and counteract, external threats to national security and other vital national interests, and it is explicitly prohibited from gathering information on Norwegian citizens on national territory.

The Police Security Service (*Politiets Sikkerhetstjeneste*) is a civilian agency, organized as a rather independent part of the police force, under the minister of justice. Its main tasks have traditionally been that of counterintelligence against foreign agencies operating on Norwegian soil, and surveillance of national citizens suspected of threatening national security and other vital national interests. During the Cold War, the main focus of the agency was to counteract Soviet and Eastern European intelligence. But the agency also conducted extensive surveillance on national citizens, especially on the political far (though not always so very far) left. Over the last decade, the tasks of the Service have both grown and changed dramatically. While it still conducts traditional counterintelligence, a fast-growing part of its work is now connected to the "new" threats. And its traditional preoccupation with the political far left has been replaced by a keener interest in the more sinister activities of the far right.

The former secretive nature of the Police Security Service was more or less blown apart in the 1990s, during which it was subjected to intensive scrutiny and debate, following a number of (real and imaginary) "scandals,"[4] and resulting in a major reorganization. It was only recently (2002) given a statutory basis, through an amendment to the 1995 Police Act, but its organization, resources, procedures, and tasks have for some time to a large extent been publicly known. Its powers to conduct operations through wiretapping, surveillance, and house searches are subject to the same legal requirements as are those of the ordinary police force, which often means that a (secret) court decision is necessary. But the Service is subjected to a far stricter oversight regime (legislative and executive) than applies to the ordinary police.

The National Security Authority (*Nasjonal Sikkerhetsmyndighet*) was established by a statutory act in 2001, as a civilian directorate under the Ministry of Defence. It replaced the former (military) Defence Security Service. Its tasks are of a preventive and defensive nature, and it does not conduct investigations or operations. It is the highest authority for issuing and withdrawing personnel security clearances, classifying and declassifying information, and for the physical and electronic securing of governmental and other sensitive premises against espionage. Though secretive, its work is seldom subject to the same potential controversy as are the operations of the two other agencies.

Oversight of the Agencies until the Early 1990s

Until the early 1990s, the structures for intelligence oversight of the Norwegian secret services were on the whole poorly developed, particularly as regards legislative oversight. The political and administrative climate was heavily influenced by the Cold War and by a broad consensus that vital national interests were best served by leaving the agencies to themselves. As in many other countries, the government effectively argued that the idea of parliamentary oversight was inherently alien to the concept of running secret services, and this was broadly and tacitly accepted by all political parties, with the futile exception of the small and marginal Socialist Peoples Party (which was itself subject to quite extensive secret surveillance). On the whole, Parliament was kept outside the "ring of secrecy," and most MPs were perfectly comfortable with this.

Dealing with the Past—the Lund Inquiry (1994–96)

This changed dramatically in the early 1990s, when new light was shed on the secret services. In a number of books and articles the services were criticized for allegedly having conducted illegal political surveillance and irregular operations, and for having had too close ties to the ruling Labour Party. This wave of criticism corresponded in time with a marked shift in the national security climate, following the breakup of the Iron Curtain. The result was a widespread public feeling that time was ripe for a major inquiry into the activities of the secret services, past and present. Demand for an inquiry gained the support both of the Conservative opposition and the Radical Socialist opposition, thereby creating a parliamentary majority, which the minority Labour government could not withstand.

The result was the Lund Commission, appointed by Parliament in 1994. The five members were headed by a judge of the Supreme Court, Ketil Lund, and included a retired general and a former radical politician. The Commission had a professional staff of eight, including historians and police investigators, and wide powers of inquiry. The mandate was to inquire into all allegations of illegal or irregular surveillance of Norwegian citizens, by any of the intelligence and security agencies, from 1945 until the present. The result was a 600-page report, presented to Parliament in the spring of 1996, which was declassified and published.[5]

In effect, this was a "truth commission," which received general acceptance on all sides of the political landscape. The Lund Commission found a lot to criticize in the agencies, particularly in the Police Security Service, but the most serious allegations were found to be unsubstantiated. For the agencies, the report was a rough encounter with the new requirements of a more transparent modern society, and it led to major reorganizations. But at the same time the report of the Commission also washed away the sins of the past, doing this so effectively as to create a basis both for national reconciliation, and for greater future legitimacy for the agencies concerned. The Lund Report is a unique historical document, and in a comparative perspective it is an example of how a thorough inquiry into the intelligence machinery can produce results that are in the long term beneficial both to the agencies and to society at large.

The Establishment of New Oversight Procedures in 1996

Just as the Lund Commission was appointed to uncover the sins of the past, a parallel process was started to establish more efficient oversight procedures for the future. In 1993 Parliament made a decision that intelligence oversight should be intensified and that Parliament itself should have a role. A special committee was appointed in 1994 to draft the legislation, and in 1995 Parliament adopted the Act Relating to the Oversight of the Intelligence, Surveillance and Security Services, thereby establishing the new Intelligence Oversight Committee, which came into operation in the spring of 1996.

The creation of the Intelligence Oversight Committee coincided with a more general reform of parliamentary scrutiny and oversight procedures in the early 1990s,[6] reflecting the political context at the time, and growing demands for increased accountability. The intensification of intelligence oversight was both part of this general trend and a result of the more specific processes that also led to the Lund Commission.

In creating the new model for intelligence oversight, the legislators were inspired by experiences and procedures from other countries, notably the other Nordic countries, the UK, Germany, the Netherlands, Canada, and Australia.[7] But the result was an original Norwegian model, reflecting national needs and characteristics. The most radical feature was that much of the oversight was moved away from the executive to the legislative branch, and the fact that oversight of the whole intelligence and counterintelligence machinery should be conducted by one single Committee, on behalf of Parliament.

The Parliamentary Intelligence Oversight Committee

The Legal Basis and Mandate of the Committee

The legal basis for the Intelligence Oversight Committee is the Parliamentary Act of February 3, 1995, and supplementary Instructions issued by Parliament on May 30, 1995. Together, they form a detailed set of rules for how the oversight procedures should be conducted, as well as establishing the Committee's powers of inquiry.

According to the Act, the activities to be scrutinized by the Committee are defined functionally, and not by reference to the three established secret agencies. If other governmental bodies conduct intelligence or counterintelligence, this will also fall within the competence of the Committee. In practice the oversight is closely related to the three agencies, and the detailed procedures in the Instructions are also tailored to each of these.

The main purpose of the Committee's oversight is to safeguard the interests of individuals under the rule of law. According to article 2 of the Act the first aim is to prevent "any exercise of injustice against any person." This is modified in the Instructions, which states that, as a general rule, the oversight should not include activities directed against persons who are not resident in Norway, nor activities "involving foreign citizens whose residence in Norway is associated with service for a foreign state." In other words, the idea is to protect Norwegian citizens on native soil and other individuals living their private lives here. Activities directed against foreign agents (and indeed Norwegians abroad) are as a main rule not covered. The Committee may however also conduct oversight in such cases, "when special grounds so indicate."

The Committee's oversight is primarily concerned with preventing "injustice," which should be read as a legal criterion, allowing it to investigate, for example, illegal surveillance or wiretapping. But the Committee shall also conduct a more discretionary test of proportionality, and may criticize any means of intervention against individuals that exceed those "required under the circumstances." Thus, the Committee may, for example, criticize the denial of a security clearance, even if it is within the legal powers of the agency concerned.

Another part of the oversight mandate according to the Act is to ensure that intelligence and security activities "do not involve undue damage to civic life," and that they are kept "within the framework of statute law, administrative or military directives and non-statutory law." The reference to "civic life" is rather vague. The reference to legal rules is more concrete: it refers to other legal restrictions on the agencies and gives the Committee the competence to raise cases that do not necessarily involve individual rights. However, one difficulty is that the rules governing the agencies are rather wide and discretionary, thus giving few criteria for any sort of extensive oversight.

According to Caparini,[8] intelligence oversight bodies generally aim to assess one of two things—either the "efficacy" of the intelligence service or the "propriety" of its activities. The Norwegian model of legislative oversight is almost entirely focused on "propriety" and leaves "efficacy" to the executive. The Committee has neither the competence nor the qualifications to evaluate the intelligence and analysis supplied by the secret agencies, nor to question their effectiveness and efficiency. Such evaluations are left to executive oversight procedures, and (to a lesser extent) to the Office of the Auditor-General.

Another restriction on the Committee's oversight is that (as the main rule) it is not concerned with operations outside of Norwegian territory. This effectively means that most activities of the Intelligence Service are not covered. The Intelligence Service may eavesdrop on the Russians as much as it likes, and should it happen to recruit agents abroad, or conduct other kinds of secret operations on foreign soil, these will normally not be reported to the Committee.

A somewhat different restriction on the Committee is laid down in the last paragraph of section 2, which states that the purpose is "purely monitory," which means that the oversight shall be ex post facto, and that the Committee may not instruct the agencies, nor be used by them for consultations (more on this later).

The Committee's oversight is primarily directed against the secret agencies as such, and not against the relevant ministries or ministers. The main purpose is to prevent injustice, and to ensure respect for the rule of law in the agencies—not to question how central government makes use of them, through instructions and political signals. This is reflected in the fact that the Committee's otherwise wide powers of inquiry do not apply to the requiring of documents and information from ministers, nor from civil servants working in the ministries. The (debatable) idea behind this is that oversight of ministers should formally be a task for Parliament itself, and not for a Committee of professionals, acting on behalf of Parliament. Should the Committee, however, find indications that the agencies have been misused for political purposes by the ruling party, for example to spy on the opposition, this would certainly be seen as falling within the heart of the oversight mandate.

Appointment and Resources of the Committee

The Committee has seven (part-time) members, including the chairman. They are appointed by Parliament in plenary session, on the recommendation of the Presidium. The term of office is five years, and the members may be reappointed. The members must be cleared for the highest security classification in accordance with national and NATO rules. The Committee is quorate when five members are present. It functions as a collective body, but inspections and investigations may be conducted by one or more of the members, assisted by the secretary.

The Committee is an external parliamentary body, which conducts its day-to-day work independently of Parliament itself, and current MPs may not be members. In this respect, the Committee differs from legislative oversight models in most other Western countries, in which the oversight bodies are composed of parliamentarians. The idea behind the Norwegian model is to combine the principle of legislative oversight with the need for more professionalized, confidential, politically neutral, and work-intensive procedures. The Committee enjoys the authority of being a "parliamentary" institution, and it reports directly to Parliament, but it functions as an independent body, removed from the daily political struggles. Parliament may in principle instruct the Committee to investigate a given case, though so far it has not done so, but it may not interfere in the way in which the Committee conducts its oversight. The model is partially copied from that of the Parliamentary ombudsman, and the members should in principle be regarded as a kind of "intelligence ombudsmen."

Just how professional and politically neutral the Committee should be has been the subject of some debate. When the first committee was appointed in 1996, the procedures allowed for each of the main parties represented in Parliament effectively to choose their own candidates, and all the members had some affiliation to a political party. Most of them had formerly held some kind of political office. This system was soon criticized, and in 1998 Parliament changed the procedures, so that new members are nominated by the Presidium (the Speakers). This in effect means that appointments are subject to broader considerations and compromises, taking into account the need for professional expertise.[9] On later occasions, three "professional" and politically neutral members have been appointed—a former diplomat, a judge, and a professor of history. At the same time, two of the original members have been reappointed, and two others chosen amongst former politicians. The result is a strange mix of "political" and "professional" expertise, which in practice seems to work rather well.

When the Committee was first appointed in 1996, there was an unwritten political understanding that the chairman should belong to the opposition. But this was abandoned in 1999, when a politically "neutral" former diplomat was appointed the new chairman. Amongst those members who are still chosen on a more political basis, care is however still taken to ensure that they reflect the main political interests represented in Parliament. Most importantly, the Committee has always had a member from the Socialist Peoples Party, a party which has traditionally been critical of the secret services, and which has itself formerly been subjected to extensive surveillance. There is a quite broad (if not complete) political consensus that this is vital in order to ensure the legitimacy of the oversight procedures.

The secretariat of the Committee is small. It consists of an office secretary and two part-time legal secretaries, drafted from the office of the Parliamentary ombudsman. Their professional training is that of handling legal cases, particularly citizens' complaints, and they are neither investigators nor intelligence experts. The Committee also has the right to engage expert assistance, but this possibility of further professionalizing oversight has only been used moderately.

The limited staff resources clearly restrict the Committee's ability to conduct more extensive inquiries and investigations as well as its ability to be proactive. There is a certain discrepancy between the tasks laid down in the mandate and the resources allocated to the Committee. To some extent this is intentional. Parliament does not suffer from lack of money, and it would have been easy within the same oversight framework to give the Committee a professional staff of five or ten persons. But this would in effect have made it a completely different institution, and would have resulted in rather more intense oversight of the agencies than Parliament deemed necessary.

Powers of Inspection and Inquiry

The Committee mainly conducts its oversight in two ways—through inspections of the agencies, and by dealing with complaints and inquiries. Of these two, the inspections are by far the most time-consuming, and arguably also the most important part of the oversight. In a comparative perspective, the strong emphasis on inspections is a particular characteristic of the Norwegian model.

The rights and duties of the Committee to conduct inspections are laid down in the Act and the Instructions, which specifies the minimum annual number of twenty inspections. Advance notice of inspections is given, though in principle unannounced inspections may also be conducted.

During inspections, the Committee may, according to section 4 of the Act, demand access to the agencies' archives, registers, premises, and installations of all kinds. All employees of the agencies shall on request procure all documents, materials, equipment, and so on that may have significance for the purpose of the inspection. The agencies are under a duty to keep archives and registers in such a way that they may be scrutinized effectively by the Committee.

Inspections of agency headquarters usually follow a regular pattern. The Committee is first briefed by the agency leadership on current general matters and presented with surveys on new cases and new major developments falling within its mandate. The parties then discuss cases currently being scrutinized by the Committee, and finally there is often a physical inspection of registers, journals, archives, or specific premises or installations.

Although the inspections follow a more or less regular pattern, the intensity and nature of the oversight conducted differs as regards the three agencies; that is, the Police Security Service is subjected to the most thorough scrutiny, followed by the National Security Authority, while oversight of the Intelligence Service is more limited.

The Committee's right to require documents from the agencies, according to section 4 of the Act, is not confined to the inspections, but may be exercised at all times. Thus the Committee may in principle demand access to any document or other piece of evidence. Especially sensitive documents are read in the offices of the agency concerned, but other documents are given in copy to the Committee.

As a main rule, the Committee's right of access to documents and information under the Act is unlimited (save from ministerial information). This is moderated in the Instructions, which states that the Committee shall not apply for more extensive access to classified information than is necessary for the purposes of the oversight, and that it shall have regard to the need to protect sources and information received from abroad. This puts the Committee under a constant obligation to evaluate what kind of information is really needed in order to conduct efficient oversight within the mandate. But it is not formally a legal restraint on the right of access, since the Instructions also state that disputes over access shall be decided by the Committee itself, subject to a right for the agency to formally protest.

During inspections of the agencies, the Committee will have discussions with the intelligence and security officials present, and the members may ask them questions on the cases under investigation. This is how the Committee gathers by far most of its oral evidence, and it is done rather informally. The Committee has the legal powers to formally summon witnesses, but these rules have so far never been applied in practice.

Complaints and Inquiries Initiated by the Committee

According to section 4 of the Act, the Committee shall "investigate all complaints from persons and organizations." This means that anyone who believes that one of the agencies may have committed an injustice against him or her may complain to the Committee, and the complaint will be looked into, as long as it falls within the oversight mandate and shows at least some likelihood of being based on facts. This is the part of the Committee's oversight function that in particular resembles the work of the Parliamentary ombudsman, although subject to rather stricter rules of confidentiality.

The number of complaints received each year has varied. During its first two years in operation, the Committee received a total of eighty-nine, but due to public misunderstanding of the nature of the oversight, half of these had to be dismissed as falling outside of the Committee's mandate. The numbers for the following years have been twenty-one (1998), seventeen (1999), fourteen (2000), twenty-five (2001), and twenty-eight (2002). The large majority of complaints concern the Police Security Service, and typically involve allegations of illegal surveillance. There are also a few complaints each year against the security authorities, concerning denials or withdrawals of personnel security clearances. So far only two complaints have been received against the Intelligence Service.

Complaints are often investigated in connection with the inspections, during which the Committee may discuss the complaint with the agency and demand explanations or access to the relevant archives and registers. Sometimes special meetings are held on a case-to-case basis. The large majority of complaints have so far been found to be unsubstantiated. If, however, the investigation reveals grounds for criticism, the Committee will express this in a written statement to the agency. The Committee has no authority to instruct the agencies to take specific action, but it may express its opinion, and may make a recommendation to reconsider the case.

According to the Act, the Committee shall also "on its own initiative deal with all matters and factors that it finds appropriate to its purpose, and particularly matters that have been subjected to public criticism." Each year a number of inquiries are initiated by the Committee itself—eighteen in 1997, fourteen in 1998, five in 1999, seven in 2000, ten in 2001, and twelve in 2002. The emphasis that special attention should be given to matters that have been the subject of public criticism reflects the fact that traditionally "scandals" concerning the secret agencies are often first uncovered by the media. In practice, all serious allegations raised by the media will be looked into by the Committee. Usually, they are found to be unsubstantiated, and when the Committee reports this to Parliament, the legitimacy of the oversight process is such that this will normally quell public criticism and distrust. In this way, the work of the Committee has so far also served to bolster the legitimacy of the agencies.

Statements and Reports

The results of the Committee's oversight are given in full statements on a case-to-case basis to the agencies concerned, in short statements to complainants, and in the annual reports presented directly to Parliament. Sometimes short statements are also issued to the press. The ability of the Committee to demonstrate the basis for its conclusions is restricted by the fact that it operates within the ring of secrecy, and does not itself have the competence to declassify secret information.

The Committee's statements to the agencies shall, pursuant to section 4 of the Act, be "classified according to their contents," which means that they are not made public nor sent to Parliament. The statements are in effect a purely internal form of communication between the Committee and the agency and sometimes also the Ministry. The Committee does not have the competence to formally instruct the agencies, but it may point out faults and failures, and if it considers that decisions made by the agency are formally invalid (on legal grounds), or contrary to principles of good administration, it shall indicate so. It may also propose improvements to existing administrative arrangements, on matters relevant to the mandate of the oversight.

Even if (or rather because) the Committee's statements to the agencies are not made publicly known, and not shown to Parliament, they are in effect probably the most important outcome of the oversight procedure. It is through these statements that the Committee may in fact actively assist the agencies in uncovering, redressing, and preventing faults and failures. This part of the Committee's work in practice functions as a kind of "internal" audit, within the ring of secrecy. By acting in an advisory, rather than an adversarial, manner this should normally help to prevent potential controversy and make it easier for the agencies to accept comments, even of a critical nature.

Statements are also given to complainants, but these are necessarily short, since the Committee lacks the competence to disclose classified information. As a general rule it may only state whether or not the complaint gave valid grounds for criticism. According to the Act the Committee may not inform the complainant as to whether he or she has been subjected to secret surveillance. The Committee may however request the consent of the agency to provide a more detailed explanation, and this has been done in several cases, in order to give the complainant and the public a satisfactory response.

The Committee's obligation to submit reports to Parliament is stated in the Act, and regulated in some detail in the Instructions. The Committee shall submit an annual main report by April 1 each year, covering its activities during the previous year, but it may also submit reports on individual cases, if it uncovers matters that "should be made known to the Storting immediately." So far this has only happened once. Any report to Parliament on an individual case necessarily gives rise to great attention, and the Committee in practice is hesitant to precipitate a crisis, unless the case is both highly important and of great urgency. But its competence to do so does give it some leverage with the agencies.

According to the Act, reports to Parliament must be unclassified. This was not a constitutional requirement, but could be seen partly to reflect a parliamentarian self-awareness that MPs are notoriously bad at keeping secrets. It also highlights the principle that the Committee conducts its oversight on behalf of Parliament, as a more professional form of scrutiny, going further and deeper into the activities of the agencies than the legislative assembly should itself do. On a need-to-know basis, Parliament usually does not really need to know, nor should it. In this way, the Committee acts "as an agent of others who cannot be as well informed."[10] It can usually submit its conclusions, but not the premises on which these conclusions rest. It may criticize an agency in a particular case, or it may exonerate it from public allegations, but often it may not explain why, nor disclose the nuances of its evaluations. This highlights the importance of maintaining the Committee's legitimacy.

The reports of the Committee are submitted directly to Parliament, and not through the executive. The Committee has, however, made it a practice to send the draft report to the agencies, so that they can assess whether the contents are unclassified. If the agency objects to a particular piece of information, on the grounds that it is classified, the Committee must remove it. But the agencies cannot otherwise interfere with the contents of the report.

In practice the annual reports are fairly comprehensive and readable. Most of the report describes the findings of the regular oversight procedures (inspections held, complaints received, the number of inquiries). Usually the Committee simply indicates the results—for example, the number of complaints that have given rise to comment. But sometimes cases are described in more detail, and usually so if the case has been the subject of public debate.

The prohibition against reporting classified information is absolute, but if the Committee finds that it is vital for Parliament to be given classified information in a specific case, it shall "bring this to the attention" of Parliament. This requires a delicate act of balancing, since the existence of such information could itself be considered classified, but it is in principle workable. It is then a question for Parliament itself whether it wants to investigate the case further. The same procedure applies "if there is a need for further investigations of factors concerning which the Committee itself is unable to make any progress." This would be the case if a thread pursued by the Committee leads from the agency concerned into the domains of the Ministry, over which the Committee does not itself have formal powers of inquiry.[11]

The reports of the Committee are published as parliamentary documents, and reviewed by the Standing Committee on Scrutiny and Constitutional Affairs, followed by plenary debate.[12] The Standing Committee may inquire further into matters raised by the Committee, and to some extent it has done so, though only twice so far by itself conducting hearings and investigations.[13] On the whole the political attention given to the reports has varied widely from year to year, reflecting the contents of each report. The regular oversight activity of the Committee is usually of limited interest to the MPs. But when the Committee reports on controversial cases, Parliament easily gets excited. So far this has happened approximately every second or third year.

The Prohibition against "Consultations"

A structural dilemma for any intelligence oversight body is the need to build up confidence in the agencies while maintaining a critical distance. Due to the lack of alternative sources, the oversight body must to a large extent rely on information supplied by the agencies, and it must function within the ring of secrecy. This makes it "vulnerable both to co-optation by the audited and to pretensions of autonomous importance."[14] For the oversight body, the danger is not only that it may become too friendly with the agencies, but also that it may be tempted to exceed the role of auditor, and instead start to give instructions and advice.

This dilemma has long been recognized by those responsible for intelligence oversight in Norway. When the need for oversight of the secret services was first put on the agenda in the early 1950s, the initiative, interestingly enough, came from the head of the Police Security Service.[15] And what he proposed was a committee that could function both as "a breakwater and an auditor," with the mandate both to oversee the service and to give advice, especially on cases that might be politically sensitive. This idea was later turned down by the Ministry of Justice, which stated that an oversight body with the double function of auditor and advisor would risk becoming "co-responsible for activities which it must later investigate."

When the Intelligence Oversight Committee was established in 1995, there was never any suggestion that it should act as an advisor or a "breakwater" for the agencies. Instead the need for critical independence was stressed, and it was laid down in the Act that the purpose should be to conduct retrospective oversight, and that the Committee cannot give instructions to the agencies, nor be used by them for consultations.

Awareness of the prohibition against consultations is high both in the Committee and the agencies, and it is unthinkable that they should seek prior approval on operations. At the same time there is a grey zone between consultations and discussions, and especially so in an oversight arrangement that relies on frequent inspections and close contact. The atmosphere during inspections is seldom adversarial, nor is it meant to be so. This is recognized in the preparatory works to the Act, and the instructions of the legislator are to find a proper balance. Experiences so far indicate that the parties have managed to do so.

The principle of retrospective oversight is difficult to maintain fully when it comes to operations that run for some period of time. Cases of secret surveillance may take years and include a number of decisions. Should the Committee have to wait until the case was finally closed, this would clearly be unsatisfactory. This is recognized in the Instructions, which state that even if the Committee should "normally" abide by the principle of subsequent oversight, it may nevertheless "require access to information on current matters, and submit comments on such matters." Again, this calls for a balance to be struck. When in 2001 the Committee presented an evaluation of the oversight arrangement to Parliament, it highlighted the "tension" between subsequent oversight and the right to inquire into current cases. The Committee pointed out that this had often required difficult decisions to be made and indicated that there had been instances of disagreement between itself and the agencies. But on the other hand it stated that it is probably impossible to regulate this in a more precise manner than is already done, and that discretionary decisions must necessarily be made based on the facts of the individual case. This was approved by Parliament.[16]

The Committee In Operation

Baptism of Fire—the Furre Case

As the Committee first went into operation in the spring of 1996, it was almost immediately thrown into its most controversial case so far. This was just after the Lund Commission had presented its awesome report on the past activities of the secret agencies, which was still being reviewed by Parliament. Tensions were high. At the same time allegations were raised in the media that the Police Security Service had been secretly surveilling the Lund Commission and investigating one of its members. The auditee had been spying on its auditors.

The allegations were scrutinized by the new Committee, which to a large extent found them to be true. The Committee's highly critical report to Parliament led to the immediate resignation of the head of the Service.[17] Soon after, the prime minister was forced to sack the minister of justice, and later on both the permanent secretary and the director general of the police department resigned.

For the Police Security Service, the Furre case was a disaster. The legitimacy of the Service was already weakened by a number of lesser scandals, and by the findings of the Lund Commission. The Furre case came on top of this, and it was commonly held that it left the Service with its spine broken. It took a major reorganization and several years of confidence building for the Service to regain a degree of legitimacy, and it was arguably not until September 11, 2001, that this process was concluded.

For the new Oversight Committee, the Furre case was at first sight a great success. Just half a year into operation, it had managed to uncover a real security scandal, and it received the full backing of a broad majority in Parliament and a united press. In hindsight, the Committee's success was not unconditional. In the agencies, and indeed amongst not a few politicians, it was a tacit but not uncommonly held opinion that the Committee had acted rashly, and had made the case more controversial than necessary. This is open to argument. But it is a fact that the Furre case made the Committee start out in an adversarial mode, which might be well suited to the handling of serious scandals, but ill suited to efficient regular day-to-day oversight of a skeptical intelligence community. It took the Committee years of consolidation to gain an acceptable degree of confidence within the agencies.

Oversight of the Police Security Service

It was a stated purpose that oversight of the Police Security Service should be more extensive than of the other two agencies, and this is also how it works. The activities of the Service are at the heart of the oversight mandate, and this is also the agency that generates most of the complaints—lately around twenty each year. And the number of annual inspections prescribed in the Instructions (six of headquarters and four of regional offices) ensures that the Committee is well acquainted with the organization. Most of the oversight concerns cases of secret surveillance, or the more general procedures for registering persons, handling sensitive information, keeping proper archives, and so on. Of the many complaints only one or two each year give rise to critical comments.

According to the reports, the Committee has put a lot of effort into checking the general procedures of the Service, especially regarding registers and archives. This kind of oversight is time-consuming and not very glamorous, but it is of practical importance, and has resulted in a number of substantial improvements.

Only a few of the many individual cases considered by the Committee are described in any detail in the annual reports, and these are usually cases which have already received some kind of public attention.

One of these cases followed the expulsion from Norway in March 1998 of five Russian diplomats suspected of espionage. The case received intense media attention, and the more so when a ministry official told the press how he had acted as a double agent, helping the Police Security Service. This coincided in time with the presentation of a White Paper on the future organization of the Service, and allegations were raised in the media that the Service had timed the expulsion, and leaked the details, in order to appear in a positive light prior to the debate on its future. These allegations were looked into by the Committee, which cleared the Service by stating in the annual report that the case had been handled according to purely professional standards.[18]

In 2001 the Committee reported on a more controversial case, involving the investigation by the Service of a journalist suspected of being a former Stasi agent, which after three years was finally dropped for lack of evidence. The Committee did not comment on the substance of the case, but it criticized several aspects of its handling by the Service, including failures of routines for seized material, deficient internal information routines, and deficient information given to the suspect and his defense lawyer.

In 2002 the Committee reported on how the Service had conducted surveillance on demonstrators during a World Bank Conference in Oslo. The Committee did not explicitly criticize the Service, but it highlighted and discussed the distinction to be made between legitimate political demonstrations and criminal behavior. In the same year the Committee also reported on its inquiry into press allegations that the Sami minority population had been subject to surveillance on ethnic grounds. The Committee was skeptical of the grounds for surveillance in two of the registered Sami cases, but it found no evidence that they were based on ethnic considerations.

After a rough start with the Furre case, both the Committee and the Service were eager to normalize relations, and in the annual report for 1997 it was stated that these were now constructive. In later reports the Committee has repeatedly praised the Service for the way in which it responds to the oversight, and there seems to have been no major disputes. According to the reports, the Service has never tried to deny the Committee access to relevant information, and usually complies fully with its comments and opinions.

Oversight of the Intelligence Service

The Committee's oversight of the Intelligence Service is rather limited, and may even be seen as somewhat marginal, in comparison to the tasks and operations of this agency. This is mainly due to the fact that most of the activities of the Intelligence Service fall outside the Committee's mandate. But it is also partly because the Intelligence Service is a very non-transparent organization, which the Committee has found it hard to penetrate and to comprehend, and because most of its operations are of a highly technical (electronic) nature.

Oversight does however take place, within the limits prescribed by the Committee's mandate. Inspections are carried out twice a year at agency headquarters in Oslo, and two or three times a year at regional offices, including operational stations. During the first four years, the remarks on the Intelligence Service in the annual reports were short, usually stating that the Committee had found nothing to criticize, and that it was still in the process of learning about the agency. But in the more recent reports the remarks have been more substantial, and some cases of particular interest commented upon.

The oversight of the Intelligence Service rests mainly on two criteria. The first is that the Service must respect the legal restraints against conducting operations and surveillance on Norwegian territory. This has so far been a rather unobtrusive kind of oversight, with the Committee posing its regular question on whether the restraints are respected, and the agency giving the routine reply of— "why yes, of course." So far no evidence to the contrary has been reported.

The second criterion rests on the Committee's mandate to check that statute law and directives are respected. This gives a somewhat wider potential for scrutiny, although lessened by the fact that the relevant rules are rather widely and vaguely formulated. In practice the Committee has focused on the requirement that intelligence activities must be under proper "national control," which has always been a fundamental principle, but one which is now explicitly stated in the 2001 Instructions for the Intelligence Service. The importance of this can be understood when considering that the Intelligence Service was, until the early 1990s, financed for the most part by the United States, and that much of its electronic signal intelligence is of military interest to NATO as a whole. In recent years the Committee has inquired into several cases concerning allegations that intelligence operations were not under national control, but so far the annual reports do not give any support to these suggestions.

In 1998 a major dispute broke out between the Committee and the Intelligence Service, over what was primarily a question of access to information, but which also concerned the more fundamental question of how far oversight should go. The row started during an inspection, when the Committee uncovered a letter that the Intelligence Service had obtained from the minister of defence in early 1997, giving it permission to withhold information from the Committee if considered necessary for the protection of national or foreign sources. Such information will normally fall outside of what is necessary for the purposes of the Committee's oversight under the mandate, but the letter was still in pretty clear violation of the Committee's rights of access under the Act. The Committee reacted strongly to the letter. A protest was sent to the ministry, followed by a request for access to certain correspondence between the Intelligence Service and foreign agencies. The Service and the ministry responded negatively.

The incident was reported to Parliament in the annual report for 1998, although just by one short sentence, since the ministry refused to declassify the case. The one sentence was however enough to arouse the attention of Parliament and the press, and after some haggling, the relevant documents were declassified and given to the Standing Committee on Scrutiny and Constitutional Affairs. During the subsequent parliamentary review a broad majority sided with the Intelligence Service, and the Oversight Committee was in effect reprimanded for having exceeded its mandate.[19] A new unwritten procedure was introduced that gives the Intelligence Service the right to decide whether information demanded by the Committee is really relevant to the purposes of oversight. In such a case the Committee retains the right to bring the question before the minister, and if need be before Parliament. This awkward procedure applies only to the Intelligence Service, not the two other agencies, and has so far not been used.

For the Committee the lack of backing from Parliament came as an unpleasant surprise. The political reaction can be explained partly by the strong position enjoyed by the Intelligence Service in parliamentary circles (the Police Security Service would never have been able to stand up against the Committee in such a way). But it also illustrated the fact that the political climate had changed by the late 1990s, replacing the earlier oversight euphoria with a concern shared by many MPs that intelligence oversight had perhaps been carried a step too far, and that the time had come to set some limits.

After the final parliamentary debate on the incident, in June 1999, a mutual need was felt in the Committee and the Intelligence Service to repair and normalize relations, which coincided in time with the appointment of several new members to the Committee. Both parties applied some effort, and in 2000 the Committee could report to Parliament that relations had "improved considerably." Since then no further disputes have occurred, and judging by the latest annual reports oversight of the Intelligence Service seems now to be of a more constructive and substantial nature than before.

A case mentioned in the latest report can illustrate this. It concerns a large new radar installation, the Globus II, erected by the Intelligence Service in Vadsø, in the far north, which went into operation in 2002. In the press there have been frequent allegations that the radar is not under national control, and that one of its main purposes is to be a part of the planned U.S. shield against nuclear missiles (the National Missile Defense, or NMD). After inquiries and an inspection of the radar, the Committee could report that its operation was under strict Norwegian control, and that it was anyway technically unsuitable as part of the NMD.

Following the 2001 presentation to the European Parliament of a report on the so-called Echelon network of electronic surveillance,[20] the Committee has discussed this issue with the Intelligence Service on several occasions. According to the reports, the Service states that it has no information on Echelon, and does not participate in any such kind of network. It has however added that many countries may have the technical capability to conduct such electronic surveillance.

On the whole, oversight of the Intelligence Service seems to have improved and matured lately. Although it will remain limited, due to the Committee's mandate, there is probably still potential for further improvement, which could well fit in with the Service's current ambition of becoming a more modern institution for the provision of a broader range of intelligence.

Executive Oversight

The executive oversight of the intelligence and counterintelligence agencies is not as regulated as are the legislative procedures, and it is mainly conducted within the traditional administrative structures, under which the agencies are subordinate to the ministries, led by the ministers, who function both as heads of their ministries and as members of the cabinet. Thus, the Police Security Service is under the control and oversight of the Ministry of Justice, the National Security Authority under the control and oversight of the Ministry of Defence, and the Intelligence Service subordinate both to the chief of defence and to the Ministry of Defence.

There is little coordination between the legislative and the executive procedures for intelligence and security oversight, and the Intelligence Oversight Committee does not receive reports or information from the executive bodies. The main reason for this is probably the rather different nature of the two arrangements. The legislative oversight process is primarily directed against preventing injustice, and focuses on the rule of law and the propriety of the agencies' activities. To some extent it may help the agencies to uncover and redress faults and failures, but its main function is to protect citizens' rights, and ensure some degree of political accountability in the system. Executive oversight arrangements on the other hand are primarily focused on the effectiveness and efficiency of the agencies and function as an internal audit. They are not designed to foster political accountability, and results very seldom reach Parliament or the public. To some extent they may create internal, administrative accountability, in the sense that officials are held to account by their superiors, or (rarely) by their ministers, but this is not the main purpose, which is to improve quality, not to administer blame.

This clear partition of functions between legislative intelligence oversight (propriety and accountability) and executive intelligence oversight (effectiveness and efficiency) is a main characteristic of the Norwegian model.

Conclusions

If the Norwegian model may be summarized in one phrase, it is: Strong oversight within limits. Apart from a certain lack of staff resources, the model created for intelligence oversight on behalf of Parliament fulfills most criteria for evaluating the strength and substance of such arrangements. It is independent, it has a pro-active capacity, the membership reflects both professional standards and the spectrum of party politics, it has good access to sensitive information as well as the ability to maintain necessary secrecy, and after the first seven years of operation it has developed a satisfactory degree of institutional maturity and expertise. It is accepted by the agencies concerned, and approved by Parliament and the press.

The limits inherent in this oversight arrangement are intentional, and reflected in the statutory mandate of the Committee. The oversight is primarily concerned with the rule of law, and the protection of the individual rights of national residents, as well as the protection of democratic governance against undue influence by the secret services. Within these limits oversight is effective, and designed not only to uncover major "scandals," but also to deal with lesser incidents of misconduct or bad administrative judgement. The preventive effect of the Committee's oversight is probably the single most important outcome of the arrangement, and it has certainly contributed to a greater awareness of the rule of law within the agencies.

The efficiency, effectiveness, and general quality of the secret services falls outside the legislative oversight model, and this is left to executive oversight procedures, which are on the whole of a somewhat "weaker" nature, as well as less visible, and less liable to result in any kind of democratic accountability.

The substance and intensity of the legislative oversight varies as regards the three secret agencies. The Police Security Service is subject to rather strong oversight, and to some extent the same applies to the National Security Authority.

Most of the activities of the Intelligence Service fall outside of the legislative procedures. The model is primarily one of counterintelligence oversight, rather than of intelligence oversight.

The present oversight model was constructed in the mid-1990s, during a period of parliamentary obsession with oversight and accountability in general, and intelligence oversight in particular. Since then there has been a certain shift in the political climate, a tacit reaction to the new oversight regime, as illustrated in the 1998–99 dispute between the Committee and the Intelligence Service. The shift is not dramatic, nor has it really reduced the capability of the Committee to conduct its tasks. But it means that the Committee cannot automatically rely on parliamentary backing, unless it demonstrates that comments and criticism are well founded. And it means that future extensions of the oversight mandate and procedures are not on the agenda.

In a comparative perspective the Norwegian oversight model is strong, and in a national historical perspective it is also at an all-time high. The main challenge today is not to extend the system further, but rather to perfect it within the existing framework, and to maintain the present high alertness and the awareness of the need for intelligence oversight and accountability.

Notes

1. Marina Caparini, *Challenges of control and oversight of intelligence services in a liberal democracy*, Paper presented at the Workshop on Democratic and Parliamentary Oversight of Intelligence Services (Geneva, October 2002)

2. The word "oversight" does not readily correspond to any Norwegian term, and indeed even in English the exact definition seems to be rather vague. In Norwegian the term most used is "*kontroll*" (control), which in Norwegian usually implies a retrospective perspective, describing an activity of scrutiny or inquiry, an audit, taking place after something has happened, with the purpose of holding someone (preferably the right person) accountable, and resulting in some kind of evaluation, followed by approval or criticism. The word "oversight" seems to cover this (though it is sometimes used differently). In this context the point should be not to read any exact meaning into the word "oversight" as such, but rather to describe what *kind* of oversight the relevant Norwegian authorities conduct.

3. The Intelligence Service Act of March 20, 1998.

4. Trond Bergh and Knut Einar Eriksen, *Den hemmelige krigen. Overvåkning i Norge 1914–1997*, Volume II (Oslo: Cappelen Akademisk Forlag, 1998), 525–38. See also Fredrik Sejersted, *Kontroll og konstitusjon* (Oslo: Cappelen Akademisk Forlag, 2002), 339–40.

5. Dok. nr. 15 (1995–1996) (Lund-rapporten).

6. Sejersted, Kontroll.

7. NOU 1994:4, 22–24.

8. Caparini, *Challenges*.

9. In accordance with Norwegian traditions, care is also taken to see that both sexes should be represented on a roughly equal basis. In the current Committee, three of the

seven members are women, two of them "politically" appointed and one "professionally" (a judge).

10. James G. March and Johan P. Olsen, *Democratic Governance* (New York: Free Press, 1995), 164.

11. So far this has only happened once; the Furre case, Dok. nr. 16 (1996–97).

12. For those few familiar with the Norwegian language, the reports can easily be found on the homepage of the Parliament, www.stortinget.no, by looking under "Saker" (cases), and then going on to "Dokumenter" (documents). The reports are normally given the number "16," and the typical *reference* will be "Dokument nr. 16 (2000–2001)."

13. In 1997 (the Furre case), Innst. S. nr. 235 (1996–97) and 2003 (the Ellingsen case), Innst. S. nr. 273 (2002–2003).

14. March and Olsen, *Democratic Governance*, 164. March and Olsen present this as a general problem in all democratic oversight procedures, but one which is particularly acute when it comes to intelligence oversight. "Special legislative committees to audit intelligence services come to see the information world from the point of view of the services."

15. Bergh and Eriksen, Den hemmelige krigen, 56, and Sejersted, Kontroll, 288.

16. Innst. S. nr. 225 (2000–2001).

17. This is the only time that the Committee has submitted a special report to Parliament. Submitting the report presented a problem, since it contained information classified at the time. The Committee solved this by making Parliament aware of the report's existence, and this created enough political pressure for the Ministry of Justice to declassify the information. The report was then handed over to Parliament, cf. Dok. nr. 16 (196–97) and Innst. S. nr. 235 (1996–97).

18. Dok. nr. 16 (1998–99), 6.

19. Innst. S. nr. 232 (1998–99).

20. The Report on the existence of a global system for the interception of private and commercial communications (Echelon), presented to the European Parliament 11 July 2001.

PART 3

The Spread of Intelligence Accountability

8

An Unresolved Game: The Role of the Intelligence Services in the Nascent Polish Democracy[1]

Andrzej Zybertowicz

> In a revolutionary situation, the institutions of security intelligence play a far more exposed, ambiguous role than they do in consolidated democratic politics. Together with ethnic minorities, they are at the centre of post-communism's moral panics and conspiracy theories, yet at the same time they are expected to protect the people and enlighten policy-makers in a period of uncertainty and disquiet.[2]

In July 2001, in the twelfth year of Poland's transformation to democracy and two months before the parliamentary elections were won by the post-communist parties, member of Parliament (MP) and former minister of interior Zbigniew Siemiątkowski[3] stated that a reform of the services designed by him should "deeply plough the structure, which had been evolving for decades, and had through informal methods captured the whole organism of the state, and until now has operated with impunity beyond anybody's control."[4] Siemiątkowski's opinion is far from being exceptional.[5] The persistence of the problem invoked in his statement is well illustrated by the fact that after completion of the reform many similar criticisms were issued by prominent political figures belonging to all factions of the Polish political scene[6]

After a decade of unexplained scandals related to the secret services and without steps to adequate legalization and accountability of the services,[7] the Polish Parliament passed a new law on civilian secret services (statute of May 24, 2002). However, the reform of the services did not meet the official targets. According to the post-communist politicians and old regime's secret services' functionaries,[8] two main intelligence organizations, the civilian Office of State Protection (*Urząd Ochrony Państwa*—UOP) and the Military Information Services (*Wojskowe Służby Informacyjne*—WSI), both covering foreign and domestic intelligence tasks, had to be dissolved. Actually, two new organizations have been established, the Agency for Internal Security (*Agencja Bezpieczeństwa Wewnętrznego*—ABW) and the Foreign Intelligence Agency (*Agencja Wywiadu*—AW). Only the UOP was dissolved;[9] the military services remained virtually unscathed. In so doing, the undercover community, it seems, has once again proved that it can resist reform projects initiated by "irresponsible" politicians.[10] This chapter aims at analysis of the accountability of security and intelligence services in Poland. One must keep in mind that the process of redesigning the services is formed by Poland's transition processes to democracy, which are plagued by the communist police state heritage.[11] In these processes, the services are both an object of change and an actor of change. In order to capture this dual role the notion of "security complex" is introduced.

The Security Complex

In order to account best for the dynamics in the relationship between the nascent democracy and its secret services, the notion of a security complex, or an undercover community, is employed. In addition to the three main organizations providing intelligence to state's authorities (the WSI, the ABW, and the AW) the security complex consists of former intelligence agencies functionaries (both of the old and the new regime), many private security and detective organizations, and many formally inactive (i.e., officially de-registered) secret collaborators of communist services currently active in business, the media, and politics.

The complex is also composed of a number of state institutions (or branches thereof) authorized to collect information via operational measures. It includes sections of the state police (especially those staffed by former communist secret services operatives), the Army's General Direction of Military Reconnaissance (*Generalny Zarząd Rozpoznania Wojskowego*), the Border Guard's Bureau of Internal Affairs (*Biuro Spraw Wewnętrznych Straży Granicznej*), the Government's Bureau for Protection (*Biuro Ochrony Rządu*—BOR), a special force within the Ministry of Finance dealing with taxation crimes, and an oversight and control section located within the Customs Service (*Służba Celna*). It must be stressed that although these institutions are legally entitled to use operational techniques and are largely staffed by former secret services personnel, there are no provisions that would allow the legislative to supervise their work.[12]

Institutional and Cultural Legacies of the Old Regime

The strength of the security complex stems from institutional and cultural legacies of the old regime. The legacies, especially those related to the policing nature of communist regimes[13] have not been, according to many independent spectators,[14] properly dealt with until now. For example, the lustration[15] law passed as late as 1997[16] and came into force two years later. This accounts for, among other things, the persistence of networks of old commitments and a lack of integrity of many public figures (the latter is commonly acknowledged in the Polish public discourse[17]). What is more, the issue of accountability for the crimes committed by the old regime is still far from being settled.

In 1990 the communist services were substantially downsized; the civilian ones from about 25,000 to about 6,000 staffers; the military ones from about 6,000 to about 1,500 employees. The communist civilian Security Service (*Służba Bezpieczeństwa*—SB) was disbanded. Large parts of its staff went into the superficially reformed state police. Many other functionaries underwent a so-called verification (vetting) procedure in order to get into the new secret services. About 4,000 of the SB functionaries ended up working in the newly established UOP, forming the majority of its total staff of about 6,000.[18]

It took until 2002 to publicly acknowledge that the noncommunist politicians, responsible for the design of the new, democratic secret services ten years ago, had actually surrendered to the strong lobby of the foreign intelligence functionaries, who in order to maintain their influence successfully pressured to maintain a post-Soviet model of the secret services in Poland.[19]

The situation has been even worse with regard to the communist military secret services. Until now, they were not subjected to any external verification. They simply verified and reorganized themselves.[20] Formerly separated military intelligence and counterintelligence were put under one umbrella, and in August 1991, following a decision of the minister of defense, the Military Information Services (WSI) were established. Until December 1995 the WSI operated according to secret military orders. The statute of December 14, 1995, addressing the office of the Ministry of Defense[21] changed this, inasmuch as it put the service under the minister's control. However, this statue did not regulate the many legal issues of the WSI activity in a comprehensive manner. Belatedly, a statute fully dedicated to military secret services passed the Parliament on July 9, 2003.[22] Despite attempts by groups of the parliamentary opposition to change this (see e.g., Biuletyn, 2003), the statute did not include any procedures of external verification or personnel audit.

There are plenty of reasons to doubt whether the WSI has fully broken with past allegiances, murky interests, and the perpetuation of the old institutional mentality. It suffices to say that Gen. Tadeusz Rusak[23] revealed in September 2003 that the scale of abuses and scandals within the WSI was so serious that he refrained from dissolving the WSI only because of the sensitive process of the country's joining NATO.[24] It seems that the military services have been reorganizing themselves in order to accomplish at least four broadly defined objectives:

1. To prevent outsiders—including democratically established control and oversight bodies—from obtaining thorough access to the services' resources
2. To present the Military Information Services as a useful ally to the NATO authorities
3. To be perceived as a useful tool for pursuing various aims by any Polish government—not necessarily consistent with any viable raison d'être
4. To obtain and stabilize the Service's upper hand in economic institutional rearrangements, including key financial flows and major privatization schemes[25]

The Present Legal Framework

The statute of April 6, 1990, established the civilian Office of State Protection (UOP), defining its organizational structure and activities and identifying its objectives very extensively. Among the tasks of the UOP, which operated from 1990 to 2002, were foreign intelligence, domestic counterintelligence, political police tasks (e.g., countering extremist groups), serious economic frauds, and drug trafficking, among others. This variety of different tasks explains why it came as no surprise to many when the UOP was accused of an unnecessary accumulation of power.[26]

After the parliamentary victory of September 2001, the winning post-communist party SLD found it necessary to abolish the UOP and form the two new services, the ABW and the AW. This was done via statute of May 24, 2002.

Concerning the military services, the need for an appropriate regulation was publicly recognized for years, but until July 9, 2003, when the statute on the WSI was passed, a comprehensive legal framework existed only vis-à-vis the civilian services. In fact, the WSI operated and based their legitimacy on various—not necessarily convergent—legal acts.[27] For, example, in July 1994, three years after setting up the "new" military services, Włodzimierz Cimoszewicz, at the time the prosecutor-general, asked the Constitutional Tribunal whether the military services are authorized to employ eavesdropping techniques. The prosecutor never received an answer to his question.[28]

Since the beginning of the transformation, the service's task was, inter alia, to screen the state institutions' personnel for all levels of security clearance. However, Parliament passed relevant legal procedures with regard to vetting only in 1999. Until then, the security agencies had a free hand to make and break political careers.

Polish civilian secret services are authorized with law enforcement powers. They can conduct criminal investigations and have powers to arrest and to search homes. In 1994, Stanisław Iwanicki, former deputy prosecutor-general, indicated that the statute of April 6, 1990, incorrectly defines the competences of the UOP, especially with regard to economic investigations.[29] Others commented that the UOP sections dealing with organized crime unduly overlapped with, and substantially weakened, parallel structures in the state police.[30] Similar views have been expressed concerning the remit of the newly established ABW.[31]

Executive Control

According to the statute of May 24, 2002, the chiefs of civilian agencies rank equally high as secretaries of the state and answer directly to the prime minister. It means that their rank is equivalent to deputy ministers. The prime minister can nominate them after consulting with the president, his cabinet's Collegium for Secret Services (*Kolegium do Spraw Służb Specjalnych*) and the Sejm Commission for Secret Services (*Sejmowa Komisja do Spraw Służb Specjalnych*). The prime minister is also responsible for the tasking of the services.

According to the statute of July 9, 2003, the director of the WSI answers to the minister of defense. The minister can nominate the WSI's director after consulting the same bodies previously mentioned. The minister is also responsible for the tasking of the WSI.

The Collegium for Secret Services is a body of the Council of Ministers (the cabinet), formed according to the statute of May 24, 2002. The Collegium is designed as a consultative and advisory body programming, overseeing, and coordinating the activity of the services. The tasks of the Collegium include generating opinions on the appointing and dismissing of chiefs of services, setting up instructions and action plans for the services, providing opinions on detailed draft budgets, and projects of legal acts concerning the services. The members of the Collegium also assess the performance of the services, including the matters of organizing the exchange of important information among various branches of the government and issues of protection of classified information. The Collegium is chaired by the prime minister and run by the secretary; it is composed of the minister of the interior, the minister of foreign affairs, the minister of defense, the minister of finance, and the national security advisor to the president. The sessions of the Collegium are also attended by chiefs of the ABW, the AW, the WSI, and by the chairman of the Sejm Commission for Secret Services.[32]

To the author's knowledge, the government does not possess independent means to check upon the work of the agencies, similar to the task of an inspector-general. However, though officially there are no individuals appointed or committees or boards established that would be mandated with control and supervision of intelligence activities, there were cases when individuals trusted by the president or the prime minister, or a relevant minister, were tasked with external, thorough scrutinizing of certain operations of the services. Such persons' mandate was not official and they were reporting to their superiors on an informal basis.[33]

According to Article 7 of the statute on the ABW and the AW of May 24, 2002, the chiefs of the agencies, no later than three months before the end of each calendar year and each within his competence, shall present the prime minister plans of action for the next year. Similar regulations affect the WSI, but the tasking and reporting takes place under responsibility of the minister of defense (article 4 of the statute of July 9, 2003).

Formally, there are two bodies responsible for the coordination of intelligence services. Apart from the Collegium for Secret Services, there is the Government Intelligence Community (*Wspólnota Informacyjna Rządu*—WIR). The WIR, as an auxiliary body of the prime minister, is designed to provide national intelligence assessments with regard to external security. These assessments are inter-departmentally agreed upon and drafted from a broad governmental perspective that cuts across ministerial boundaries.[34] The chief of the AW chairs the WIR.

Additionally, the Supreme Chamber of Control (*Najwyższa Izba Kontroli*—NIK; a body reporting only to the Sejm) is entitled to perform auditing. The scope of this is limited to financial probity of the civilian services. The issue of any sensitive types of operations that might require explicit approval by members of the executive is, it seems, formally unregulated.

Executive Control Assessed

In 1994, Krzysztof Kozłowski[35] declared that the "tasks for our services are formulated neither by the prime minister, nor the president, nor the Parliament; therefore in the services' work there is plenty of chaos."[36] In 1995 the then chief of the WSI announced that "we do not have a center which would coordinate the activity of military and civilian services."[37] In 1996, the former director of the UOP counterintelligence department declared that "successive prime ministers could not make their own cabinets to announce in a systematic and not incidental manner—the tasks for the UOP, both short and long-term." To him, the services requested in vain that the tasks need to be specified.[38] In November 2001, Jerzy Dziewulski, an MP of the SLD party, claimed that "actually the services work beyond control. They task themselves and fulfill the tasks, also for their own needs."[39] Col. Zbigniew Nowek, chief of the UOP between 1997 and 2001, opposes Dziewulski strongly.[40] However, in 2003 a former functionary of the UOP wrote: "An outsider would be very astonished, provided s/he knew, how low the levels of the hierarchy are which take the liberty to pick tasks for themselves."[41] In sum, it appears that in Poland the secret services have been reformed and their powers were unleashed before their mission was properly identified.[42]

The key point in dealing with the issue of executive control in post-communist states is that one cannot help but move back to the still unsettled heritage of the police state. More precisely, what are the consequences of the fact that numerous individuals active in present political life were functionaries and/or secret collaborators of communist secret services? Can one rule out the possibility that various branches of the government and the Parliament are staffed with the former/present marionettes of the services to an such extent that the relation between the principal and agency has already become blurred or even reversed?

For example, in the administration of prime minister Leszek Miller (in office since autumn 2001), at least twelve undersecretaries of the state have formally, under the present lustration law, acknowledged former ties to communist secret services. The head of the prime minister's chancellery is presently accused of having committed the so-called lustration lie;[43] that also applies to at least four current MPs of the ruling coalition and another undersecretary of state. Two other MPs of the SLD have previously acknowledged their relationship to the services.[44] The prime minister's team of advisors included no less than five former communist services functionaries and/or secret collaborators.[45]

The year 2003 witnessed a series of big scandals originating from within the current government and its nearest political milieu (note in particular the notorious case of the so-called Lew Rywin corruption proposal[46]). These scandals pose big problems for the executive as, on the one hand the rule of law has to prevail, but, on the other hand, revealing scandals would also, at least partially, admit the executive's responsibility of failing to keep the services under effective control. Moreover, the services do not remain passive. In December 2003, at a closed meeting of the Sejm, the ABW chief, Andrzej Barcikowski, delivered a classified speech in which (according to media reports) he criticized the Polish media as being subject to manipulations of various lobbyist groups hostile to governmental projects. The speech has almost unanimously been interpreted as a premeditated political move, aiming, among other things, to threaten the media, which uncovered (with exceptional persistence) many scandals in which the cabinet and/or the ruling party members were involved.[47]

Parliamentary Oversight

Despite widespread recognition of the severe heritage of the old system's secret services, it was not until April 1995 that, by virtue of the amended Sejm resolution[48] of July 30, 1992, the parliamentary Commission for Secret Services was set up. The tasks of the Commission include assessing projects of legal acts concerning the services, providing opinions on the directions of their work, issuing opinions on appointments of particular persons as chiefs and deputy chiefs of the services, and examining the chiefs' annual reports. The Commission assesses draft budgets for the services and examines reports on budget implementation. It also analyzes the cooperation between the services and other bodies of state administration and examines complaints concerning activities of the services.

The Commission is a standing committee composed of no more than nine members, all members of Parliament. The composition of the Commission is determined by the plenary body, upon request of the Presidium of the Sejm submitted after consultations with the Council of Seniors. The chairmen of parliamentary caucuses or groups of at least thirty-five deputies submit candidates for members of the Commission to the Sejm Speaker.[49] The members are chosen proportionally according to parliamentary representation of their parties in the Sejm.

In 2003 the Commission had under contract four paid experts, mostly former high functionaries of the services, and a permanent administrative staff of three people. The Commission can interview witnesses, but it lacks investigative powers. The chiefs of the agencies are often summoned and appear.

The membership of the Commission is published.[50] All members undergo security vetting prior to and during their tenure. In 2001 during the initial selection the post-communists attempted to ban an opposition MP, Col. Konstanty Miodowicz, from the Commission, because of his former work in the UOP as a director of counterintelligence. Eventually, after a series of publicized clashes, a consensus to allow his membership was reached.[51] It is noteworthy that the Commission's chairman may be chosen only among the opposition members. At first, among the nine members of the present Commission, five of them were representing the ruling coalition.

Some of the MPs on the committee possess experience in dealing with the services. Among representatives of the opposition, one can identify a former minister of the interior (Antoni Macierewicz), former chief of the counterintelligence of the UOP (Miodowicz), and a former acting National Prosecutor who, at the time, was in charge, among other things, of issuing warrants for employing operational techniques (Zbigniew Wasserman). On the ruling coalition side is only Maj. Marian Marczewski, who graduated from two militia academies and was working in the traffic militia before 1990.

As far as the relationship of the oversight body to the plenary legislature is concerned, one can refer to a publicized case where the speaker of the Sejm prohibited the Commission from having a meeting devoted to a hot issue[52] during the Sejm plenary session, despite the fact that meetings of other commissions during plenary sessions are commonplace.[53]

The Commission meets fairly often. During the last term of the Sejm, from October 2001 until January 2004, it met eighty-nine times. When the Commission investigated the issue of an illegal international arms trade pursued by the Military Information Services in the first half of the 1990s, the Commission had over twenty meetings debating this issue in the first half of 2003.[54] Even so, according to Wasserman, there are many other sensitive issues (controversial, though not extremely pressing), that cannot be examined due to lack of time. All sessions of the Commission are secret.

Parliamentary Oversight Assessed

The Commission's first challenge came in December 1995, when the UOP, at the time a department within the Ministry of the Interior, made an allegation that the then prime minister Józef Oleksy, a former communist official, had been spying, first for the KGB and later for Russian Intelligence. Investigative powers of the Commission were very limited and the conclusions reached did not satisfy either side to the dispute. Another problem is that members of the Commission tended to have personal relationships with the objects of their oversight. Lucyna Pietrzyk, a policewoman, who was in the subcommission investigating the Oleksy case, was employed by the Ministry of the Interior within which the UOP operated at the time.

A similar problem has surfaced in recent years. Miodowicz, a member of the Commission in the two last terms of the Sejm (i.e., since 1997), was publicly accused of being an "undercover functionary" assigned to a civilian job. These accusations have never been clearly and officially rejected as false. In turn, Miodowicz stated that the subcommission investigating the Oleksy case included secret collaborators of the communist services.[55] This allegation was never duly substantiated nor discarded as false.

Instances like these cannot help but cast doubt on the independence of the oversight. In 2002 one of the most reputable spectators of the Polish political scene has noted that some members of the Sejm Commission are:

> [P]ersons either completely without authority, or people very deeply connected to the services, sometimes in a discrediting way, and without a distance necessary for decent and independent assessment. The present composition of the Commission is extremely fatal. This Commission lacks creditability, and it rather induces political unrest instead of real control.[56]

Although one may find these words unduly harsh, similar opinions are often expressed.

The opposition in the present Parliament claims that the Commission is dominated by party politics and provided many examples when its initiatives were simply voted out by the representatives of the ruling coalition. It also appears that the most sensitive investigations have been responsive to events (usually raised by the media[57]) rather than programmed well in advance. According to Miodowicz, the present scope of democratic supervision of the services has deteriorated if compared to the situation a few years ago.[58]

The main difficulty for the Commission stems from the fact that the services obviously play a power game over their "territory." The working relations with the intelligence agencies are not satisfactory. According to the opposition members of the commission (most notably Macierewicz and Wasserman) the agencies attempt to frustrate the due course of the most sensitive investigations. Wasserman said that the chiefs of the agencies often present their own interpretations of the laws on the legislative oversight in order to prevent the Commission's access to some kinds of data: "Actually, they let us know what they want us to know."[59] Wasserman claims that the actual powers of the Commission are very limited, because it may issue opinions and recommendations only. The only efficient instrument available for the opposition members of the Commission is of an informal nature—to brief the media in order to arouse the pressure of public opinion on the chiefs of the services. This seems to work, at least to a certain extent.

All objections notwithstanding, the recent public image of the Commission seems to be quite good. There are many examples where the Commission was invoked as the appropriate body for the clarification of controversial issues during the pungent clashes of opinions over the conduct of the intelligence agencies.[60] This is partly due to the proactive stance of the opposition members of the Commission.

In general, it holds true that the strengths and weaknesses of the system of control and accountability stem from the poor running of the Polish state. It is riddled with corruption, partisan politics, incompetence, and an immature civil service. Speaking in systemic terms, the main lines of conflict lie along the informal, oligarchic, parasitic power and influence groups exhibiting a façade of Polish democracy, versus dispersed groups committed to the rule of law, democracy, and civil society.

Undoubtedly, there is legislative intelligence oversight in Poland. Is it strong or weak in the sense Lawrence Lustgarten and Ian Leigh express?[61] They characterize strong oversight by the following: The body concerned: (1) is independent from the executive; (2) has a proactive capacity; (3) has a membership that reflects the spectrum of party politics; (4) has full access to information about the security or intelligence agency's activities; (5) has the ability to maintain secrecy where necessary; (6) has institutional expertise; and (7) has adequate support staff. Let us deal with these items now.

1. The Polish Sejm Commission is formally the body independent from the executive.
2. Its proactive capacities are granted.
3. Its membership reflects the current balance of power in the Sejm. The proportionality of membership accounts for the majority of the ruling coalition members in the Commission and the actual, often mechanical, voting out of many initiatives of the opposition members, therefore diminishing

the Commission's proactive capacities. Since the government controls its own parliamentarian base, it also influences the Commission.

4. According to the opposition the access to information is far from satisfactory. The Commission has no subpoena powers.

5. The members of the committee are vetted.

6–7. These conditions seem to be largely fulfilled, though all experts of the Commission are former employees of the services. One may doubt whether they are able to maintain a critical distance from their former employers and colleagues.

All the same, one may wonder whether, at least under the present post-communist predicament, the seven conditions proposed have enough "resolving power" to adequately portray specific post-communist predicaments; for example, to differentiate between skillful formal-bureaucratic performance focused on paying lip service as opposed to actual adherence to principles of the rule of law.[62]

Conclusions

The Polish secret services have not been used for brutal wars abroad nor for partisan repression at home. Instead, they have been abused in an unsystematic and politically very pluralistic fashion. The undercover community has shown itself to be a sort of pool of resources for the pursuit of party politics and the unfolding of oligarchic power networks that managed to anarchize the Polish state.

One could hardly say that the move from a closed and repressive apparatus toward a democratically accountable government service is completed. It is increasingly often asserted that Poland does not have an intelligence policy that is truly in the interest of society.[63] However, it seems that the tearing down of the inappropriate practices is beyond the power of any democratic institution in present-day Poland. The main safeguards that prevent the use of the agencies by the members of the government against their domestic political opponents are the Sejm Commission and those groupings within the parliamentary opposition that tend to preserve a rather tough anti-communist stance. Another safeguard is the general sensitivity of the public toward these kinds of abuses. However, all this largely depends on the attitude of the private media. Since the end of 2002, the media (except the public TV, which is under informal, yet firm, control of the present government) has become much more proactive in responding to various abuses of power.

It becomes more and more clear that another thorough reform is needed not only of the services and other official parts of the security complex, but also of the oversight system. Without achieving this, the services cannot become an instrument that may be systematically employed for pursuit of the public good.

Fourteen years since the beginning of the systemic transformation, the balance between advantages and disadvantages of continuation of the secret services personnel is far from being settled. The game over the shape of the Polish democracy is not finished yet. In fact it is not even clear who has the upper hand.

Notes

1. This chapter relies mostly upon open sources, i.e., legal acts, official documents, data available in the media and accessible via the Internet, including the official websites of the secret services and the Sejm (the lower house of the Polish Parliament). It also draws from data accessible at a website run by an anonymous group of former officers of the now dissolved Office of State Protection (www.republika.pl/uop12lat). In addition, the author interviewed the former chief of the UOP, Col. Zbigniew Nowek, and two opposition representatives in the Sejm Commission for Secret Services, Antoni Macierewicz and Zbigniew Wasserman. What is more, the author talked to a number of former and active politicians (MPs and government ministers included), and to a few former and present secret services staffers as well as activists of anarchist organizations (targeted by the services). The latter sources prefer to anonymous.

2. K. Williams and D. Deletant, *Security Intelligence Services in New Democracies: The Cases of Czech Republic, Slovakia and Romania* (London: Macmillan and School of Slavonic and East European Studies, UCL, 2000): 1.

3. Social democratic party (*Sojusz Lewicy Demokratycznej—SLD*). He was also postcommunist cabinet coordinator of the secret services. Since 2002, he has been director of the newly established Foreign Intelligence Agency (*Agencja Wywiadu—AW*).

4. Z. Siemiątkowski, interviewed by M. Barański (*Nie*, July 26, 2001): 5.

5. See, e.g., M. Dukaczewski, interviewed by A. Walentek (*Życie Warszawy*, December 4, 2001); A. Kapkowski, interviewed by R. Walenciak (*Przegląd Tygodniowy*, February 18, 1998): 3.

6. See, e.g., A. Celiński, interviewed by M. Barański (*Trybuna*, April 26, cited in *Gazeta Wyborcza*, April 28, 2003a, b): 2; J. Hausner, Akt oskarżenia (*Polityka*, June 21, 2003): 38–40; A. Macierewicz, Kursanci z Moskwy i Tel Awiwu (*Nasza Polska*, March 20, 2002): 1, 13; Z. Wasserman, interventions in a discussion (*Nowe Państwo*, No 1, January 2002): 16–20; Z. Wasserman, interviewed by M. Stychlerz-Kłucińską (*Tygodnik Solidarność*, August 15, 2003): 6–7.

7. The number of scandals revealed to the public is huge. One prominent example is the case of the so-called Colonel Lesiak group, a special team organized within the UOP and tasked with infiltration and disintegration of some of right-wing political groupings in the first half of the 1990s (see, e.g., Marszałek 1998, 1999). Another symptomatic case is illegal international arms trade pursued by the Military Information Services in the mid-1990s, revealed only in 2002 (see, e.g., Marszałek 2002, 2003). This case was investigated by the Sejm Commission for Secret Services, which produced a report confirming press accounts and accused the WSI of many irregularities including cheating by one prime minister. The Commision discovered that networks used in this illegal trade originated in the 1980s. (see Raport speckomisji . . . 2003).

8. See, e.g., *Opcja, przyszłość polskich służb specjalnych* (Warszawa: Instytut Problemów Bezpieczeństwa; SLD—Rada Krajowa, Zespół ds. Cywilnej i Demokratycznej Kontroli Służb Specjalnych, 2001).

9. After the UOP was dissolved, about four hundred employees were fired, i.e., 9 percent of the total of the Office's personnel.

10. See, e.g., J. Paradowska, Pod niespecjalnym nadzorem. *Polityka*, April 13, 2002): 25–26.

11. See M. Łoś and A. Zybertowicz, "Is Revolution a Solution? State Crime in Communist and Post-Communist Poland (1980–1995)" in *The Rule of Law after Communism*, eds. M. Krygier and A. Czarnota (Aldershot: Ashgate, Dartmouth 1999), 261–307.

12. See Regulamin Sejmu Rzeczypospolitej Polskiej, "Uchwała Sejmu Rzeczypospolitej Polskiej z dnia 30 lipca 1992 r. Załącznik do obwieszczenia Marszałka Sejmu Rzeczypospolitej Polskiej z dnia" (29 maja 2002 r. *Monitor Polski*, No. 23 pos. 398, 2002, art. 142).

13. See M. Łoś and A. Zybertowicz, "Is Revolution a Solution? State Crime in Communist and Post-Communist Poland (1980–1995)" in *The Rule of Law after Communism*, eds. M. Krygier and A. Czarnota (Aldershot: Ashgate, Dartmouth 1999), 261–307; M. Łoś and A. Zybertowicz, *Privatizing the Police-State: The Case of Poland* (London: Macmillan, New York: St. Martin's Press, 2000).

14. See, e.g., T. Lis, *Co z tą Polską* (Warszwa: Rosner & Wspólnicy, 2003); A. Zybertowicz, "Sztuka zapominania: państwo policyjne jako nierzeczywistość," in *Świat historii*, ed. Wojciech Wrzosek (Poznań: IH UAM, 1998), 429–39; compare T. Rosenberg, *The Haunted Land* (New York: Vintage Books, 1996).

15. The Polish lustration law obligates individuals holding high public offices to reveal their work for or secret cooperation with the communist secret services. The individuals' declarations are published in the Official Journal of the Government (Monitor Polski). The law does not lead to any negative consequences for individuals who have stated truth. The consequences arise only for those who lied, i.e., only for those individuals whom the Court of Appeal has legitimately found to have provided untruthful declarations. Their names are published and these individuals cannot occupy public posts for ten years.

16. Ustawa z dnia 11 kwietnia 1997 r. o ujawnieniu pracy lub służby w organach bezpieczeństwa państwa lub współpracy z nimi w latach 1944–1990 osób pełniących funkcje publiczne (Dz. Us. 1997, No. 70 pos. 443).

17. See, e.g., T. Lis, *Co z tą Polską* (Warszwa: Rosner & Wspólnicy, 2003).

18. See Łoś and Zybertowicz 2000, 127; compare Siemiątkowski 1998, 108.

19. Z. Siemiątkowski, a Sejm speech presenting the cabinet's project of secret services reform delivered on March 13, 2002, www.sejm.gov.pl; accessed January 4, 2004.

20. See, e.g., J. Maloj, Machina (nadal) postsowiecka (*Nasza Polska*, January 21, 1998); see other thirteen articles of the author published in this weekly between February and May 1998; A. Zybertowicz, *W uścisku tajnych służb: upadek komunizmu i układ postnomenklaturowy* (Komorów: Antyk, 1993): 52–56.

21. Ustawa o Urzędzie Ministra Obrony Narodowej z dnia 14 grudnia 1995 r. (Dziennik Ustaw 1996, No. 10, pos. 56).

22. Published in Dz. Us. 2003, No. 139, pos. 1326.

23. Chief of the WSI from 1997 to 2001.

24. Poland joined NATO in 1999. See T. Rusak, interviewed by E. Łosińska (*Dziennik Polski*, September 12, 2003); compare J. Jakimczyk (Jednostka 3362. *Rzeczpospolita*, July 16, 2003).

25. See, e.g., W. Cieśla and J. Jachowicz, Big Brothers, czyli wojna agentów (*Gazeta*

Wyborcza, November 2–3, 2002): 12–15; W. Frasyniuk, Interviewed by R. Laudański, (*Gazeta Pomorska*, August 14, 2003); A. Gargas, Fozz z wojskowymi w tle, (*Gazeta Polska*, June 18, 2003); S. Janecki, Wojskowe Służby Interesów, (*Wprost*, December 28, 1997): 22–3; I. Leszczyńska and G. Indulski, Generalicja zgarnia kasę (*Newsweek Polska*, November 23, 2003): 22–24; R. Zieliński and MNS, *Akademia przekrętów* (Super Express, edition AB, January 16, 2001): 3.

26. Compare A. Antecki, Firma (*Tygodnik Powszechny*, December 7, 2003): 1, 4.

27. The relevant regulations were (in Polish): Ustawa z dnia 21 listopada 1967 r. o powszechnym obowiązku obrony Rzeczypospolitej Polskiej (Dz. Us. 1992 r., nr 4, poz. 16 ze zmianami); Ustawa o Urzędzie Ministra Obrony Narodowej z dnia 14 grudnia 1995 r. (Dz. Us. z 1996 r., nr 10, poz. 56); Ustawa o ochronie informacji niejawnych z dnia 22 stycznia 1999 r. (Dz. Us. nr 11, poz. 95); Rozporządzenie Rady Ministrów z dnia 9 lipca 1996 r. w sprawie szczegółowego zakresu działania ministra obrony narodowej (Dz. Us. nr 94, poz. 426); Rozporządzenie Prezesa Rady Ministrów z dnia 19 września 1997 r. w sprawie szczegółowego rozdziału kompetencji oraz zasad współdziałania w zakresie ochrony gospodarki narodowej między UOP a WSI (Dz. Us. nr 116, poz. 774); Uchwała Trybunału Konstytucyjnego z dnia 16 stycznia 1996 r. (Dz. Us. nr 14, poz. 80).

28. T. Kosobudzki, *Bezpieka w MSZ: Służby specjalne w polityce zagranicznej RP w latach 1989–1997* (Kielce-Warszawa: Elipsa, 1998): 152.

29. S. Iwanicki, Gangi próbują kupować urzędników (*Rzeczpospolita*, August 18, 1994): 12.

30. I. Janke, Tajni potrzebują ciszy (*Życie*, December 21–22, 1996): 13; I.T. Miecik, Ośmiornica czy krewetka (*Polityka*, June 24, 2000): 10; compare A. Antecki, Firma (*Tygodnik Powszechny*, December 7, 2003): 1, 4.

31. See e.g. J. Wilczak, Niesłychanie tajna służba (*Polityka*, June 14, 2003): 27.

32. See e.g. official website of the ABW: www.abw.gov.pl; accessed August 21, 2003.

33. Personal communications (in April and July 2003) with two individuals related to the services who remain anonymous.

34. See the official website of the AW—www.aw.gov.pl/english/szef-agencji/wir-czym-jest.html.

35. First chief of the UOP and then minister of the interior in 1990–91.

36. Cited J. Jachowicz and K. Kęsicka, Tajne kontrolowane (*Gazeta Wyborcza*, November 22, 1994): 4.

37. Malejczyk 1995, 13.

38. K. Miodowicz, interviewed by A. Kublik et al. (*Gazeta Wyborcza*, February 24–25, 1996): 10.

39. J. Dziewulski, interviewed at an Internet chat, 2001, http:/czateria.interia.pl/gosc?cid + 633&F = 5; (accessed August 30, 2003).

40. Interview with the author on June 11, 2003.

41. A. Antecki, Firma (*Tygodnik Powszechny*, December 7, 2003): 5.

42. See A. Antecki, Firma (*Tygodnik Powszechny*, December 7, 2003): 1, 4.; K. Williams and D. Deletant, *Security Intelligence Services in New Democracies: The Cases of Czech Republic, Slovakia and Romania* (London: Macmillan and School of Slavonic and East European Studies, UCL, 2000); A. Zybertowicz, *W uścisku tajnych służb: upadek komunizmu i układ postnomenklaturowy* (Komorów: Antyk, 1993); M. Łoś and A. Zybertowicz, *Privatizing the Police-State: The Case of Poland* (London: Macmillan, New York: St. Martin's Press, 2000).

43. See note 15.

44. See the website of the lustration prosecutor: www.rzecznikip.gov.pl.

45. See E. Olczyk and M. Subotić, Wszyscy ludzie premiera (*Rzeczpospolita*, January 24, 2002); A. Kublik, Kto dzwonił do mediów? (*Gazeta Wyborcza*, September 17, 2003): 1.

46. See e.g. Skórzyński, ed., *System Rywina, czyli druga strona III Rzeczypospolitej* (Warszawa: Świat Książki and Rzeczpospolita, 2003).

47. See e.g. K. Kozłowski, To służbami grają (*Tygodnik Powszechny*, December 7, 2003): 1; A. Macierewicz, Kursanci z Moskwy i Tel Awiwu (*Nasza Polska*, March 20, 2003): 1, 13.

48. Legal act of law rank regulating inner workings of the Sejm.

49. See the English part of the AW official website—www.aw.gov.pl/english/kontrola/sejmowa-komisja-ds-sluzb-spec-1.html; accessed August 24, 2003.

50. See http://orka.sejm.gov.pl/SQL.nsf/skladkom4?OpenAgent&KSS; accessed July 11, 2003.

51. See B. Kittel and A. Marszałek, Chcą i nie chcą Miodowicza (*Rzeczpospolita*, November 8, 2001); KNYSZ, Służby bez nadzoru (*Gazeta Wyborcza*, August 1, 2002): 7.

52. In February 2002 the president of Orlen, a petrol company co-owned by the state, one of the largest in Poland, was detained in a spectacular way (instantly publicized) by the UOP. Though he was freed that very same day, the next day he was fired as the company president. A trusted hand of the sitting government has been placed in his position. This was interpreted as an abuse of a secret service to achieve an economic purpose. Later on the Warsaw district court has found the use of the UOP in this case was unlawful (see, e.g., Sakiewicz 2002).

53. See KNYSZ, Służby bez nadzoru (*Gazeta Wyborcza*, August 1, 2002): 7.

54. See the Commission's subpage on the Sejm website: www.sejm.gov.pl.

55. See PW, Oskarżenia agenturalne (*Gazeta Wyborcza*, April 7, edition 2, BYT, 2000): 5.

56. J. Paradowska, Czysta czystka (*Polityka*, August 17, 2002): 28–30.

57. Obviously, this was the case of the illegal arms trade pursued in the 1990s by the WSI; the investigation stemmed from a newspaper article (Marszałek 2002) and concluded that serious abuses were actually completed by the WSI.

58. Cited J. Wilczak, Niesłychanie tajna służba (*Polityka*, June 14, 2003): 26.

59. Communication of July 12, 2003; compare J. Widacki, Interviewed by A. Kublik (*Gazeta Wyborcza*, April 16): 16.

60. See, e.g., A. Celiński, interviewed by M. Olejnik on the Radio Zet on December 30, 2003 (cited www.wiadomości.wp.pl; accessed December 30, 2003).

61. Laurence Lustgarten and Ian Leigh, *In From the Cold: National Security And Parliamentary Democracy* (Houndsmill, Hampshire, 1994): 461–62).

62. Compare W. Kozieł, "Ewolucja systemu kontroli i nadzoru nad służbami specjalnymi w Polsce," in *Bezpieczny obywate—bezpieczne państwo*, eds. J. Widacki and J. Czapska (Lublin: KUL, 1998): 121–29; D. Rowicka, "Służby specjalne w Polsce—nadzór i kontrola," in *Bezpieczny obywatel—bezpieczne państwo*, eds. J. Widacki and J. Czapska (Lublin: KUL, 1998): 107–20; S. Zalewski, *Służby specjalne w państwie demokratycznym* (Warszawa: Akademia Obrony Narodowej, 2002).

63. See e.g. A. Antecki, Firma (*Tygodnik Powszechny*, December 7, 2003): 1, 4; J. Jakimczyk, Podzwonne dla UOP (*Rzeczpospolita*, July 19, 2002): A8; K. Kozłowski, Koniec UOP, początek niewiadomej (*Tygodnik Powszechny*, July 7, 2002): 3; J. Widacki, interviewed by A. Kublik (*Gazeta Wyborcza*, April 16, 2002): 16–17; compare www.uop12lat.republka.pl.

9

Executive and Legislative Oversight of the Intelligence System in Argentina

Eduardo E. Estévez

This chapter addresses the main features, concerns, and ongoing progress concerning the intelligence system and legislation of Argentina[1] in its search for democratic legitimacy. Since the recovery of democracy in 1983, there has been both public and political concern about the role of intelligence. This feeling was due to the history of military rule in Latin America and particularly to the role played by intelligence agencies ". . . in short, integrally associated with the human rights abuses which characterize most authoritarian regimes most of the time."[2]

In efforts to revamp the intelligence sector and establish strong legitimacy, it was necessary to leave behind the history of abuses, lack of controls, and distrust. During the decades of building democracy, the main efforts focused on the development of a legislative framework able to trigger a reform process. In November 2001, the National Congress passed the National Intelligence Law establishing the national intelligence system. The law defines the organization, activities, objectives, and scope of the intelligence policy; creates a national intelligence agency, a criminal intelligence agency, and a military strategic intelligence agency; establishes a mechanism to authorize interceptions of communications in conjunction with the judiciary; and sets the standards for parliamentary oversight,[3] including secret budget and expenditure control.

A key senior advisor of the Senate recently described five essential prerequisites that guided congressional debate on the intelligence legislation: (1) to have a legal framework capable of generating a context for developing intelligence activities characterized by professionalism and excellence; (2) to ensure that the efficiency of intelligence activities do not collide with the principle of full protection of human rights; (3) to define clear penalties applicable to the cases in which fundamental rights of the inhabitants have been violated, at the same time creating specific congressional mechanisms to guarantee a permanent oversight of these activities; (4) to ensure that such legal frameworks be representative of the consensus reached by all the actors involved in such activities, in order to prevent the law from being ignored on those issues for which consensus was unattainable; (5) to reach a balance and distribution of roles that enable a clear identification and description of specific functions and powers of each one of the components of the intelligence system.[4] Argentina's new legislation on intelligence services constitutes a step toward the consolidation of democracy.

Intelligence Sector Legislation and Agencies

A triad of laws governs the intelligence sector:

- National Intelligence Law No. 25520 of 2001
- Internal Security Law No. 24059 of 1992, dealing with internal intelligence
- National Defense Law No. 23554 of 1988, concerning military intelligence restrictions

The legal framework also entails other norms:

- Decree No. 950 of 2002, providing regulations for the provisions of the National Intelligence Law
- Decree No. 1088 of 2003, approving the bylaw applicable to intelligence personnel
- Decree No. 1273 of 1992, providing regulations for the provisions of the Internal Security Law
- Personal Data Protection Law No. 25326 of 2000
- Decree-Law No. 5315 of 1956 and Law No. 18302 of 1969, establishing a regime for "Reserved or Secret Expenditures"

Argentina has several intelligence agencies[5] at the national level, including civilian, military, and police/security forces components. Within the executive there are the following organizations:

- Secretariat of Intelligence, the main agency, subordinate to the presidency of the nation, responsible for collecting and producing foreign and domestic intelligence and counterintelligence

- National Directorate for Criminal Intelligence, a coordination body concerned with intelligence efforts related to domestic security
- National Directorate for Strategic Military Intelligence, responsible for the production of military intelligence

The following organizations are under the military services:

- J-2 Intelligence, Joint Staff of the armed forces
- Army Intelligence, including a G-2 within the army general staff and a Military Intelligence Collection Centre, with several small units all over the country
- Naval Intelligence Service
- Air Force Information Service

The following belong to the police and security forces:

- National Gendarmerie Intelligence Service
- Argentine Coast Guard Intelligence Service
- Intelligence elements of the Argentine Federal Police
- An intelligence element of the Federal Penitentiary Service

Intelligence Reform in the Wake of Democratic Consolidation Process

Argentina's new legislation on the intelligence system has to be analyzed in the context of the ongoing process of democratic consolidation. Beginning in 1983, this process included several important legislative actions taken in related fields, such as the National Defense Law of 1988 and the Internal Security Law of 1992. These two pieces of legislation, which played a crucial role in solving the military problem, contain a few sentences on specific intelligence activities and structures. As shall be seen in the following discussion, these precedents opened a window of opportunity for a longstanding and intermittent debate about the role of the intelligence sector in a democracy.

The National Defense Law links the concept of national defense exclusively to the use of the armed forces, in a deterrent or an effective way, to confront external aggression, and recognizes a distinction between national defense and internal security, being the last concept to be defined by a special law. Article 15 relates to intelligence and prohibits the military intelligence agencies from conducting activities related to domestic political affairs; it establishes that the highest-level intelligence agency is in charge of producing national defense intelligence. This article also states that military intelligence production is to be carried out by an agency comprising the intelligence agencies of the armed forces, under the authority of the minister of defense.

The Internal Security Law constitutes a significant improvement in terms of a legal framework for domestic security with relevant content related to intelligence. For the first time in Argentina, this law established the foundation of the system for planning, coordination, control, and support of the national police effort committed to guarantee internal security. The law defined internal security as the:

> factual situation under the rule of law in which liberty, life and property of the inhabitants, their rights and guarantees and the full validity of the institutions of the representative, republican and federal system established by the national Constitution are protected (article 2).

A cabinet minister has authority for the direction and coordination of the activities undertaken by the federal police and the security forces'[6] intelligence components. Furthermore, to avoid uncertainty about the role of intelligence in internal security, article 16 provides for a Directorate of Internal Intelligence, the organ through which the minister exerts power in this field. A significant provision of this law applies to congressional oversight. Title VII provides for parliamentary control of internal security and intelligence, creating for the first time in Argentina a permanent congressional Joint Oversight Committee on Intelligence and Internal Security, composed of six senators and six deputies with the mission to supervise and control all internal security and intelligence activities and organizations.[7]

Although the area was not at the top of the agenda of controversial issues, the main topics of debate were the scope of congressional control over intelligence activities and agencies as well as legislation governing the intelligence sector. Some controversy resulted from the fact that although article 46 of the National Defense Law provided for the drafting of several related bills, including one to govern the intelligence system with the addition of congressional oversight, it was only after fourteen years that consensus was reached and an intelligence law was passed by Congress in 2001.

As Garreta explains, from the 1960s until the National Congress passed the intelligence law, a secret normative framework for state intelligence, designed by the armed forces and based upon the so-called national security doctrine, was functional but neither democratic nor public.[8] Meanwhile, since 1983, an intelligence sector with doubtful legitimacy, though headed by a civilian appointed by the president, was characterized by duplication between the several intelligence agencies, denoting a lack of coordination and featuring a squandering of resources. Intelligence activities progressively began to act in support of judicial investigations and the discretion toward secret expenditures increased without any justification.

The evolution toward an intelligence law allows a brief description of several waves of bills. The first wave of bills on intelligence systems arose in the early 1990s. At that time, the desire was to establish a political and legal basis for intelligence agencies and activities under firm democratic control and supervision, in order to remove the ambiguity, autonomy, and distrust that surrounded their operations in society.[9] In June 1990, Deputy Victorio Bisciotti of the Radical Party entered a bill under the name of "Information and Intelligence Organic Law," while in September 1991, Senator Eduardo Vaca of the Peronist Party entered a bill called "National Intelligence System." By mid-1993, the congressional committee with authority to oversee intelligence and security activities and agencies created by the Internal Security Law came into existence several months after this law was passed. The committee was created in reaction to a scandal known as "ideological surveillance."[10]

A second wave of bills sprouted during 1994 and 1995, particularly those submitted by minority legislators. At the same time an initiative backed by the majority and the executive was evolving in the Senate. After reaching a partial consensus, an intelligence bill was approved by the Senate in September 1994. By late 1995, the lack of consensus about the scope of congressional control, among other topics under discussion, frustrated the approval by the Chamber of Deputies of the intelligence bill earlier approved in 1994 by the Senate. Meanwhile, two terrorist bombings hit the country. The first one was on March 17, 1992, against the Embassy of Israel, the second one on July 18, 1994, against the *Asociación Mutual Israelita Argentina* (AMIA), a Jewish community center building. A special joint congressional committee created in September 1996 to follow up the judicial investigations contributed through hearings and reports to an extended debate on the need for intelligence reform. There was also a political perception that sectors of the main intelligence agency—the former state intelligence secretary—had impeding attitudes or omissions regarding the investigation of these terrorist bombings.

A third wave of bills arose during 1997 and 1998, all of them characterized by a strong emphasis on parliamentary controls. In parallel to the various intelligence system bills, other related bills were drafted by legislators intending to rule on specific topics such as secret budgets, parliamentary oversight and controls, external controls such as ombudsmen, and judicial controls and responsibilities. A motive for these initiatives was an almost illegal practice systematically applied by the executive during the 1990s, consisting of an increase in secret expenditures far from the figure yearly approved as a secret budget by Congress. Finally, the new millennium began with active but silent parliamentary work of consensus building, the final result being the enactment of a law in November 2001.

General Concepts and Characteristics Governing Intelligence Activities

National Intelligence Law No. 25520 of 2001 established the juridical and functional basis of the national intelligence system.[11] In view of the implications for the intelligence sector itself, it is very important to mention the set of terms defined in the law (article 2), including national intelligence, counterintelligence, criminal intelligence, strategic military intelligence, and the national intelligence system. *National intelligence* is defined as the activity involving the collection, systematization, and analysis of specific information related to facts, threats, risks, and conflicts affecting foreign and domestic security. This compares with the term *criminal intelligence*, which is linked to specific criminal activities that, due to their nature, magnitude, foreseeable consequences, dangerousness, or mode, affect the freedom, life, and property of individuals, as well as their rights and guarantees, and the institutions of the federal, republican, and representative system established by the constitution.

The three agencies comprising the national intelligence system[12] are the Secretariat of Intelligence, the National Directorate for Criminal Intelligence, and the National Directorate for Strategic Military Intelligence. The first agency—replacing the state intelligence secretary—which holds the status of the highest agency of the system (article 7), has the function of producing national intelligence (article 8) and has as its general mission the direction of the system (article 7). The second agency is responsible for the production of criminal intelligence (article 9), and the third produces strategic military intelligence (article 10). It is noteworthy that the law prohibits the creation, establishment, and functioning of associations, institutions, networks, and groups of persons, either of physical or juridical status, that plan and/or perform intelligence functions and activities (article 11).

After a nonbinding consultation with the Joint Committee for the Oversight of Intelligence Activities and agencies of the National Congress (article 15) the president appoints the secretary of intelligence, who has a cabinet minister rank. The removal process is similar to the one applicable to any secretary of state, in that the president may require his or her resignation at any time. The heads of the National Directorate for Criminal Intelligence and the National Directorate for Strategic Military Intelligence are appointed by the minister of their respective jurisdictions following a similar procedure established for any national director of the executive.

Exercising Executive Control and Coordination—Intelligence Policy and Tasking

The National Intelligence Law gives control and coordination powers over the national intelligence system to the executive. The principal source of external guidance for the intelligence system is right at the top of the executive branch. This is a significant improvement in comparison with past practices, where the autonomy of intelligence agencies allowed them to determine their own requirements.

Through Title IV, "National Intelligence Policy," the law provides for the control and accountability arrangements for executive control of intelligence. According to article 12, the president determines the strategic outlines and general objectives of the national intelligence policy. For this purpose he may convoke an inter-ministerial advisory council. For consulting purposes and when he considers it pertinent, he may also invite representatives of the armed forces, security forces, or Argentine federal police (article 14).

While the Secretariat of Intelligence is under the presidency of the nation, the National Directorate for Criminal Intelligence is under the Interior Security Secretariat (article 9). This Secretariat is part of the Ministry of Justice, Security and Human Rights. The National Directorate for Strategic Military Intelligence, in accordance with the provisions of article 15 of the National Defense Law, is under the Ministry of Defense. The Secretariat of Intelligence has powers to conduct and articulate the activities and the functioning of the system and to coordinate activities within the framework of national defense and internal security laws through officials appointed by the ministers of those areas, whose position must not be lower than under-secretary of state (article 13.5). Concurrently, the Secretariat of Intelligence shall issue the rules that may be necessary for the functioning of the national intelligence system (article 4, decree No. 950). The notion itself of an intelligence system comprising the top agencies implies that national intelligence assessments can be interdepartmentally agreed upon, mainly between the Ministries of Defense and of Justice, Security, and Human Rights, respectively, through the heads of their intelligence agencies. In fact, as discussed, the secretary of intelligence has to coordinate these activities.

Regarding national intelligence assessments, production of national intelligence is the responsibility of the Secretariat of Intelligence, as determined by article 8 of the law. Furthermore, according to article 15 of the National Defense Law, the intelligence agency at the highest level, which is today the Secretariat of Intelligence, would be the agency in charge of producing national defense intelligence. Article 13.8 of the National Intelligence Law gives the Secretariat of Intelligence authority to coordinate the preparation of a national strategic intelligence assessment as well as a collection plan. The minister of justice, security, and human rights and the minister of defense have, respectively, authority over the intelligence agencies within their departments. Considering the fact that these agencies are at the same time part of the national intelligence system, these ministers do not necessarily exert much influence in the daily activities of these agencies.

The National Directorate for Criminal Intelligence, pursuant to article 48 of the law and in accordance with the provisions of article 16 of the Internal Security Law, ought to play a significant role in the national intelligence system in terms of the functional direction and coordination of intelligence activities of the so-called national police effort—including the national police and security forces, and the twenty-three provincial police forces—in all matters related to internal security. Decree No. 1273 is clear about the responsibilities of the head of the Criminal Intelligence Directorate, outlining in article 5.6 the scope of the direction and coordination functions regarding the activities of the intelligence elements already mentioned. These functions include the planning, setting of priorities, preparation, and formulation of requirements regarding collection of information and intelligence production. In the field of military intelligence, article 6 of Decree No. 950 gives powers to the National Directorate for Strategic Military Intelligence to coordinate actions regarding the armed forces intelligence agencies. For the purpose of producing strategic operational intelligence and tactical intelligence needed for the planning and conducting of military operations and specific technical intelligence, the military intelligence agencies of the army, navy, and air force armed forces are respectively under direct control of the chief of each force.[13]

There is one type of intelligence operation that requires explicit approval by members of the executive. The secretary of intelligence can request a written and grounded judicial approval to carry out interceptions of communications for intelligence or counterintelligence activities.[14] For these operations, the Secretariat of Intelligence has a Directorate for Judicial Observations, the only organ of the state legally allowed to perform these duties under permission or instructed by competent judicial authorities (article 21). In principle, relations with foreign intelligence services are one of the specific duties of the Secretariat of Intelligence; under article 13.4, the secretary of intelligence is responsible for the direction and articulation of relationships with the intelligence agencies of other nations. Within the executive there are no specialized independent means of checking upon the work of the intelligence agencies, such as an inspector-general office, a commissioner, an executive oversight body, or a supervisory committee.

As explained in the following discussion control, oversight, and accountability arrangements comprise other notable elements within the legislative and the judiciary. Although it appears to be an infrequent mechanism, citizens are able to raise complaints against any national intelligence system agent or agency to the Joint Committee. Furthermore, as a constitutional right, the judicial option has been always at disposition. Independent supervision is a key feature of a democratic intelligence sector; therefore, the lack of review mechanisms in the executive is a weakness of the whole concept developed by the Argentinean legislators. The absence within the law of any reference to those executive mechanisms may be a consequence of the considerable importance granted to parliamentary control by the drafters. There may also have been a lack of confidence on the ability or proclivity of the executive to review its own activities, having considered the risks associated with the exercise of political/partisan influence over those mechanisms.

Legal Constraints and Classified Information

A set of safeguards to prevent the use of the intelligence agencies by government officials against their domestic political opponents and affairs are clearly established by law. Title II of the National Intelligence Law provides for the protection of rights and guarantees of the inhabitants of the nation. Its article 3 states that ". . . the functioning of the national intelligence system must adjust strictly to those provisions under chapters I and II of the national constitution and the laws and regulations in force."

Intelligence agencies are forbidden to:

- Perform repressive activities, have compulsive powers, fulfill police functions, or conduct criminal investigations unless so required by justice or when so authorized by law
- Obtain information, collect intelligence, or keep data on individuals because of their race, religion, private actions, and political ideology, or due to their membership in partisan, social, union, community, cooperative, assistance, cultural, or labor organizations, or because of legal activities performed within any field
- Exert influence over the institutional, political, military, police, social, and economic situation of the country, its foreign policies, and the existence of legally formed political parties
- Influence public opinion, individuals, media press, or any kind of associations whatsoever.[15]

As stated in article 4.4, agencies are not allowed to reveal or divulge any kind of information acquired when performing their functions and related to any individual or company, whether public or private, unless so required by justice.

Article 16 specifies that intelligence activities and agencies, their personnel, documentation, and databases, shall be assigned a classified security grading in accordance with the interests of internal security, national defense, and foreign relations and that the access to such information shall be authorized in a case-by-case basis by the president or the official to whom this authority has been expressly delegated.

Those members of the intelligence agencies, as well as any person who, due to his responsibilities or circumstances, has access to intelligence information, are obliged to maintain secrecy and confidentiality; those who infringe this obligation will be subject to penalties.[16] In this regard, article 13 of Decree No. 950 states that by way of an internal resolution each agency of the system shall specifically record the formal and written notification of these responsibilities for each agency member. Article 2 of Decree No. 950 clearly specifies that the intelligence agencies shall frame certain activities—obtaining information, collecting intelligence, or keeping data on individuals—as inexcusable under the provisions of the Personal Data Protection Law, specifically its article 23.[17] The fulfillment of these provisions shall be a matter of directives and controls by the head of each agency. Domestic intelligence activities raise major concerns among politicians as much as in the society; however, provisions contained in the law regarding criminal intelligence are great improvements on establishing limits to intelligence collection from within.

Consistent with constitutional guarantees,[18] article 5 of the National Intelligence Law stipulates that telephone calls, mail, telegraph, facsimile, or any other system for sending objects or transmitting images, voice, or data, as well as any kind of information, files, registries and/or private documents or documents to which the general public have no access are inviolable unless so required by justice. The decision to include limitations to the intelligence activities was an issue that underwent several ups and downs during the legislative debate. Having selected to draft a detailed bill, the group of legislative advisors that prepared the first drafts were able to inscribe several clauses, all of them ending in a full title of the law devoted to the protection of the rights and guarantees of the inhabitants. These sets of operational principles represent a clear advantage in terms of the exercise of democratic control over the intelligence sector.

Budgeting Process and Reporting

The executive, the Joint Congressional Oversight Committee, and the General Accounting Office are involved in the process of the budget and control of secret expenditures. The first step of the yearly processes for approval of the intelligence budget was accomplished in accordance with article 38, which stipulated that the national executive power shall include in the ruling of Law No. 24156 on financial administration and control systems of the national public sector, a new line named "intelligence" under the topic "services for defense and security," grouping the whole budget corresponding to the intelligence activities in whatever jurisdiction it may have originated. Although on legal grounds, secrecy is maintained for obvious reasons, the global figure is public and is subject to a budget process similar to that of any other department or agency. Decree No. 950 also establishes that both the National Directorate for Criminal Intelligence and the National Directorate for Strategic Military Intelligence shall submit their budget requirements to its superior hierarchy, and shall be responsible for the spending of the specific budget for intelligence.

The process for auditing of intelligence expenditures within the government is ruled by article 39 of the National Intelligence Law, which states that these expenditures made during the fiscal year shall be recorded in a monthly affidavit signed by the responsible officials belonging to the respective organism or office; that shall be considered a receipt by the general accounting office.

The intelligence agencies report to the ministries as established by law. Article 13 states that the Secretariat of Intelligence shall provide to the Ministry of Defense the information and intelligence needed to contribute to military strategic intelligence production, as set forth by article 15 of Law No. 23554, and to the Interior Security Council the information and intelligence needed to contribute to criminal intelligence production, as set forth by article 10, paragraph (e) of Law No. 24059.[19] Article 13.9 of the National Intelligence Law specifies that the Secretariat of Intelligence shall prepare the annual report of intelligence activities to be presented to the Joint Congressional Oversight Committee. Based upon article 33, the executive—the Secretariat of Intelligence—has to submit to the Joint Committee the national intelligence plan and the curricula of the National Intelligence School. For the purpose of congressional budget and expenditure control and oversight, the executive is obliged to submit to the Joint Committee all the information needed, as set forth by article 37. Each year the executive reports to Congress on its administration policies, programs, and activities of the previous fiscal year. This public report has a two- to three-page long chapter prepared by the Secretariat of Intelligence. This practice began in the mid-1980s. In the chapters on the defense and justice, security and human rights ministries, respectively, there should be contents related to their intelligence offices.

Achieving Ministerial Responsibility in Practice

Although the new law was intended to supersede the tendency to centralize the intelligence community, it does not solve this challenge because of the diffuse roles granted to the heads of the Ministry of Justice, Security and Human Rights and Ministry of Defense within the intelligence system itself. Indeed, the roles and responsibilities of the three intelligence agencies are clearly described. The scheme provides that the two minor agencies be accountable predominantly to the major agency—who holds the status of the highest agency of the system— leaving aside the natural accountability of an office to the head of the department where it belongs. The secretary of intelligence is indeed the chief advisor to the president on intelligence matters, being at the same time the head of the system. This special relationship, which is not different from that existing before the enactment of the National Intelligence Law, reflects a centralized system in which the producer and consumer roles are not clearly shaped.

The defense and domestic security legislation in force has several clauses related to intelligence; it appears that the whole intelligence community comprises not only the intelligence system established by the National Intelligence Law, but also what can be called "subsystems," one for internal/criminal intelligence and another for military intelligence. The creation of a criminal intelligence agency meets the need to give full legal recognition of intelligence within the state to delineate the interface between intelligence policy and domestic security policy. The history of abuses, repressive state, and internal dirty wars indicated that any exclusion or blurring concept of domestic intelligence could pose a threat to society. In fact, applying the principle of separation of law enforcement and intelligence poses the problem of excluding those intelligence activities carried out by a government for the purposes of gaining information and analysis to be aware of the general situation of domestic security/insecurity and holding them unaccountable. Executive civilian control over those activities is a prerequisite in order to avoid intrusion in privacy from, misuse of, and abuses by police intelligence. Within the boundaries of domestic security policy, civilian control is achieved through the coordination and tasking of the domestic intelligence elements. In this case, the mission of those intelligence activities carried out within the country, within its society, is strictly limited to those legitimate and legally accepted and defined objectives, as stated by the National Intelligence Law. The new system can be considered a combination of a centralized-prone pattern at the top, with a decentralized-prone pattern at the immediate second level, in which the principle of division of labor between the intelligence agencies[20] is effective. As a hybrid, a silent struggle may take place for the actual control of those specialized intelligence agencies between the various ministers with jurisdiction over agencies in charge of intelligence functions as well as the secretary of intelligence.

The concept of civilian ministerial responsibility over the intelligence agencies has not been exercised fully in the fields of domestic and military intelligence. Issuance of directives and control over personnel, budget, and expenditures has not been a priority although there were legal foundations for this several years before the National Intelligence Law was enacted. A fifty-year tradition of a strong and centralized national intelligence agency under the presidency, and the frequent interruptions of democratic rule, are significant reasons that explain this behavior.

During the transitional government of the congressionally appointed President Eduardo Duhalde (January 2002–May 2003), the Intelligence Secretariat was headed first by Carlos Soria, former chairman of the Joint Special Committee in charge of monitoring the judicial investigations of the terrorist bombings against the embassy of Israel and the AMIA building. Subsequently, another congressman with experience in the fields of defense, security, and intelligence legislation, Miguel Angel Toma, was appointed to that post. According to the press, these changes were confirmation that the agency continues to respond to the aspirations and fickleness of political interests, rather than to the needs of its important strategic role.[21]Notwithstanding these factors, the National Intelligence Law is an important improvement because its clauses upgrade the already existent agencies focused on criminal and military intelligence respectively.

Legislative Oversight: the Joint Committee for the Oversight of Intelligence Activities and Agencies

The National Intelligence Law created the Joint Committee for the oversight of intelligence activities and agencies of the National Congress (article 3). The role of the Joint Committee is specified in legislation[22] and in the Committee's internal rules of procedures. Essentially, its oversight role includes the following: the legality of intelligence activities, the policy that guides the intelligence system, the management and administration of the system and its agencies, the system's effectiveness, personnel education plans, the secret budget and expenditures, previous data on telephone interception operations, and complaints from members of the public about the agency or its personnel. It is obliged to report to Congress and to the executive. The Committee includes fourteen legislators, seven appointed by the Chamber of Deputies and seven by the Senate. The president, the two vice-presidents, and the secretary of the Joint Committee are chosen by simple vote of its members, with a term of office of two years, rotating between each one of the two chambers. Tradition dictates that the presidency of the Committee is held by a member of the majority. There is no special procedure to veto prospective members or to remove members of the Joint Committee other than not having or losing the political confidence of its wing peers, particularly the president of the wing. All legislators are eligible to be members of the Joint Committee; there is no security vetting before or during appointment. The joint status of the congressional committee under study poses a weakness in terms of the relationship with the chambers. For example, the Joint Committee is not directly involved in the lawmaking process—and cannot report bills to the floor—except for the intelligence secret budget included in the administration's overall annual budget bill. Senator Mario Daniele[23] (Justicialist party; province of Tierra del Fuego), member of the Joint Committee, is aware of the difficulties of this new beginning regarding gaps or areas of difficulty in practice; he mentions the institutional weaknesses that the country has suffered as legislators attempt to provide mechanisms of suitable control.

Powers of the Joint Committee

The National Intelligence Law grants a set of formal powers to the Joint Committee. Article 32 allows this committee to ascertain that the functioning of the intelligence agencies complies with the constitutional, legal, and statutory norms in force, verifying the strict observance and respect for individual warranties stated by the national constitution as well as the strategic outlines of general objectives of the national intelligence policy. According to article 33, parliamentary control comprises mainly the analysis of the national intelligence plan, the consideration of the secret annual report on intelligence activities prepared by the Secretariat of Intelligence, and the elaboration and submission to the executive and the Congress of an annual secret report[24] furnishing opinions in relation to any legislative project on intelligence activities. It also includes receiving denunciations made by individuals or associations regarding abuses or illegal acts committed by intelligence agencies and investigating them, as well as controlling the curricula of the National Intelligence School. The intelligence agencies are obliged to submit to the Joint Committee upon its request every internal regulation, doctrine, and organic-functional structure (article 35).

Overseeing Secret Budget and Expenditures

A key feature promoted by legislators was legislative control and oversight of intelligence secret budget and expenditures. As mentioned above, the law sets out specific powers related to this matter. The Joint Committee is competent to oversee and control the secret budget assigned to the national intelligence system agencies. For this purpose the Committee may intervene in the discussion of the national budget bill proposed by the executive to Congress; the executive is obliged to submit every document as needed, particularly the amounts approved or expended by each agency and a classified appendix comprising the purpose, program, or subject of the expenditures. In spite of the lack of congressional experience in the exercise of secret expenditures oversight, the Joint Committee has full legally granted powers to exert effective democratic control over the intelligence sector. Time will show if the "power of the purse" principle is applicable to Argentinean congressional culture.

Parliamentary Investigations and Other Features

The investigative experience of the legislative has been scarce, scandal-driven, and unsystematic. In the field of intelligence, the main precedent is the action undertaken by the Joint Special Committee in charge of monitoring the judicial investigations of the terrorist bombings against the embassy of Israel and the AMIA building. During the period 1997–1999, two public reports were issued that included recommendations on intelligence reform. Yet there has been no opportunity to test the investigative powers of the Joint Committee based on article 32 of the National Intelligence Law. These powers allow the Joint Committee, for example, to initiate an investigation based on a complaint or on conclusions of their own work. As mentioned by Senator Daniele, once the Committee was established, the first task carried out by legislators and advisors was the drafting of internal rules of procedure of the Joint Committee; at the present time the Joint Committee is fully prepared to handle and store sensitive information. To fulfill the authority granted by article 34 to check and analyze information regarding the interception of communications and to ensure that such warrants are consistent with judicial requests, the Joint Committee established a special subcommittee by internal ruling.

As with every congressional committee, the internal rulings of the Joint Committee stipulate that there should be weekly meetings of a secret nature. An administrative secretary chosen by its president and appointed by vote of its members runs the daily work of the Joint Committee. Each Committee member can appoint an advisor who will be a congressional staff member. The Joint Committee can also hire administrative personnel—four to eight people— selected from within the congressional personnel payroll. The internal ruling of the Joint Committee calls for the permanent education of these advisors in those tasks to be performed by the Committee.

Challenges to Legislative Oversight

The Joint Committee for the Oversight of Security and Intelligence Agencies and Activities was created in 1993 and remained active until 2001 when it was abolished with the enactment of the new law. The previous congressional experience lacked independence from the executive and with the new law was granted powers that gave full access to information about the security or intelligence agency's activities. The National Intelligence Law provided for a minimum scheme for the work of the Joint Committee based on these requirements:

- To request the organic–functional structures of the agencies of the national intelligence system, as well as all the regulations in force—including intelligence and counterintelligence doctrines
- To require periodic reports on the secret budgetary and expenditures execution of each intelligence agency
- To request the set of intelligence requirements (essential elements of information; other intelligence requirements), the plans for collection of information, and other documents concerning analysis of information
- To ask for periodic reports on the following: operations of intelligence and counterintelligence, protecting the sources and methods; all interceptions of private communications; other activities of intelligence in support of judicial investigations; and counterintelligence and counterespionage activities and operation

Consistent with articles 33.4 and 37.4 of the law, the Joint Committee annually submits a secret report to the executive, as well as to both chambers of Congress. Article 36 states that no public document issued by the Joint Committee must reveal information that may harm intelligence activities and affect domestic security and national defense. Astonishingly, the law makes no reference to a public report to be periodically issued by the Joint Committee. As of this writing, the Joint Committee had not yet issued its first annual report, which is in preparation.

At this writing, the Joint Committee has not been active long enough to raise conclusions about its pros and cons. Although its membership reflects the spectrum of political parties, in terms of check and balances the prevalence of the majority may lessen the work of the Joint Committee with the presidency of the Committee being held by a member of the Justicialist party. It is important to note that the powers to exercise control and oversight of intelligence budget and expenditures granted by law have no precedent in the modern history of the country. As Senator Daniele says, only after the enactment of the 2001 National Intelligence Law 25520 can it be affirmed that the needed powers are available to engage fully in parliamentary control. The proactive capacity of the Joint Committee has yet to be proven.

Recent Trends

A resolution issued by the Anti-corruption Office[25] asked for more transparency in the management of secret accounts and considered that intelligence legislation has weaknesses as far as requirements of registry of expenditures, specialized control, public access to information, and in relation to the judicial control of the legality of those acts as well as to access on the part of the judges to relevant information for their cases.[26] It is important to mention that this resolution included a draft proposing several amendments to the 2001 National Intelligence Law 25520.

In May 2003, President Nestor Kirchner (elected in 2003) posted Sergio Acevedo—a member of Congress representing the province of Santa Cruz, which is that of the president—as intelligence secretary. Recently, Acevedo stressed the need to exclude the agency from acting in support of judicial investigations and to assign this role to criminal intelligence. He considered this a matter of legislative reform.[27] As a relevant precedent, President Kirchner exercised, by decree, executive control on the declassification of information concerning the judicial investigation of the AMIA bombing, allowing several top intelligence officials to answer any judicial inquiry. By October 2003, a "secret reform" of the intelligence secretariat was leaked to the press. According to a newspaper report,[28] it consisted of a dismissal of 160 agents, to be followed by a new internal structure and profile and by new curricula and professors for the National Intelligence School. Also, to avoid past practices of increasing secret expenditures, the executive would submit to Congress the real figure for the 2004 secret budget, in compliance with the National Intelligence Law. According to the same report, the directorate for Judicial Observations, belonging to the Secretariat of Intelligence, and in charge of the interception of communications, would be transferred to the judiciary. For this purpose, in the near future the president will submit a bill to Congress.

Conclusions

Voices of warning have been raised concerning ". . . [t]he possibility [that] exists that democratically elected civilians may not in fact be interested in controlling the intelligence apparatus in the new democracies."[29] Argentina has gone through a long process to develop a legal and democratic framework for the intelligence sector. A remarkable political will was present notwithstanding the serious political and economic crises that the country suffered during recent years. Several conclusions can be made about following the approach suggested for this study:[30]

- Intelligence agencies are established by legislation. Their powers and limits are clearly defined.
- The most feared intrusive technique—interception of private communications—is under executive and judiciary control.
- Legal restrictions on collection of information regarding the inhabitants become safeguards for the rule of law and human rights protection.
- Transparency appears for the first time associated with the intelligence sector because the law unveils several aspects of intelligence activities previously unknown either to executive officials and legislators or to the public.
- Secret budgets and expenditures are subject to legal accountability mechanisms to be performed by a congressional committee.
- Parliamentary oversight has been formally revamped and since the new law a Joint Committee addresses intelligence activities and organizations with significant powers.

The new legislation has not been in force long enough to make an evaluation of its benefits or weaknesses. The severe social and economic crisis suffered by Argentina after December 2001 appeared to be a worst-case scenario for achieving results in the field of congressional oversight on intelligence. The improvements in the intelligence legislation must not be seen as a panacea. Taking into account that the two ministerial intelligence agencies are in an embryonic stage, the intelligence system is still under construction. In any case its history is still to be written.

Nevertheless there are several aspects not covered by legislation, such as an independent supervision mechanism at the executive level, a detailed process for raising complaints, and a specific procedure for granting authorization to conduct other intrusive techniques. There are other aspects to change, such as the predominance of the executive over the intelligence sector in spite of the new legislation. Surely a better law is desired; but the 2001 National Intelligence Law 25520 was the one approved after a broad-spectrum political consensus was reached. The ability to exercise all those functions granted by law will be an indicator not only of the political will to oversee the intelligence sector, but also of the maturity of Argentina's democracy. It still remains to be proven if there exists political willingness among legislators to exert effective oversight and among executive officials to improve intelligence reform.

Several Argentinean authors, all sharing similar involvement in the legislative debates since the 1990s,[31] agree in their writings and speeches that this period is a unique opportunity to shape a new intelligence culture, leading to a new and democratic interface between policy and intelligence anchored in confidence, professionalism, mutual learning, and adaptability, with clear roles and responsibilities and under strict controls. The intelligence sector of the new century appears to be markedly different from previous decades and from that of the period of military rule. Nevertheless, there is a long way to go to establish a new culture and practices in the intelligence sector in general and in the oversight function in particular.

Notes

1. According to article 1 of the National Constitution, Argentina adopts the federal republican representative form of government. The president of the nation is the head of the nation, head of the government; and he is politically responsible for the general administration. Article 44 [Legislative Power] states that the legislative power of the nation shall be vested in a Congress composed of two chambers, one of deputies of the nation and the other of senators for the provinces and for Buenos Aires City.

2. Thomas C. Bruneau, "Controlling Intelligence in New Democracies," *International Journal of Intelligence and Counterintelligence* 14 (3) (June 2001): 331.

3. The terms "oversight," "review," and "control" are used hereafter as stated by Marina Caparini in *Challenges of Control and Oversight of Intelligence Services in a Liberal Democracy*, paper presented at the Workshop on Democratic and Parliamentary Oversight of Intelligence Services (Geneva, October 2002), 5; and Hans Born, *Democratic and Parliamentary Oversight of the Intelligence Services: Best Practices and Procedures*, paper presented at the Workshop on Democratic and Parliamentary Oversight of Intelligence Services, (Geneva, October 2002), 9–10.

4. Jaime Garreta, "El Diseño de un Nuevo Marco Jurídico Regulatorio para la Actividad de Inteligencia del Estado en la Argentina," *Security and Defense Studies Review* 2 (2), (2002): 270.

5. In accordance with their authority to collect information or not, these agencies can be classified into two types: organs, those agencies with no collection means; and organisms, agencies with collection means which can perform all the steps of the intelligence cycle.

6. The National Gendarmerie and the Argentine Coast Guard.

7. Article 35 specified that: "The committee shall verify that the performance of the agencies and organizations referred in article 33 is adjusted strictly to the constitutional, legal and regulating norms in force, stating the strictly observance and respect of the National Constitution individual guarantees, as well as of the measures contained in the Human Rights American Convention, known as 'San José de Costa Rica Agreement' and included in our legal arrangement through the law No. 23.054."

8. Garreta, El Diseño, 269.

9. Eduardo Estevez, *Argentina's Intelligence after Ten Years of Democracy: the Challenge of Reform and Congressional Oversight*, paper, Intelligence Resource Project, Federation of American Scientists (Washington, D.C., 1993).

10. An order to update intelligence files given by the Ministry of Interior and executed by elements of national and provincial security forces was leaked to the press, triggering that decision as a matter of democratic control.

11. The law comprises fifty-three articles arranged in ten titles—general principles, protection of rights and guarantees of the inhabitants of the nation, intelligence agencies, national intelligence policy, classification of information, interception and seizing of com-

munications, personnel and education, parliamentary control, criminal provisions, and transitional and complimentary provisions.

12. Defined as ". . . the group of functional relations of the intelligence agencies of the national state, under the direction of the Secretariat of Intelligence for the purpose of giving assistance to decision-making in the field of foreign and domestic security of the nation."

13. Article 10, 2001 National Intelligence Law No. 25520.

14. Title VI—Interception and Seizing of Communications, articles 18 and 19.

15. Article 4.

16. Under articles 222 and/or 223 of the Penal Code (article 17).

17. This article states that "Processing of personal data for the purposes of national defense or public security by the armed forces, security forces, police departments or intelligence agencies, without the consent of the parties involved, shall be limited to those events and data categories necessary for strict compliance with the missions legally assigned to them for national defense or public security purposes, or to fight against crime. In such cases, files shall be specified and identified to such effect, and they shall be classified in categories, according to their degree of reliability."

18. Article 18 of the National Constitution specifies: "The domicile may not be violated, as well as the written correspondence and private papers; and a law shall determine in which cases and for what."

19. The mentioned paragraph (e) allows the Internal Security Council created by that law to ". . . require of the intelligence organizations, either civilian national or provincial, and of the security forces and police, all necessary information and intelligence, which must be supplied."

20. As described by Born, 2002, 5.

21. Editorial, *La Nación*, July 14, 2002.

22. Title VIII, 2001 National Intelligence Law 25520.

23. Interview, Buenos Aires, August 15, 2003.

24. This includes: (a) analysis and evaluation of the activities, functions, and organization of the National Intelligence System regarding the implementation of the National Intelligence Plan; (b) description of the oversight and control activities performed by the Joint Committee when fulfilling its functions, as well as the explanation of the grounds for performing them; (c) recommendations for improving the performance of the National Intelligence System.

25. An independent office of the Ministry of Justice, Security and Human Rights.

26. Officina Anticorrupción, "Resolución del 11 de abril de 2003. Ministerio de Justicia, Seguridad y Derechos Humanos," Buenos Aires 2003, 1–3.

27. Interview with Sergio Acevedo, *La Nación*, September 8, 2003, 9.

28. Anonymous, "Echaron a más de 160 espías de la SIDE," *La Nación*, October 19, 2003, 9.

29. Bruneau, "Controlling Intelligence," 23.

30. Ian Leigh, *Democratic Control of Security and Intelligence Services: A Legal Framework,* paper presented at the Workshop on Democratic and Parliamentary Oversight of Intelligence Services (Geneva, October 2002), 8–17.

31. Such as Jaime Garreta, Pablo Martínez, Marcelo Saín, José Manuel Ugarte, and the present author.

10

The Role of the Security Services in Democratization: South Korea's Agency for National Security Planning

Jonathan Moran

This chapter analyzes the system of oversight and accountability with regard to the National Intelligence Service (NIS).[1] The NIS is the premier intelligence/security organization in the Republic of Korea (hereafter South Korea) with responsibility for internal and external national security. The NIS was formerly known as the Agency for National Security Planning and before that began operation as the Korean Central Intelligence Agency.

An analysis of oversight and accountability of intelligence cannot be undertaken without setting the NIS in its political, legal, and historical context. This context highlights the remarkable progress of reform of the security establishment in South Korea since democratization. A sustained period of military-backed rule lasted from 1961 to 1987. The sheer size of the security establishment, erected in the service of an extensive definition of national security, led some observers to question the possibility of democratization. However a democratization process, instituted in 1987–88, has been successful—there have been repeated National Assembly elections, local autonomy was introduced in 1995, and Korea's fourth presidential election in succession took place in 2002. As part of this process the military and security establishment has been subjected to legal and organizational reform and to popular scrutiny.

However, this context also highlights the powerful position that the intelligence service held in Korean politics, a position that is still evident. Although democratic reforms have constrained the formerly extensive role of the security services in some areas, the NIS continues to play an evident role in the Korean polity. There is reason for this: requirements for national security with regard to North Korea are a factor in the significant NIS role in domestic affairs. The continuing external threat from North Korea has ensured that security issues and thus intelligence organizations have remained central in post-authoritarian politics. However, NIS legal and paralegal operations are in evidence in the overall political process and are evident in the mainstream political process. A number of political corruption scandals in South Korea appear to involve NIS personnel at both high and low level. These legal and paralegal activities highlight the need for effective oversight.[2]

An analysis of the context of South Korean politics highlights the fact that problems with intelligence agency operations cannot be traced to weak oversight alone. The strength of the executive, the extensive national security legislation, the role of "network" or unofficial politics, and the politics of national security are other factors which provide the context for NIS power and a lack of oversight that the existing system of parliamentary oversight cannot be expected to remedy.

Context

To understand the role of intelligence agencies and their oversight it is necessary to understand the role of political power and its effect on law in South Korea. The development of political power in South Korea saw the creation of a powerful intelligence establishment. This dominated the development of law in South Korea.

South Korea became a sovereign nation in 1948. A period of democracy lasting from 1948 to 1961 ended in a military coup. From 1961 to 1987 the military effectively ruled South Korea. During this period the role of the intelligence establishment was massively expanded. National security was a priority. North Korea and most domestic dissent was regarded as a national security threat.

Following the military coup of 1961, which terminated the democratic period of Syngman Rhee (1948–1960) and Chang Myon (1960–61), the South Korean concept of national security drew on the Japanese notion of "Rich nation, strong army"—industrial development as the guarantor of military capability, social cohesion, and thus national security. Labor was repressed and excluded. Businesses were also controlled and threatened in the development of "national capitalism." Other civil society groups were tightly regulated, as was the media.[3] In the early 1970s South Korea's "managed democracy" was replaced by a national security state due to a domestic political crisis coupled with the worsening external situation (increased North Korean activity and Nixon's planned withdrawal from direct U.S. involvement in East Asian security). The need to marshal society in the Heavy Industry "Big Push" of the 1970s, another component of national security, also played a role.[4] The existing large security establishment was expanded and its power increased, a power that remained intact until democratization.

Thus during the 1970s, the state erected a national security infrastructure of incredible scope and power centered around a strong executive. The security ideology of Park Chung Hee, which involved disinformation, propaganda campaigns, and the militarization of society remained an influential one even after his death. Groups opposing national development and the adoption of a strong front toward North Korea—and the two were often viewed as combined—were defined as subversive; for example, labor and student organizations. The subsequent repressive regime of Chun Doo Hwan (1980–1987) built upon this system. The military remained the backbone of the political system, and the intelligence apparatus operated throughout the political system.[5]

The legal system developed in the shadow of national security politics. Laws did not function as guarantors of individual or collective rights. Law was subordinated to political authority and the strategy of the moment. The National Security Law (NSL), inherited from Syngman Rhee, contained an extensive definition of national security, with severe penalties for generously defined "anti-state" activity. Most anti-government actions and expressions could be construed as "aiding the enemy"—that is, North Korea. A series of subsequent laws set strict limits and penalties on a wide range of political behavior which could be deemed a threat to national security, or—very closely linked to this—a threat to social/political order.

Despite this unpromising context South Korea democratized in 1987. Remarkably successful economic development had given rise to various groups in civil society such as the middle class and strengthened others, such as trade unions, student groups, and activist groups. Although still weak compared to the strong, pervasive state, these groups could at times effectively mobilize to force political change: Sustained protests by the civilian opposition forced Chun Doo Hwan to institute a genuine democratization process.[6] President Roh Tae Woo was elected in 1987; followed by Kim Young Sam, elected in 1992; Kim Dae Jung, elected in 1997; and Roh Moo-hyun, elected in 2002.

The Development of the National Security Establishment

In terms of organization, following the military coup of 1961 the existing intelligence establishment was reorganized and expanded, with military agencies providing the backbone. The Korean Central Intelligence Agency (KCIA), founded in 1961, had responsibility for domestic and international intelligence-gathering and anti-subversion, and stood as the main organization investigating crimes of subversion as defined in the NSL and other security legislation. Built up from the 3,000-strong Army Counter Intelligence Corps, by 1964 the KCIA had 370,000 employees.[7] It grew into a power base in its own right during the late 1960s and 1970s, with each of its directors challenging for influence in the government structure. In 1979 the then head of the KCIA, Kim Chae Kyu, assassinated President Park Chung Hee (in power from 1961 to 1979), after which the KCIA underwent a name change to the Agency for National Security Planning (ANSP) and reform under President Chun Doo Hwan. Its authority re-emerged in the 1980s, though this time not as an independent power grouping but under the president's wing, as it had been in the early 1960s.[8] The agency in its various forms has had twenty-seven directors, twenty of whom have come from the military.

Chun Doo Hwan's military coup in 1980 led to an increased role for military intelligence in the form of the Defence Security Command (DSC), Chun's initial power base. Chun had headed the DSC under President Park Chung Hee and used it as a platform from which to mount a coup in 1979–80, following Park's death.[9] Modeled on the example of centralized political organization set up by the Nationalist Chinese in Taiwan, the DSC had been created to monitor activities inside the military itself and to prevent external subversion of the military. In practice, through its Directorate 2, the DSC expanded into the surveillance of political parties, universities, and the media.[10] Almost every media organization contained DSC officials.[11] Finally, in 1970 the Combat Police Organization Law established a combat division to counter infiltration and engage in riot duties. Although subsidiary to the military and intelligence agencies, the division constituted a powerful grouping within the state.[12] Generally, "the police constitute(d) a highly centralized national paramilitary force directly linked to the President of the Republic."[13] Chun Doo Hwan expanded the combat police from 20,000 to 120,000 during the 1980–1986 period.[14]

External Threat—North Korea

South Korea faced a consistent external threat from North Korea (Democratic Peoples Republic of Korea). Following the termination of the Korean War in 1953, the North embarked on a series of probing missions, involving commando raids on the South Korean presidential residence, the Blue House, in 1968, digging tunnels under the DMZ in the 1970s, and terrorist attacks in the 1980s both abroad and on South Korean airlines. In addition, lower-level North Korean infiltration has included spy missions, the establishment of long-term agents in the South, and the funding of political movements and individuals sympathetic to the North. This external threat cannot be underestimated as a variable affecting intelligence operations and reform.

Reform and Democratization: Reducing the Remit of the Security Services

Following democratization, reforms were aimed at the security/intelligence establishment. Under President Roh Tae Woo (1988–1993) the ANSP was gradually weaned away from domestic overt and covert operations. In 1988 the agency removed its agents from the Seoul Criminal Court and Supreme Court.[15] Seventy percent of the top echelon were replaced by younger, more professional officers, a process continued by Kim Young Sam.[16] Outside pressure also contributed to reform. The 1988 National Assembly elections had seen the ruling party lose its majority. Opposition parliamentarians pressured the government to accelerate reforms, which aided those reformers in the ruling party itself. Though the ruling party regained its majority in 1990, other figures continued the pressure to reform, particularly the thirty or so generals and ex-security-service figures who had joined the opposition following democratization.[17] These actors attempted to bring the ANSP under parliamentary scrutiny, which would go some way toward the establishment of an effective oversight committee.

The NSL was reformed in 1991 to limit the applicability of some of the more extensive prohibitions on political activity, since much normal political activity had been classed as a threat to national security under the NSL. Further, after six years of negotiations (1988–1994) between the opposition and the government, the National Security Planning Agency Act stripped the agency of powers to investigate crimes defined in article 7 (praising or sympathizing with "anti-state" groups) and article 10 (failing to inform the authorities of "anti-state" group activities under articles 3, 4, and 5.1) of the National Security Law, which had given impressive scope for Agency investigations of domestic political and social groups. (However, these powers were restored with the support of the executive in 1997.)

Parliament was also empowered to review the ANSP's budget, important because according to opposition reports it spent nearly 2 percent of the national budget in 1992.[18] Under Kim Young Sam an Intelligence Committee was established in the National Assembly to supervise the ANSP's budget and planning.[19] Kim also continued the reforms aimed at weaning the ANSP from excessive domestic political intelligence activities. After assuming office, Kim named Professor Kim Deok of Hankuk University of Foreign Studies as ANSP director. Kim

Deok recalled agents inside social, political, and economic organizations, instructing them to keep to their legally defined activities[20] and further reduced their remit of domestic operation.[21] In 1992, Lee Jong Chan, former officer in the ANSP and then ruling party presidential candidate, had said: "The NSP has to change from being a SAVAK to a Mossad," that is, to a professional agency with a demarcated legal-institutional footing.[22] This had certainly been the theoretical result of the reform processes initiated since 1987, but the extent to which this occurred in practice will be examined in later sections.

The election of Kim Dae Jung as president in 1997 facilitated more change. An opposition politician of long standing, Kim Dae Jung had been the target of the intelligence agency in the 1970s and 1980s, and had been sentenced to death for anti-state activities. Kim appointed Lee Jong Chan as ANSP director. Lee was a reformist politician who had previously been an ANSP official. Lee replicated the reforms of Kim Young Sam in the early 1990s. With executive backing, Lee removed top officials and encouraged others to tender resignations. As a result, nearly twenty-five top officials left the ANSP. Other officials were reshuffled. In 1999 the ANSP's name was changed to the National Intelligence Service (NIS). Lee began a process of organizational change, attempting to further move the ANSP away from domestic operations and criminal investigation and toward intelligence gathering and the analysis of international (North Korea and others) developments and threats.

Roh Tae Woo reduced the DSC's influence and made its command a less prestigious post.[23] DSC agents were withdrawn from the National Assembly in 1988.[24] As with the ANSP, opposition pressure increased the reform drive. The DSC was first subjected to parliamentary scrutiny in 1988, and then again in 1993, this latter process led by a ruling party politician who had once been interrogated and tortured by DSC agents. Kim Young Sam intensified the reforms, immediately replacing the commander of the DSC and moving the DSC under the jurisdiction of the Defence Ministry, rather than the presidency, and planning a reduction in the DSC's staff from six thousand to under five thousand.[25] From 1993 the DSC did a successful job of dismantling the Hanahoe and Aljahoe societies. These were semi-secret groups based around military class and regional ties. Forty other unofficial societies inside the military were dismantled.

Reform of the intelligence bureaucracy thus involved the demarcation and limitation of the operational area of intelligence activities, a necessary task since the remit of the ANSP and DSC had been so broad in the past. Reforms were instituted from the presidency, and through pressure by the opposition and some ruling party politicians themselves, some of whom had formerly been in the intelligence services or military. There is no doubt these reforms have had a substantial effect in contributing to the political opening of the system. Not only were security agency operations limited in law, they are open to challenge. Perhaps one sign of the changes lies in the number of former members of the military and ANSP who have joined opposition parties and who can comment and provide evidence on intelligence operations. The ruling party has also predictably taken in former members of the ANSP but also former radicals who were subject to the agency's attentions in past decades. Further, the actions of the ANSP have become more open to scrutiny by the media. As the subsequent sections will demonstrate, some security service operations have been exposed through a series of public scandals involving the presidency, the ANSP/NIS itself, and the political elite.

These scandals highlight the fact that there are important areas of NIS structure, remit, and operations, which could be the subject of reform. While the debate over reform often provokes political disagreement, the idea that the NIS requires some level of reform often stretches across the political spectrum.

The Current Situation

The NIS

The basic structure of the NIS consists of one director, three deputy directors, and an executive director. The executive director heads administrative support. The three deputy directors each head one of the three major sections of the NIS: international affairs; North Korea affairs; and domestic affairs. Each section is itself divided up into relevant bureaus. For example, the domestic affairs section has an anti-communism bureau, investigating long-term DPRK agents inside the South (and an economic department within the anti-communism bureau); a political department, which gathers intelligence on political fund gathering (a source of corruption and links to the DPRK) and public/political individuals; and a media department, which collects information on TV and newspaper companies and output.

Each section is responsible for collecting information, planning and coordination, threat assessment, and counterintelligence and criminal investigation. The NIS has powers to get information from ministries and other government agencies. It has criminal investigation powers in areas related to national security. In practice this is a wide remit, since laws covering national security, such as the National Security Law and the Military Security Protection Law, are wide in scope. The NIS has between seven and nine thousand members. The decline in numbers from the 1960s and 1970s reflects the decrease in military influence over the Korean political system. In previous decades the direct control and surveillance of economic and political and social institutions and actors was evident. The KCIA was a major political actor in its own right. Over recent decades, and particularly since democratization, the size of the intelligence establishment has been reduced.

The NIS works with the Supreme Public Prosecutor's Office, whose Public Security Department deals with national security and espionage cases. South Korea operates a U.S.–influenced system of criminal investigation in that the police and NIS cooperate with an independent prosecutorial organization. The Prosecutor General's office reports to the National Assembly on violations of the NSL.

The NIS is separate from the military. The military has its own intelligence agency, the Defense Security Command (DSC). Both agencies may work together when necessary. The Defense Ministry nominates the head of the DSC, whom the president normally accepts. In 2003 for the first time the recommendation was rejected, as the president felt the nominated head did not agree with the president's plans for intelligence reform.[26] The NIS is separate from the police. Where the agency and the police conflict the agency has priority.

Executive Control

The nature of executive control cannot be understood without reference to the South Korean Constitution. The executive (the presidency) has significant power. The power stems from the scope for executive decisions, particularly in the area of appointments to government and the legal system. The legislature (the National Assembly) has limited powers, although it can check the executive in certain areas. The judiciary is to some extent overshadowed by the executive. Whilst in national terms the presidency can become a "lame duck" administration due to perceived policy failure, crisis, and National Assembly and media pressure, the executive remains a powerful force in the day-to-day operations of government and state administration.

The main problem is that executive control of the NIS is strong in formal and informal terms. The head of the NIS is appointed by the executive (the president). Until recently the legislature (National Assembly) had no role in this. The legislature now holds confirmation hearings but cannot block an appointment. The NIS head can be removed by the president. The head of the NIS is a legal person. The president receives intelligence briefings directly from the director-general of the NIS. The president appoints a national security advisor, a cabinet-level post, which is not subject to assembly approval.

What is also important is that the heads of the Office of National Tax Administration (ONTA), the National Police Agency (NPA), and the NIS were/are not only appointed by the executive, they remain/ed personally close to the executive. These posts remain executive appointments. The minister of justice is also appointed by the executive and this official controls/influences whether the prosecutor-general launches investigations. Thus the higher reaches of the national security establishment are approved by the executive, and decisions on criminal investigations related to national security are undertaken by individuals appointed by the executive.

In informal terms the executive wields great influence over the NIS. There is little or no transparency or accountability of the executive in its control of the NIS. Despite Kim Young Sam's policy of moving the ANSP away from domestic political matters, the ANSP (renamed the NIS) was accused of attempting to smear Kim Dae Jung before he was elected in 1997, and ANSP officers were convicted of corruption-related offenses involving the activities of important figures in the executive and legislature.[27] A recurring problem is the use of the NIS by the president or his family members for illicit purposes. Such scandals have been evident in all presidencies in the democratic era (1987–2002). Kim Ki-seop, head of policy planning and coordination in the NIS under President Kim Young Sam (1993–1997), worked with the president's second son to facilitate political influence peddling,[28] while the former director of domestic intelligence at the NIS and his subordinate were convicted of offenses concerned with bribery and exercising undue influence on behalf of a business figure during the Kim Dae Jung administration (1998–2003).[29]

The NIS still targets political opponents of the executive such as politicians, political activists, the media, and trade unionists.[30] The NIS has been found to have illegally telephone-tapped media figures, National Assembly politicians, presidential advisors, and businessmen. Recently, the opposition Grand National Party alleged that the NIS ran three thousand telephone taps per day.[31]

There are few agreed standards of performance for results or compliance with law and policy. Parliament, parts of the media, and interested civil society groups currently see this as an area in need of reform.

Thus Korea does not face the problem sometimes evident in other nations whereby the intelligence agency is effectively out of government control. Indeed, the government is in one sense a source of the problem in that executive control of the NIS is evident, and thus the main checks in existence are from the executive itself. The executive, through the minister of justice, can encourage the prosecutor's office to initiate investigations into senior NIS figures. In addition, until it was abandoned by President Kim Dae Jung in 2000, a special police unit, headed by the senior presidential secretary for civil affairs, could initiate investigations of presidential family members, senior government, bureaucratic, and political (including opposition) individuals. This would cover their inappropriate relationships with NIS officials. Incoming President Roh planned to revive the unit.[32]

The current arrangements do not constitute a clear structure of accountability, either politically or in terms of measuring agency efficiency. The relations between the executive and the agency often remain personalized and secret. What one might term network politics is influential. There is a lack of clarity in roles and responsibilities and reporting. This is a subject of repeated calls for reform.

Policy and Tasking

As mentioned, the fact of tight executive control of the NIS does not make sure the agency functions properly; indeed, some pressures for intelligence agencies to act improperly actually come from the executive or individuals close to the executive. The work of the agency is influenced by executive/ministerial/policy formal and informal networks, and the relations involving the agency may be personalized and thus operate around formal channels.

The NIS is responsible for national intelligence assessments. National intelligence assessments do not generally stem from interdepartmentally agreed-upon assessments; some organizations and individuals are important in influencing national intelligence assessments. These include the executive, certain advisors, senior officials in the NIS itself, military intelligence, and other influential individuals who may not occupy a relevant post but are important advisors. The NIS has been criticized in terms of some assessments of North Korean activity, but the NIS is a competent agency in terms of preventing internal and external subversion, and this must rest on an efficient intelligence gathering and tasking operation.

Bilateral relations are authorized by the executive and supervised by the executive. However, the extent to which these relations are not organized along professional lines was evident in the scandal surrounding the development of links with North Korea. The former head of the NIS was given an eighteen-month suspended sentence for his role in facilitating an illegal cash transfer to North Korea to encourage North Korea to host an inter-Korean summit.[33]

There is no clear framework for the direction of intelligence agencies' work related to the needs of government and its "customers." A national security model is influential: the executive is central in deciding intelligence priorities as well as the NIS itself. The NIS has an impressive record in countering external and internal subversion. Although there have been examples of penetration of South Korean society by agents working for the North, and examples of terrorist attacks and other incursions around the border, overall the record of the NIS and its predecessors has been effective by any reasonable standard. NIS work responds efficiently to executive priorities and to its own well-developed perception of national security. The question is whether these priorities are always appropriate.

National Security Legislation—Too Wide a Remit?

Some controversies over intelligence agency activities in democracies rest on whether the actions of the agencies in question are legal.[34] In South Korea the central controversy is the very wide legal scope provided for NIS actions by the relevant national security laws, such as the National Security Law[35] and the Military Security Protection Law.

The main law covering the powers of the intelligence agencies is the NSL. This law is very wide in scope and covers an extremely wide definition of offenses, which the NIS is empowered to investigate. Provisions of Article 7 of the NSL are held to be in contradiction to the International Covenant for Civil and Political Rights, to which South Korea assented in 1990.[36]

In addition many NIS operations do not appear to require internal administrative authorization. The most intrusive measures do not require the minister's signature. They require approval from the relevant senior official within the domestic or foreign branch of the NIS. The NIS also undertakes acts that its officers know to be illegal, such as telephone tapping and opening of individuals' mail.[37]

Theoretically there is supposed to be regular feedback on the use of powers within the NIS. However, one of the main complaints concerning the NIS is that the senior management are often circumvented by internal unofficial networks of agents whose loyalty is based on regional and school alumni ties, both of which are extremely important in South Korea.[38]

Thus, in terms of the laws governing national security, there are not clear limits that balance ministerial control but also protect against political abuse. This is the case in legal terms and also unofficially. Legally, the NIS is bound to the executive; legally, the executive has great political power. Legally, the NIS has great power. Unofficially the executive has significant influence over the NIS, and the NIS itself has significant influence in terms of investigative and other actions. This raises non-legal political and security judgments as to the appropriate levels of accountability. Where external agencies such as the Constitutional Court have made judgments about the infringement of human rights they appear to be effectively ignored.

Independent Supervision

At present independent supervision of the NIS is weak. There is an Intelligence Committee in the National Assembly, which oversees the main issues relating to NIS operations (see the discussion that follows). However, there are no independent committees or boards mandated to control and supervise NIS operations. There is a government proposal to place the NIS under the remit of the Board of

Audit and Inspection, but this alone is not sufficient to ensure that professional standards are maintained and efficient methods of operation are developed. Significantly, many of the noticeable debates concerning the role of the NIS arise from a nonspecific source such as National Assembly members, media reports, and the actions of civil society groups.

Legislative Oversight Bodies

The National Assembly: Toothless Tiger?

Parliamentary oversight of the NIS has been—and still is—weak. As mentioned previously, the heads of the Office of National Tax Administration, the National Police Agency, and the NIS were not only appointed by the executive and remained personally close to the executive, their appointment and operation was without effective sanction from Parliament. There was no confirmation hearing for the head of the NIS before the National Assembly until 2003, and the executive can still proceed with the appointment despite National Assembly opposition. The National Assembly Intelligence Committee can call the nominated head before it for a hearing but, like the full National Assembly, cannot block his nomination. Other senior NIS appointments are not subject to National Assembly confirmation hearing.

The Parliamentary Oversight Committee

The National Assembly's Intelligence Committee was formed in 1994. It is a standing committee with twelve members. Numbers and functions are determined by Assembly regulations. The Committee has both ruling and opposition party members; currently the Committee is composed of six ruling party (Millennium Democratic Party) and six opposition (Grand National Party) members. The head is from the ruling Millennium Democratic Party. The members elect the chairman, who controls proceedings and officially represents the Committee. The Committee examines bills relevant to national security and provides commentary on these. It also holds hearings for individuals nominated for senior positions in the NIS.

The Committee can interview members of the NIS. The results are not made public. The exception has been the 2003 interview with the nominated head of the NIS. The Committee does not have the power to subpoena witnesses.

The Committee receives reports from the NIS on intelligence matters. These include reports on the national security situation both domestically and with reference to North Korea. There has been criticism of the quality of intelligence presented to the Committee:

There used to be a lot of second and third rate information first reported in the media and then repackaged and delivered to the committee. —GNP Intelligence Committee member Hong Joo-pyo[39]

In terms of inspecting premises, Intelligence Committee members or other National Assembly figures apparently have limited scope to investigate interrogation centers used for national security investigations. For example, the interrogation chambers in the Seoul District Prosecutor's Office were established in 1989. They were only inspected twice in 1996 by National Assembly members and after the death of a detainee.[40]

Despite its short history and limited remit/powers, the Committee has developed a higher profile on intelligence issues, including examination and comment on various issues. Recently this culminated in the Committee producing a formal report that was backed by a unanimous vote rejecting the nomination of Ko Young-Koo as head of the NIS. The Committee also suspended its operation in protest at this and one other nomination for the senior positions in the NIS, who they view as having a history of academic sympathy with North Korea.[41] However, the Committee reflects the weakness of the National Assembly generally in relation to the executive. It is limited in calling the executive and the Intelligence Service to account. Its powers of independent investigation are limited, and it has little effective control over NIS budgetary matters. However, the Committee is in its relative infancy.

Judicial Oversight by the Constitutional Court

The Constitutional Court was established in 1988 as a result of the democratization process and acts as a body of judicial review. The court interprets the constitution and interprets statutes in terms of their constitutionality. The court has nine justices, serving terms of six years, which may be renewed. A topic of concern is the fact that the Constitutional Court's decisions are not adhered to in practice. Since 1988 the court has struck down in whole or in part 269 statutes. However, approximately fifty of these have not been changed by the National Assembly. This figure includes more than twelve laws in the last two years.[42]

The Constitutional Court declared in an appeal judgment in 1992 that the provision on the NSL which allows detention of suspects for fifty days before charge was unconstitutional. The National Assembly has never reformed the NSL in accordance with this or many other judgments on criminal investigation, which the court calls unconstitutional.

Other Bodies and Mechanisms

Presidential Truth Commission

The Presidential Truth Commission on Special Deaths was established by then President Kim Dae Jung in 2000. The legislation establishing it and providing it with powers was approved by the National Assembly. Its mandate ran until 2003 when its term expired. The Commission examined eighty suspicious deaths under previous authoritarian governments, many allegedly involving the intelligence agencies. This commission had more power than the Intelligence Committee. However, it did not have power to subpoena witnesses or government officials. Nevertheless, fifty-three cases were completed, including twenty-four convictions of agents of the KCIA and ANSP (previous forms of the NIS). Twenty cases were left unresolved. According to members of the Commission, the police, military, and NIS were uncooperative in producing relevant witnesses and documents.[43]

National Human Rights Commission

Kim Dae Jung established a National Human Rights Commission, which examines relevant legislation, comments on it, and generally raises the profile of human rights issues. However, it was ignored concerning the 2002 Terrorism Prevention Bill, which it argued was unnecessary considering the existing wide provisions of the NSL. This bill fell because of the subsequent presidential election. There are also concerns at the commission's lack of proactive power.[44]

Civil Society

South Korea has a tradition of vigorous civil society activity. Many civil society groups have highlighted the lack of accountability of the Korean political system generally, and of the National Intelligence Service in particular. Such groups include the left-leaning Peoples Solidarity for Participatory Democracy (PSPD) and Lawyers for a Democratic Society. The media, including mainstream newspapers, have continually highlighted issues concerned with NIS accountability, efficiency, and probity (including the role of serving and former NIS officers in corruption scandals).[45]

In international terms, a range of organizations have focused their attention on the operation of the NIS and the NSL, including Amnesty International and Human Rights Watch. Amnesty International has particularly focused on the use of the National Security Law and has produced a series of reports highlighting the issues of the law's extremely wide remit, its use to control political dissent, and the cases of individuals sentenced under the NSL.

Civil society agencies in effect function as an ad-hoc form of accountability. These groups, particularly the media, have often successfully pressured for investigations and prosecutions, on issues such as corruption and human rights. Of course civil society activity itself raises general and specific problems: Civil society groups are self-appointed; they are not themselves rigorously accountable. Further, civil society groups are not a permanent regularized system of accountability designed to address specialist issues such as organizational efficiency, organizational development, and professional evaluation.

Conclusions

The issue of NIS accountability to government and the public functioned as a major issue in Korean politics before the 2002 presidential election and in its aftermath.[46] The issues of corruption and illegal telephone tapping were high on the agenda and the subject of media and civil society and opposition political comment. The new president, Roh Moo-hyun, promised reform of the NIS and its operations. Thus, the continuing debate about intelligence reform highlights the issues of NIS organization and accountability addressed in this report.

South Korea has made important progress in the areas of human rights, reform of the actions of police and intelligence agencies, and oversight and constructive criticism of these agencies. This is particularly impressive given South Korea's political and legal history, which saw the military and the security and intelligence establishment wield enormous power from the 1960s until the late 1980s. Despite the criticisms made in this chapter, the reforms that have taken place in South Korea are, in this context, especially remarkable.

However, at present the system of oversight of the NIS within the executive, the legislature, and the judiciary is weak. There is no credible independent structure of oversight. The main official oversight body is the National Assembly's Intelligence Committee. This body has a cross-party membership and has often been vigorous in its criticisms. However, its powers are limited, it cannot reasonably be characterized as proactive, and its institutional capacity is limited. The Committee's powers should be strengthened.

Outside the legislature accountability and oversight could be increased by strengthening existing bodies. During the presidential campaign it was suggested that the Bureau of Audit and Inspection (BAI) could be involved in the managerial and financial evaluation of NIS operations.[47] The BAI is an independent constitutional agency, which undertakes financial and performance audits of central and local government agencies, government invested agencies, and agencies that request audits. It reports to the executive and the National Assembly, and it can recommend remedial action and reparation. However, this alone will not be sufficient to develop a system of efficient tasking and coordination, and BAI involvement should be restricted to matters of general public sector efficiency. The BAI should not have access to classified intelligence product.

Procedures could be developed to ensure that Constitutional Court decisions on national security related matters are given priority. The National Human

Rights Commission's powers could be strengthened, so that its recommendations of national security–related matters are binding.

Internal NIS reforms could further enable accountability to be developed; for example, developing the service as an intelligence gathering and analyzing agency, rather than an agency involved in criminal investigation. This should reduce some of the controversies over NIS accountability by taking away controversial areas of operation.

Ko Young-hoo, current NIS head, has stated: "It is not desirable for the intelligence body to abandon all of its investigative authority, but the right to investigate domestic related security crimes will be discarded."[48] Thus powers to investigate domestic subversion and the violation of security-related laws may be transferred to the NPA and the Public Prosecutor's Office(s). Other areas of operation are being taken away from the NIS remit. For example, a new national crisis bureau is to be established to collect and analyze information on national crises and prepare prevention and reaction plans. Although NIS officials will play a significant role, this was a task previously undertaken solely by the NIS.[49] In addition, the police are to expand their intelligence gathering and analysis functions to identify possible areas of social and political conflict and develop responses to these.[50]

But other more fundamental reforms are needed. These include legal reform to the NSL to introduce a reasonable definition of national security; for example, along the lines of that operating in Canada (See chapter 6 in this volume).

Further, at present the problem is that the level of accountability of the NIS is fundamentally affected by South Korea's system of government, political culture, and legal environment. These structural factors will govern the development of accountability and oversight. South Korea's political system overshadows structures of accountability that may develop. That is, the power of the executive is officially and unofficially strong. The president makes high-level intelligence appointments, has a close relationship with senior NIS officials, receives direct information, and makes input on intelligence operations. The NIS is closely bound to the executive, both formally and informally. Thus, while pressure to reform the NIS often comes from the executive immediately after an election, this perpetuates the problem. Indeed, the current president, Roh Moo-hyun (now facing impeachment over corruption and other issues), continued the pattern of executive interference, dismissing a deputy head of the NIS in late 2003. The need to reform the powers of the executive is one reason there is recurring debate about the possibility of moving to a cabinet system of government in South Korea. Civil society and the media remain important areas of unofficial oversight and accountability that complement the weak executive and parliamentary systems. Relying on the media/civil society groups and campaigns, however, is not an effective or stable system of oversight.

Last but not least, an analysis of accountability of South Korea's intelligence services has to be understood in the current political and regional situation. South Korea faces a very real security threat from North Korea. This threat operates on a number of levels—a clear conventional threat, a middle-level threat from insurgencies, a threat from terrorist operations, and a more subtle threat from espionage and subversion through agents and political movements in the South. It is this context that must always guide judgments about accountability and reform of intelligence in South Korea.

Notes

1. Website of NIS is www.nis.go.kr/app/eng/index [accessed March 19, 2005].
2. And also within East Asian political culture itself. Although there has been extensive debate concerning the extent to which Western normative concepts of rights can be applied to Asian nations (the "Asian Values" debate) the East Asian region *does* have an indigenous discourse asserting rights of expression and association and so forth.
3. Yunshik Chang, "From Ideology to Interest: Government and Press in South Korea 1945–1979," in *Korean Studies: New Pacific Currents*, ed. Dae-Sook Suh (Centre for Korean Studies, University of Hawaii, 1994).
4. Joungwon Kim, *Divided Korea: the Politics of Development* (Cambridge, MA, and London: Harvard University Press, 1976); and C. I. Eugene Kim, "Emergency Development and Human Rights: South Korea," *Asian Survey* 18 (4), (1978): 363–78; and S. J. Kim, *The State, Public Policy and NIC Development* (Seoul: Dae Young Moonwhasa, 1989); Edward A. Olsen, "Korea Inc: the Political Impact of Park Chung Hee's Economic Miracle," in *The Two Koreas in World Politics*, eds. Tae-Hwan Kwac', Wayne Patterson, and Edward A. Olsen (Institute for Far Eastern Studies, Kyungnam University, 1983).
5. Young Whan Kihl, "Korea's Fifth Republic: Domestic Political Trends," *Journal of Northeast Asian Studies* 1 (2) (1982): 38–55.
6. For an account of the South Korean democratization process see Chalmers Johnson, "South Korean Democratization: the Role of Economic Development," *Pacific Review* 2(1) (1989); and S. J. Han and Y. C. Park, "South Korea: Democratization at Last" in *Driven by Growth: Political Change in the Asia-Pacific Region*, ed. J. W. Morley (New York: ME Sharpe,1993).
7. Kim, *Divided Korea*, 234.
8. Jonathan Moran, "The role of the Security Services in Democratization: An Analysis of South Korea's ANSP," *Intelligence and National Security* 13 (4) (1998): 1–33.
9. Kim, *The State*, 1989.
10. *Far Eastern Economic Review* 1(4), 1993.
11. Author interview with K. Kaliher, Chief of Research, Office of the Special Advisor to the C-in-C, United Nations Command, 8.11.1994. The opinions expressed were personal and not official. The DSC was dominated by members of the *Hanahoe* society, led by Chun.
12. S.Y. Lee, "The Call for Reform of the Korean National Police Force," in *Korean Public Administration and Policy in Transition Vol. One—Governmental Institutions and Policy Process*, eds. K.W. Kim and Y. Jung (Seoul: Korean Association for Public Administration/Jangwon, 1993), 303.

13. Lee, *Call for Reform*, 307.

14. Kim, *The State*, 264.

15. U.S. Department of the Army, *"Intelligence Agencies,"* in *Army Area Handbooks: South Korea* (n.d.), Washington, D.C.

16. *Far Eastern Economic Review* 30.12.1993–6.1, 1994.

17. Author interview with K. Kaliher, Chief of Research, Office of the Special Advisor to the C-in-C, United Nations Command, 8.11.1994. The opinions expressed were personal and not official.

18. *Far Eastern Economic Review*, 30.12.1993–6.1.1994.

19. Chin Mi-kyung, *Political Change in South Korea: the Kim Young Sam Era*, paper presented to the 4th Korea Seminar, University of Newcastle, February 1994, 11.

20. *Far Eastern Economic Review*, 11.3.1993.

21. Author interview with K. Kaliher, Chief of Research, Office of the Special Advisor to the C-in-C, United Nations Command, 8.11.1994. The opinions expressed were personal and not official.

22. Quoted in *Far Eastern Economic Review* 15.10.1992.

23. Author interview with K. Kaliher, Chief of Research, Office of the Special Advisor to the C-in-C, United Nations Command, 8.11.1994. The opinions expressed were personal and not official.

24. U.S. Department of Army, Intelligence Agencies..

25. *Far Eastern Economic Review*, 28.10.1993.

26. Anonymous, "President vetoes choice for military intelligence," *Joongang Ilbo*, 23.4.2003.

27. Moran, *Security Services in Democratization*, 11–12.

28. Moran, *Security Services in Democratization*.

29. Won-bae Kim, "Intelligence officials get prison fines," *Joongang Ilbo*, 1.2.2002.

30. Confidential author interview with trade union federation official, Seoul, February 1999. Plus subsequent media reports and Amnesty Reports e.g. Amnesty International, "Republic of Korea (South Korea) Summary of Concerns and Recommendations to Candidates for the Presidential Elections in December 2002," *ASA 25/007/2002*, 2–5.

31. Sang-il Lee, "GNP releases more papers, says scale of taps was vast," *Joongang Ilbo* 2.12.2002.

32. "Reverting to a bad practice," *Joongang Ilbo*, 14.2.2003.

33. M. Ser, "Court rejects appeals in cash-for-summit case," *Joongang Ilbo*, 29.11.2003.

34. Laurence Lustgarten and Ian Leigh, *In From the Cold: National Security and Parliamentary Democracy* (Oxford: Clarendon, 1994).

35. Available at: www.kimsoft.com/Korea/nsl-en.htm. Web Editor's note: This is an unofficial translation of the National Security Law. The sole purpose of this translation is to make the main gist of the law available to non-Korean readers. The readers are forewarned that this English version is neither an accurate nor a legal representation of the law. Several sections and paragraphs dealing with purely prosecutor matters are omitted. Some of the legal terms used here may not be precise or legally correct. This translation covers up to 1994. The NSL was redrafted in 1994 to remove the ANSPs role in investigating crimes under a.7 and a.10 AND in 1997 to restore the ANSPs role in investigating crimes under a.7 and a.10.

36. National Security Law, article 7 ("Praising or Sympathizing") [1] "Up to seven years in prison for those who praise, encourage, disseminate or cooperate with anti-state groups, members, or those under control, being aware that such acts will endanger national security and the democratic freedom" (unofficial translation).

37. Confidential author interview with trade union federation official, Seoul, February 1999.

38. Regional ties and networks have played a powerful role in Korean politics, particularly the "T-K faction" a group of army officers, bureaucrats and other officials from Kyongsang province. Military officers were also bound into alumni networks by graduating in the same year from the Korean Military Academy. See Se-Jin Kim, *The Politics of Military Revolution in Korea* (Chapel Hill: University of North Carolina, 1971) and Mark L. Clifford, *Troubled Tiger: Businessmen, Bureaucrats and Generals in South Korea* (New York: East Gate Press/ME Sharpe, 1994).

39. Jung-min Lee, "Intelligence Committee ends strike," *Joongang Ilbo*, 5.6.2003.

40. Chung-hoon Chang, "Interrogation chambers to be closed," *Joongang Ilbo*, 16.11.2002.

41. Jung-min Lee, "Intelligence Committee ends strike," *Joongang Ilbo*, 5.6.2003 and Seoung-hee Park, "Roh rebuked for choice of leader at spy agency," *Joongang Ilbo*, 24.4.2003.

42. Cited in a review by National Assembly member Hee-ryong Won, of the opposition Grand National Party.

43. N. Wook, "Commissions find tough going at end of Kim term," *Joongang Ilbo* 16.8.2002 and N. Wook, "Death probe unit has no regrets," *Joongang Ilbo*, 16.9.2002.

44. Amnesty International, "Republic of Korea (South Korea) Summary of Concerns and Recommendations to Candidates for the Presidential Elections in December 2002." ASA 25/007/2002, 18; and Amnesty International, "Republic of Korea (South Korea) Terrorism Prevention Bill," 25/003/2002 and Amnesty International, Korea (Republic of) in *Amnesty International Report 2003* POL/10/003/2003 [available at www.amnesty.org].

45. Author interviews with member of the PSPD, Seoul, March 1999.

46. J. Nam and Sang-il Lee, "Both candidates vow to curb NIS," *Joongang Ilbo*, 3.12.2003.

47. Nam and Lee, Ibid.

48. Korea Herald, "Controversy erupts over National Security Law" *Korea Herald*, 23.4.2003.

49. C. Yoon, "Police to expand intelligence units," *Joongang Ilbo*, 29.7.2003.

50. Yoon, Ibid.

11

Controlling the Hydra: A Historical Analysis of South African Intelligence Accountability

Kevin O'Brien

In the post-Soviet era, many states experienced massive changes with the end of the bipolar aegis that had gripped the world. One of these states was South Africa, which clearly underwent a revolution: in its society, its politics, its strategic posture and position, and its very system of governing. One of the areas where this is most evident is that of national security and intelligence, as has been indicated by the continued evolution of the security and intelligence structures of the Republic of South Africa (RSA). This change was first acknowledged on October 21, 1994, when Minister of Justice Dullah Omar announced—in conjunction with the release of a government White Paper on Intelligence—the intended new structure of South Africa's secret services. This was followed in December 1994 by three new acts restructuring the intelligence and security services, as well as the mechanisms for control, coordination, oversight, and accountability. These changes were crucial to the furthering of a peaceful settlement between the former apartheid government and the former liberation groups. The new intelligence dispensation that was established in 1994 aimed, in addition, to develop solutions for many of the problems cited in other intelligence and security services.[1]

In representing a transitional state, moving from (in its case) white-minority rule to universal suffrage and multi-party democracy, South Africa retains a legacy from its past which has led to it both rejecting certain paths and options due to their (imagined or real) association with that past, while retaining other aspects of the past in the current dispensation. South Africa's intelligence oversight and accountability mechanisms today evolved out of the intelligence dispensation that existed under the apartheid regime; as such, they have both unique characteristics for a democratic system and the failings and foibles of a transitional state following liberation.

Understanding South Africa's intelligence dispensation today requires an appreciation of where it has come from.[2] The evolution of South Africa's intelligence oversight and accountability parameters and structures has been neither linear nor constant. At times in South Africa's republican (since 1961) history, it has had strong and clear executive accountability, while at other times the executive has sought actively to blur the lines (at the least) between its command-authority and command-responsibility and the activities of the intelligence services; this has been the case both before and since the 1994 transition.

During the period 1978 to 1990, under the leadership of first P. W. Botha and later F. W. de Klerk, South Africa was a security state. While nominal political authority and power rested with the elected cabinet ministers, the State Security Council (SSC) was the true center of power; executive/cabinet responsibility for intelligence and its three main agencies (South African Police Security Branch, Directorate of Military Intelligence [DMI], and Bureau of State Security [BOSS, later the National Intelligence Service]) was governed by the SSC through a number of pieces of legislation (the most important being the 1972 Security Intelligence and State Security Council Act), and military intelligence (DMI) dominated. Indeed, while in some ways apartheid-era intelligence was characterized by poor coordination of intelligence, corruption, mismanagement, and poorly defined briefs, in other ways a highly efficient intelligence and national security system was developed, in which all government efforts were driven by the Total National (later Counter-revolutionary) Strategy and the National Security Management System which underpinned it,[3] which oversaw the war against the liberation movements.[4] The relationship of Parliament to the intelligence brief was virtually nonexistent under apartheid—with the National Party's total dominance of governing, there was virtually no parliamentary oversight of intelligence under apartheid.

While that transitional period can now be said to be over, many of the problems of the transition remain. One clear legacy is its impact on not only the state but also on the state of mind of the individuals responsible for intelligence and security matters. There has been a lack of trust inherent in the new dispensation: lack of trust between individuals (not just "old guard" and "new guard" but also between the various individuals affiliated with one liberation group or party who now find themselves working together), lack of trust in the institutions (serious concerns exist over the functions of the National Intelligence Agency, as will be discussed), and lack of trust in the intelligence itself—deriving from both of the other two points and, perhaps worst of all, leading to (at times) a total politicization of the intelligence process, with both the intelligence product becoming politicized and the political leadership developing parallel-but-independent intelligence structures because of their own professed lack of trust in the state structures.

In this sense, while the institutions of oversight and accountability for the intelligence function would appear to be strong on the surface, upon further examination these can be found to be weak and problematic at best. That being said, serious moves—in the form of new legislation and the establishment of new oversight-and-accountability-related mechanisms—are being made currently to make up for such serious shortfalls. In all of these senses, therefore, South Africa is today—more than ten years into the post-apartheid era—faced with a continuing sense of fractiousness, factionalism, lack of trust, and even corruption in its intelligence structures. Nevertheless, it is both a product of the decisions that were made concerning its (the intelligence structures) transformation at the end of apartheid, and in far better shape than many other intelligence communities that have undergone transformation.[5]

The Transition Post-Apartheid: the "New Approach"

The end of apartheid was—in many senses—brought about by the intelligence services of both sides. At beginning of the 1990s, President F. W. de Klerk used the NIS to oversee the negotiation process with the African National Congress (ANC), resulting in the new political dispensation that came from the Conference on a Democratic South Africa (CODESA), the Transitional Executive Council (TEC) and—following the April 1994 elections—the Government of National Unity (GNU).[6]

Most of the new policies and legislation emerged out of the discussions between the NIS and ANC intelligence during the time of the TEC (formed in November 1993 to govern and oversee the period up to the elections and the transfer of power, as well as negotiations on the interim constitution), whose Sub-Council on Intelligence originated much of the dispensation discussed here: This was especially important because the future scope and focus of South Africa's intelligence community was not covered in great detail in the interim constitution, unlike the military and police, which were.[7] At the same time, a Joint Coordinating Intelligence Committee (JCIC) was established within the TEC, which gave the TEC oversight of the intelligence services' operations while day-to-day control was left to the individual department heads, much as with the military and the police.[8] The JCIC was authorized to oversee the coordination of the intelligence services, to investigate the activities of any service that appeared to contravene its mandate, and to provide intelligence information to the Transitional Executive Council (TEC) and its other sub-councils. The reason behind the changes in the intelligence and security structures were partly a result of the general government restructuring following the transition, but as well to allow for the integration of the ANC intelligence, along with all other intelligence services in the country, into the new national intelligence structures.

The Sub-Council on Intelligence agreed that as part of the continued approach to the philosophy of intelligence, certain principles and practical requirements were to be included in the mandates of the services for purposes of control and accountability: allegiance to the constitution, subordination to the rule of law, a clearly defined legal mandate, budgetary control and external auditing, an integrated national intelligence capability, political neutrality and the separation of intelligence from policy making, a balance between secrecy and transparency, and the absence of law-enforcement powers.[9] These were in addition to the four principle mechanisms for oversight and control of the intelligence services that would be built into the new structures: the appointment by the president of inspectors-general to oversee the services, the establishment of a parliamentary committee on intelligence, the implementation of a code of conduct for the intelligence services, and a strict limit in definition of the briefs of each service. In order to ensure that those agencies tasked with carrying out the intelligence and security work of South Africa would be able to execute their tasks with minimal interference and question, three final guidelines were established within the government. First, the services must accept as primary the authority of the government and other democratic institutions of society, as well as those bodies constitutionally mandated to participate in and monitor the determination of intelligence priorities. Second, the services must be assured that no changes to their operational doctrines, structures, and procedures would occur unless approved by the government and the people. Finally, the services would bind themselves to the new agreements through a mutually agreed set of norms and a code of conduct.[10]

Given the history of South African intelligence interference in society, it is not surprising that the new dispensation outlined a new "philosophy of intelligence" as its foundation for change. Noting that:

> . . . prior to the election of a democratic government, security policy was formulated by a minority government. Its ability to detail what was in the national interest was therefore flawed. Moreover, since the minority government was faced with a struggle for liberation, this issue dominated the question of security and, consequently, the activities of the statuary instruments that served it . . . the role of the state's security apparatus was over-accentuated with virtually no institutional checks and balances . . .

the new government believed that:

> reshaping and transforming intelligence in South Africa is not only a matter of organisational restructuring. It should start with clarifying the philosophy and redefining the mission, focus and priorities of intelligence in order to establish a new culture of intelligence.[11]

Given South Africa's apparent prosperity and order against the backdrop of the rest of sub–Saharan Africa, it is an attractive target—whether for illegal immigration or more serious threats—to others in the region; thus, a number of external security issues impact on the domestic security of the RSA. The 1994 White Paper on Intelligence recognized this ("new global political, social and economic problems are filtering South Africa's borders"), while also expressing strong concerns about increased "foreign intelligence activities in South Africa."[12] In addition, the twinned issues of domestic reconciliation coupled with internal development were crucially linked to the abilities of the intelligence agencies in South Africa to provide warning and assessment information to the government. However, the politicization of the intelligence process, in many respects, coupled with the continuing lack of national reconciliation—even now, a decade after the end of apartheid—has meant that the intelligence processes in the country, including the agencies, command and control, and oversight and accountability, have been stunted and indeed, in some cases, stillborn in their abilities to truly serve the national interest.

Through all of these negotiations, it was hoped that eventually, as Mike Louw (then director-general of the NIS) stated, South Africa could have "an intelligence service at peace with itself."[13] In order to accomplish this, Louw went on to say, "the watchwords must be control, accountability and supervision. Too many people equate us with other secret organizations. We need to establish our own identity."[14]

Models Examined: The "Mixed Bag" of Western Oversight Models

As part of their determination to restructure the new intelligence dispensation—and particularly its oversight and accountability functions—the South Africans studied a number of comparative examples, entirely derived (it would appear) from Western intelligence communities: Canada, Australia, the UK, and the United States, a notable fact considering the Marxist-Communist legacy of the ANC/SACP alliance and many of the leading figures in the new South Africa.

Overall, the Central Intelligence Agency Act and the British Security Services Act and Intelligence Services Act were most often held up as being indicative of problems with legislation and oversight in this area, as compared to the Canadian and Australian models that were most often seen as the correct approach. The South Africans' favorable comparisons to both the Canadian and Australian models were frequent in both discussions and in the literature and legislation, with the Canadian Security Intelligence Service Act and the Australian Security Intelligence Organization Act frequently cited by the officials involved in the policy-formulation process in South Africa.

Legislation and Statutes (1994–2003)

The principle pieces of legislation that concerned the new structures were the National Strategic Intelligence Act, the Intelligence Services Act, the Intelligence Services Control Act (originally introduced as the Committee of Members of Parliament on an Inspectors-General of Intelligence Act), and the 1994 White Paper on Intelligence. In addition, aspects of the 1995 South African Police Services Act, the 1996 National Crime Prevention Strategy (NCPS), and the 1995 White Paper on Defence: Defence in a Democracy, are relevant to any examination of the new national security structures.

These tenets—and the roles of the services, oversight and accountability— were outlined further in several amending acts passed by Parliament between 1998 and 2003, with a variety of aims, generally bringing South African intelligence into the twenty-first century. These included the Intelligence Services Control Amendment Act (Act 42 of 1999), the most relevant to the issue of oversight as it updated the Intelligence Services Control Act (Act 40 of 1994, as amended to Act 31 of 1995); the second Intelligence Services Control Amendment Act (Act 66 of 2002); the General Intelligence Law Amendment Act (Act 66 of 2000); the new Intelligence Services Act (Act 65 of 2002), which revisited and rewrote significant parts of the 1994 Intelligence Services Act; the National Strategic Intelligence Amendment Act (Act 67 of 2002), which further amended the 1994 National Strategic Intelligence Act; the General Intelligence Laws Amendment Act 2003 (Bill 47 of 2003, at the time of writing not passed by Parliament); and Regulation of Interception of Communications and Provision of Communication-related Information Act (Act 70 of 2002).

The Place of the Intelligence Services in the New Constitution

Although the intention of the parliamentarians who wrote the legislation, and who participated in the Constitutional Assembly's debates on the new constitution, originally was to have the mandates, areas of responsibilities, and a code of conduct for the intelligence services written into the new constitution (similar to sections on the national defense force and the police service), it was decided that the constitution would support only the existence of intelligence services, and defer to the legislation governing these services in this area only. As such, while the SANDF and SAPS are the only statutory security services in South Africa under the terms of the constitution, the president was authorized under sections 187(1) and 196(1) to establish "what intelligence services are required." However, this lack of a clear definition of South Africa's intelligence services, as compared to a concrete delineation of the police and defense force, is indicative of the problems that the constitutional assembly encountered in debating the role of the intelligence services and their placement in the constitution: when comparing the final constitution to the interim constitution, there has been a devolution of clarity in defining the roles, mandates, and related issues of the intelligence services. These should have been clearly defined in the constitution, especially given not only their specialized capabilities but also the fact that ongoing events relating to the post-transition intelligence services have clearly indicated that problems exist in their use by the executive. Minimally, there should have been a well-defined link between the constitution and the code of conduct for intelligence personnel contained in the White Paper on Intelligence. Although these missions were clearly defined in the Acts of Parliament relating to intelligence, these same acts allow sufficient latitude for these services to be utilized by the executive and its directorship as desired in particular situations.

To counter this possibility, section 185 of the constitution indicates that the intelligence services must be monitored, coordinated, and controlled largely in conjunction with those principles laid out in the National Strategic Intelligence Act, the Intelligence Services Act, and the Intelligence Services Control Act, including multi-party parliamentary oversight of the services, civilian oversight through an inspector-general, and coordination of all intelligence (including defense and police) activities in South Africa. Furthermore, the security services have been prohibited, under section 187(7), from attempting to influence, positively or negatively, the political process.

Ultimately, it was determined that the new mission of the South African intelligence community (see figure 11.1) would be to safeguard the constitution; uphold individual rights enunciated as fundamental rights in the constitution; promote the interrelated elements of security, stability, cooperation, and development, both within South Africa and in the region of Southern Africa; assist in the achievement of national prosperity while making an active contribution to global peace and other globally defined priorities for the well-being of humankind; and promote South Africa's ability to face foreign threats and to enhance its competitiveness in a dynamic world.[15]

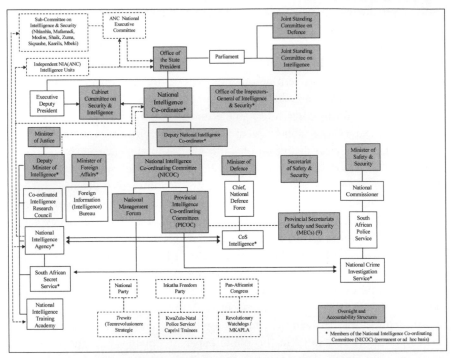

FIGURE 11.1   RSA Intelligence Structures 1996

The Services and Functions

In order to fulfill the missions laid out for the new South African intelligence community, a finite definition of national intelligence was first devised in order to provide parameters for both the restructuring of the community and the new (or continued) operational mandates of these agencies. National intelligence functions include counterintelligence, foreign intelligence, crime intelligence, military intelligence, and domestic intelligence. In addition, the president is further authorized to approve "special activities" by the South African intelligence community. In order to avoid the problems that occurred under the apartheid regime, the National Strategic Intelligence Act clearly defined these new briefs and what they mean for each agency.[16] Specific services are responsible for each of these functions within their own area of operations.

The Domestic Intelligence Capability

The National Intelligence Service was disbanded on January 1, 1995; in its place was established, under section 3(1) of the Intelligence Services Act, the National

Intelligence Agency (NIA). It comprised those former members of the NIS, ANC Intelligence, the Pan-Africanist Security Service, the Transkei Intelligence Service, the Bophutatswana Internal Intelligence Service, the Venda National Intelligence Service, and any other members of any intelligence service either attached to a political organization or operating in the independent homelands or self-governing territories.[17] Although the new agency included members from all of these services, a percentage of these former members instead became members of the new South African Police Service rather than intelligence.[18]

While many would have thought that the NIS should have been disbanded due to its links with the old order, many in the ANC argued for its retention due to a number of factors, the most important being the NIS contribution to the compromises that led to the settlement between the government and the ANC. As well, the NIS possessed assets and capabilities that the ANC would not want to lose, including sources; information on both the white right wing and extremists in political rivals such as Inkatha; technological capabilities; and greater professional training than those in the ANC. Finally, while it was not stated openly, the NIS also possessed information of great interest to the ANC: information on the ANC itself, its leaders and cadres, which it accrued through the placement of "moles" and other penetration exercises into the ANC and PAC ranks. The NIS could have inflicted considerable damage on the Government of National Unity by loosing this information.[19] The structure was left intact through a mutual agreement reached between the NIS and ANC prior to the elections so that the "constant flow of intelligence should not be disrupted" in order to ensure "a balance between continuity and change."[20] Similarly, the principle of "effective management" was established to ensure that those serving at the upper management positions would be competent and not simply political appointees; this would also prevent the disruption of the intelligence process by affirmative action programs.[21]

The mission of the NIA—as the domestic intelligence service—was defined in the White Paper as being to "conduct security intelligence within the borders of the Republic of South Africa in order to protect the constitution," with an overall focus being "to ensure the security and stability of the State and the safety and well-being of its citizens."[22] This means that the NIA carries out counter-intelligence and counter-terrorism operations domestically, acting alongside the SAPS to detect, deter, and prevent terrorism, insurgency, foreign espionage, and other activities that could undermine the state.[23]

In addition, the former Crime Combating and Investigation Division of the South African Police, established in April 1991 with the merger of the SAP Security Branch and the Crime Investigation Division, was disbanded in July 1994. In its stead, the South African Police Service National Crime Investigation Service

(NCIS) was created, solely concerned with crime intelligence and no longer with issues of national security.[24]

The Foreign Intelligence Capability

At the same time, the foreign intelligence-gathering department of the NIS was separated and constituted under section 3(1) as the South African Secret Service (SASS), to further its mandate as defined in section 2(2) of the National Strategic Intelligence Act. SASS has a complimentary role to the NIA: to "conduct intelligence in relation to external threats, opportunities, and other issues that may affect the Republic of South Africa, with the aim of promoting the national security and the interests of the country and its citizens."[25] SASS is also the ultimate mechanism for collecting and disseminating strategic intelligence, in cooperation with elements of the other agencies, for the National Intelligence Coordinator.[26]

Foreign intelligence is also provided by the Foreign Intelligence Bureau of the Department of Foreign Affairs, through its interaction with both agencies (NIA and SASS) for sourcing and coordination of foreign intelligence.[27]

It was hoped that dividing the operational mandates of the old National Intelligence Service between its foreign and domestic roles would "promote greater focusing, effectiveness, professionalism, and expertise in the specialized fields of domestic and foreign intelligence."[28] There were still cohesive ties between the two services in that the directors-general of the NIA and SASS must consult with each other on all decisions regarding operations and plans for the services. The first head of the NIA was the former deputy head of the ANC Department of Intelligence and Security, Sizakele Sigxashe, while the first head of SASS was the former director-general of the NIS, Mike Louw; many of the former NIS department heads retained their positions, with the addition of the DIS and PASS personnel.[29]

SANDF Defense Intelligence

Within the new South African National Defence Force (SANDF), formed in April 1994 following the national election, the intelligence division was greatly downsized and brought under civilian oversight, while remaining under the purview of the defence secretary. It included former members of military intelligence (DMI), ANC military intelligence, intelligence personnel from the Azanian People's Liberation Army, and the intelligence components of the Defense Forces of Transkei, Bophutatswana, Venda, and Ciskei. Its operational mandate is to:

gather, correlate, evaluate, and use foreign military intelligence, and supply foreign military intelligence relating to national strategic intelligence to [the National Intelligence Coordinating Committee] . . . gather, correlate, evaluate and use domestic military intelligence excluding covert collection except when employed for service referred to in section 227(1)(e) of the constitution . . . and institute counter-intelligence measures within the National Defence Forces.

Military intelligence is specifically forbidden from the covert collection of non-military foreign intelligence under section 2(4)(a) of the National Strategic Intelligence Act.

Ultimately, Defense Intelligence—like all other intelligence agencies—is subject to accountability and oversight in the forms of the parliamentary Joint Standing Committees on Defence and Intelligence, the inspectors-general of the SANDF and Intelligence, and other mechanisms provided for in the new intelligence dispensation such as the National Intelligence Co-ordinating Committee.

Electronic Intercepts/Communications Intelligence

In 2002, a new Electronic Communications Security (Pty) Ltd was established under the Electronic Communications Security (Pty) Ltd Act (Act 68 of 2002), which provided "for the establishment of a company that will provide electronic communications security products and services to organs of state," under oversight. The "Comsec" (as the ECS(P)L is referred to in the Act) is mandated to:

> (a) protect and secure critical electronic communications against unauthorized access or technical, electronic or any other related threats; (b) provide, with the concurrence of the National Intelligence Agency . . . verification services for electronic communications security systems, products and services used by organs of state; (c) provide and co-ordinate research and development with regard to electronic communications security systems, products, services and any other related services; (d) perform any other function not inconsistent with this Act that is necessary for the effective functioning of Comsec.[30]

Comsec is also governed—under the direction of the minister of intelligence services—by a board and a CEO.[31]

Executive/Cabinet Responsibility for Intelligence

A National Co-coordinating Mechanism?

One of the legacies from apartheid for the national intelligence function has been the retention of a national coordinating mechanism for intelligence and security.

Rather than fully disband—and reject—the old apartheid structures, the GNU decided to keep and reform the national coordinating structures, at both the national and provincial levels. While questions remained as to the need for such a system, it soon became apparent that the country's level of violent crime—including criminal violence, the "taxi wars" of the mid-1990s, and increasing politico-religious-criminal activities such as Muslim vigilantes in the Western Cape Province—and external infiltration meant that the GNU was concerned to retain the ability to share intelligence quickly across the national and provincial structures. A more cynical view would also say that once the ANC came into control of much of the national security apparatus which had existed under apartheid, it was loathe to give it up.

Whatever the case, the reforms to the old structures meant that a newly formed Cabinet Committee on Security and Intelligence (CCSI), in cooperation with other cabinet committees, would direct security policy; within this structure, it was plain from the transition of power that the old securocrats had been removed and new individuals appointed at all managerial and ministerial levels by the GNU. The new National Intelligence Coordinating Committee (NICOC) was authorized to oversee the coordination of the intelligence services, to investigate the activities of any service that appeared to contravene its mandate, and to provide intelligence information to the TEC and its other sub-councils. It reports to the president through the CCSI and comprises the National Intelligence Coordinator, the director-general of each service (including the NCIS and Defense Intelligence) and, on an ad hoc basis, the inspectors-general, the deputy directors of each services, and parliamentary representatives. NICOC has the following specific and inherent functions, among others:

- To advise the government on threats or potential threats to the security of the country and its citizens
- To advise the government on policy relating to the conduct of intelligence at national, regional, and local levels
- To coordinate the conduct of all intelligence functions and the collective intelligence resources of the country and relations with foreign intelligence services
- To report and to make recommendations to the Cabinet Committee on Security and Intelligence and to the Parliamentary Joint Standing Committee on Intelligence and Security as required
- To prepare and interpret a national intelligence estimate for consideration by the cabinet[32]

Similar to NICOC, at the provincial levels there exist Provincial Intelligence Coordinating Committees, chaired by provincial coordinators. In conjunction with the position of the provincial Members of Executive Councils (MECs) for Safety and Security, and Provincial Secretariats for Safety and Security coordinating and overseeing SAPS activities at the provincial level, a clear national security structure emerged, which (as noted earlier) reflects closely the apartheid-era NSMS structures. It was felt that a strong national security system was required to ensure coordination, accountability, and the continuous flow of essential intelligence to the executive.

A further mechanism for such coordination, but outside the formal chain of responsibility, was established through the appointment of an advisory board for the directors-general of both the NIA and SASS as mandated in section 31 of the Intelligence Services Act. The function of these bodies is to advise the director-general on the use of their powers.[33]

In addition to these formalized structures of coordination, a number of agreements were reached between the security services on sharing intelligence in pursuit of domestic security issues. The most important of these was a memorandum of understanding concluded between SAPS, the NIA, SASS, and the SANDF on May 10, 1996, which would ensure the sharing of information relating to combating organized crime. Included in the memorandum is a provision to establish a National Management Forum attached to NICOC, which will coordinate the anti-crime strategy between the security agencies.[34]

Finally, for accountability purposes, the civilian services are directly responsible to the Office of the State president, originally through the deputy minister who reported to the minister of justice (although this has now been replaced by a minister of intelligence); in the case of Defence Intelligence and the NCIS, responsibility flows respectively through the SANDF chief of staff (Intelligence) and the defence secretary in consultation with the minister of defence, and the SAPS national commissioner in consultation with the minister of safety and security and secretary for safety and security to the president.

Parliamentary Oversight of Intelligence: the Parliamentary Joint Standing Committee on Intelligence and the Inspectors-General of Intelligence

Within Parliament, an oversight committee was established in September 1995. This committee, designated the Joint Standing Committee on Intelligence (JSCI), is similar to the Canadian Security Intelligence Review Committee (SIRC) in its functions (see chapter 6 on Canada in this volume). The Committee was originally composed of eighteen members appointed by the president, proportionally representative to the seating of the various parties in Parliament. Subsequent legislation led to a change in the numbers and composition of the Committee to be more proportionally representative of Parliament,[35] while demanding that all members received security clearance from the NIA.[36]

The role of the Committee is to receive reports of the services from both the auditors and other evaluators of the services, make recommendations on both legislation related to the services and the activities of the services themselves, and to order investigations and hold hearings on matters relating to intelligence and national security. It also monitors the activities of the services with regard to human rights and other rights entrenched in the constitution. Its jurisdiction covers not just the NIA and SASS, but also—most notably—Defense Intelligence and the NCIS; it reports directly to the president, and through him to Parliament.[37]

This Committee was seen as one of the most significant changes in Parliament following the 1994 elections. In the apartheid Parliament, committees were closed to the media and to the public—their proceedings were secret and their decisions were publicly disclosed only after they had been taken. In the democratic Parliament, however, all but the Joint Standing Committee on Intelligence are held in the open, with journalists reporting on their proceedings and decisions, and the public, including advocacy and monitoring groups, are entitled to attend hearings.[38] While the JSCI hearings are not public, this overall move toward openness and transparency is remarkable nonetheless.

The Committee's mandate is quite broad and intrusive. Although section 4 of the Intelligence Services Control Act authorizes the Committee's access to any and all information that it may require in its investigations and duties,[39] the same section also authorizes the services to withhold from the Committee information on any person or body engaged in intelligence or counterintelligence activities, information which could reveal the identity of a source, or any knowledge of intelligence or counterintelligence methods carried out by any service if that information could also reveal a source.[40] This absolute protection of sources is one of the key political compromises that led to this point: as both sides prior to the 1994 elections engaged in espionage activities against the other, it is assumed that each side had (and may continue to maintain) sources in the other camp. Thus, any revelations regarding the nature of sources at this point in time could greatly damage the negotiated compromise achieved within the services themselves.[41] In the Intelligence Services Control Amendment Act 2002, the Committee's oversight purview was expanded from "intelligence and counterintelligence functions" to now include "the administration, financial management and expenditure of the Services."[42] In addition, the Committee was also authorized to "for the purposes of the performance of its functions, require Minister responsible for a Service, the Head of a Service, the CEO or the Inspector-General, to appear before it to give evidence, to produce any document or thing and answer."[43]

Questions were raised early on, however, on the sanctity of the Committee's secrecy, given that a number of parties sitting on the committee were deeply implicated (to varying degrees) in allegations of links to so-called "third-force" and other destabilizing activities aimed at the new democratic process; this was especially the case with Deputy Minister of Safety and Security Joe Matthews, the Inkatha Freedom Party (IFP) representative on the JSCI, who was closely linked with IFP attempts at resurrecting their intelligence capacity.[44]

A recent and welcome move has also been the requirement for the Committee to "within two months after 31 March in each year, table in Parliament a report on the activities of the Committee during the preceding year, together with the findings made by it and the recommendations it deems appropriate, and provide a copy thereof to the president and the Minister responsible for each Service"; it was furthermore required to "furnish Parliament, the president or such Minister with a special report concerning any matter relating to the performance of its functions."[45]

Further, a code of conduct has been written into the Intelligence Services Act as an additional mechanism of oversight and accountability. This code emerged out of discussions between the ANC and NIS in which the ANC wanted detailed guidelines with real regulatory powers which spelled out the rights of operatives, how to handle sources, and so on. The NIS argued that this would make intelligence work extremely difficult, possibly even endangering operations and agents; it wanted a code which would bind agents as little as possible.[46] The compromise, written into the purview of the minister responsible for the intelligence brief, became the code of conduct. It includes provisions that all members of the secret services shall adhere to the basic principles of their profession, as well as the policies, regulations, and directives of their respective services; shall respect the norms, values, and principles of a democratic society including the basic human rights of individuals; shall strive to be responsible in the handling of information and intelligence, and shall at all costs prevent the wrongful disclosure of national security interests; shall commit themselves to the promotion of mutual trust between policy-makers and professional intelligence workers, as well as cooperation with all the members of the intelligence community; and will conduct themselves in their personal life in a manner which will not prejudice their organization, their profession and fellow craftsmen, or the facilities entrusted to them.[47] Breaches of this code and other guidelines were laid out very specifically in the Intelligence Services Act;[48] should violations or misconduct occur, the director-general of each service is mandated with presidential authority to "charge any member with misconduct," to establish a board of inquiry following an unsatisfactory explanation from the individual in question, and to sentence that individual should he or she be found guilty; these powers could be used extra-territorially should the offense occur outside of South Africa's borders but still fall under the purview of the Intelligence Service Act.[49] Finally, the code had the function of authorizing intelligence officers to disobey any orders that contravened either the code or other statutes on operational capabilities.[50]

At the same time the Intelligence Services Control Act created the positions of inspectors-general for the services (NIA, SASS, Defense Intelligence, NCIS), to whom the director-general of each service is accountable. The Office of the Inspectors-General includes an investigation arm, a legal section and an information resource center. The inspectors-general are to review the activities of the intelligence services and to monitor their compliance with policy guidelines and other established mandates and principles. They are allowed full access to documents, budgets, reports, and all other classified information; each director-general is mandated to ensure that all matters of interest and concern having to do with the services is brought to the immediate attention of the inspectors-general.[51]

A worrying sign overall is that in the eight years of the new intelligence dispensation, the post has only been occupied twice briefly, with each incumbent resigning soon after taking office. This, in addition to the continued "tinkering" with the mandate and role of the inspector-general (IG) in the legislation, would appear to indicate a serious concern over this one key—indeed, crucial—area of oversight.

The role of the IG changed further with subsequent legislation: first, in a serious change from the previous, the Intelligence Services Control Amendment Act 1999 stated that there would now be "one or more Inspectors-General of Intelligence," rather than the previous dictate of "for each Service an Inspector-General."[52] It also stipulated that the IG could be approved by "at least two thirds" of the members, rather than the previous "majority of at least 75 per cent"—relating clearly to the failures to appoint an IG successfully.[53] The IG's purview was also expanded in section 6 of the Act as being "to receive and investigate complaints from members of the public and members of the Services on alleged maladministration, abuse of power, transgressions of the laws and policies referred to in paragraph (a), corruption and the improper enrichment of any person through an act or omission of any member."[54] In relation to this, it was stipulated that an IG "shall have access to any intelligence, information or premises under the control of the Service in respect of which he or she has been appointed. . . . No access to intelligence, information or premises . . . may be withheld from an Inspector-General on any ground."[55]

These problems were thrown into an even starker light when the subsequent Intelligence Services Control Amendment Act 2002 deemed that there should only be one inspector-general of intelligence—once again pointing to the difficulty in appointing even one, let alone multiple IGs. The IG's overall mandate was again expanded "(a) to monitor compliance by Service with the constitution, applicable laws and relevant policies on intelligence and counter-intelligence; (b) to review the intelligence and counter-intelligence activities of any Service; (c) to perform all functions designated to him or her by the president or Minister responsible for a Service."[56] In addition, the complaint mechanism from the public was strengthened—the IG's mandate was expanded to also include the ability to order investigation by and to receive a report from the head of a service.[57] Finally, the IG also now had to submit "certificates . . . [and] reports" to both the minister and the Committee pursuant to their functions; this was reflected, for the heads of services, in the requirement that they now must "in respect of every period of 12 months or such lesser period as is specified by the Minister responsible for that Service, submit to that Minister a report on the activities of that Service during that period, and shall cause a copy of such report to be submitted to the Inspector-General."[58] Furthermore, "each Head of a Service shall report to the Inspector-General regarding any unlawful intelligence activity or significant intelligence failure of that Service and any corrective action that has been taken or is intended to be taken in connection with such activity or failure."[59]

Finally, the auditor-general and the Standing Committee on Public Accounts monitor the relevant intelligence budgets, while the constitution provides for protection against state abuse through the public prosecutor and the Human Rights Commission.[60]

The new legislation also made a number of other amendments. The General Intelligence Law Amendment Act (Act 66 of 2000), among other amendments, included the establishment of an Intelligence Review Board, which—consisting of three to five persons appointed by the minister—was mandated to "consider and approve any application by a former member to disclose information or material" relating to their former employ, thus ensuring that a statutory body would be in place to consider how former employees had used their knowledge gained during their employment with the intelligence services.[61]

The new Intelligence Services Act (Act 65 of 2002), which revisited and rewrote significant parts of the 1994 Intelligence Services Act, established the new National Academy of Intelligence under the same legislation as the intelligence services,[62] as well as the Intelligence Services Council on Conditions of Service, which makes recommendations to the minister on the development of policies on conditions of service and human resource matters. It also established clearly the powers of the minister of intelligence services. Finally, it proposed "Offences" for all employees of the intelligence services.[63]

Finally, in 2003, an additional General Intelligence Laws Amendment Act 2003 (Bill 47 of 2003, at this writing not passed by Parliament) was tabled, which—among other things—regulates the interception and monitoring of communications (further to the Regulation of Interception of Communications and

Provision of Communication-related Information Act—Act 70 of 2002) and the newly established Office for Interception Centers.[64] It establishes an Appeals Panel process responsible to the minister of intelligence services;[65] and, most importantly, further supports the Intelligence Services Council, answerable to the minister and the president, "to promote measures and set standards to ensure the effective and efficient performance and implementation of policies on human resources within the Academy or the Intelligence Services, as the case may be, and to make recommendations to the Minister."[66] All in all, it is clear from the legislation tabled through the turn of the century that the parliamentarians were attempting to come to grips with not just some of the more serious problems that South African intelligence had faced during the 1990s (see the following section) but also with those aspects of the original acts—passed immediately at the end of apartheid and subject to the influences of the time—which had proved lacking over the last decade (see figure 11.2).

Danger of politicization of intelligence

While there are many pressing problems that must be addressed, the greatest appears to be the ongoing concerns over the politicization of the intelligence process and the development of parallel (political) intelligence structures.

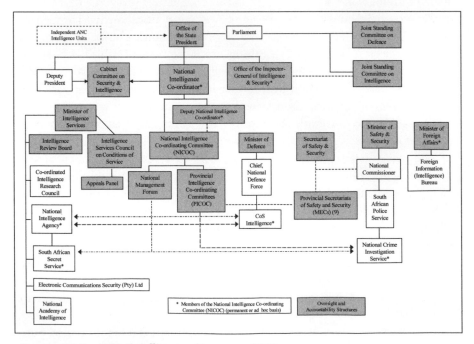

FIGURE 11.2   RSA Intelligence Structures 2003

It is clear that the new intelligence structures in South Africa are the product of great ncgotiation and discussion; while these appeared to achieve initial successes, over the course of the mid- to late 1990s, the scandals, questionable (and sometimes outright illegal, as in allegations of NIA spying on the leadership of the National Party and the SAPS in the mid-1990s) activities, and ongoing failure to secure all the instruments of oversight has meant that South Africa's intelligence services are very much in crisis—and show little sign of recovery. During the 1990s, South African intelligence suffered from numerous scandals—including accusations of "bugging" each other; spying on political opposition parties; spying on friendly governments' diplomatic missions; the unlawful and suspicious deaths of at least two leading intelligence figures; allegations of collusion with the so-called "third force" of former apartheid and former ANC intelligence and special forces operatives engaged in destabilizing the country; collusion with the country's top bank-robbers, themselves alleged to be former members of an ANC Special Forces unit; and other scandals.[67]

As mandated in the 1994 Intelligence Services Act, the directors-general of each agency are responsible for ensuring not only that all national security intelligence, collection methods, sources, and the identities of members are protected to the fullest extent from unauthorized disclosure, but as well to ensure that "no action is carried out that could give rise to any reasonable suspicion that the Agency or Service . . . is concerned in furthering, protecting or undermining the interests of any section of the population or any political party or organization."[68] This politicization is really notable in three regards:

- Aiming to match the current political climate, both through the placement of ANC loyalists in key positions within the intelligence services and from those within the services wishing to simply meet the anticipated expectations of the political leadership (the least problematic of the three).
- (Somewhat following from the first) ensuring factional integration within the intelligence services between old enemies. Early on in the integration process, there were strong concerns regarding not only the independence of the public service from ANC party policy, but as well an increasing degree of dissatisfaction within the public service and an increasing number of resignations. Reports of "factionalism" within the NIA emerged, indicating that similar problems that existed within the ANC during exile have not been solved, but rather enhanced with the power such individuals and factions have found in their new positions; this is in addition to the not-surprising division between the old and new guards. These problems appear to persist.[69]
- Finally, the development of parallel intelligence structures for political purposes due to a total lack of trust in the national intelligence functions—

perhaps the most worrying.[70] An ANC document published in the mid-1990s, analyzing the success of the GNU, recommended that a number of small, mobile, professional intelligence units be set up to "detour deficiencies within the official ranks of the NIA and the information flow that runs through NICOC to the government."[71] This is seen as providing a means to get around the lack of trust and suspicions that exist in the national structures.[72]

Overall, this raises serious questions regarding the separation of policy surrounding intelligence from that of ANC party policy itself: the two must remain separate and distinct for obvious reasons. As one government source stated to the author in the late 1990s:

> No government can rule effectively without having the power to ensure that the leadership of the government departments will act according to the political will of the government. The old civil service was full of personnel who had no commitment to fulfill the will of the new government—should we have left them in an untransformed civil service?[73]

Ironically, this has led—it could be argued—to the re-emergence of the dominance of "securocrats" within the South African government, albeit this time ANC ones.

Conclusions

Is South Africa to be held to higher standards than other countries? A severe critique—and this is a severe critique—would say yes, if for no other reason than that the architects of South Africa's new intelligence dispensation stated that they would hold themselves to far higher standards than not only the system that they looked to replace, but also international standards for the field. The professions of the ANC intelligence professionals in the period before and during the TEC process, as well as those sentiments enunciated in the White Paper on Intelligence, were toward the highest standard of quality, transparency, accountability, control, and oversight; regrettably, any clear assessment of the current state of South Africa's intelligence dispensation would note failings (and worse) in each of these areas.

In assessing the South African experience and dispensation, only a barely passing grade should be granted to South Africa in terms of the strength of its accountability and oversight mechanisms for intelligence. The intelligence services are barely independent from the executive—indeed, in some senses they could be seen as slaves to the executive's policies and interests. The oversight mechanisms remain fragile and bare; while Parliamentary oversight has strengthened over the last decade—in terms of its membership, staff, access, and proactivity—the continuing failure to appoint a lasting inspector-general for the intelligence services is a glaring void in oversight.[74]

If a balance can now be found between the ANC domination of the government and public service—which bears with great importance on the absolute necessity for clear coordination and accountability within the security services—and the concerns of the professionals who serve in these agencies, a peaceful and stable environment will be developed for an equitable future within the country's intelligence community. As has already been seen from the decade of the new dispensation, clear problems exist in coordination between services and cooperation not only with each other but also with the political leaders of the day. This problem must be solved to ensure a peaceful future both within the services and within South Africa itself.

Notes

1. This chapter results in part from interviews conducted with official and private sources in South Africa, Canada, Britain, Australia, and the United States during 1994–2000. As most of these interviews were confidential in nature, I have tried to indicate general sources for such information in this chapter. Where this has not been possible, no reference will be cited.

2. An extensive understanding of the *apartheid* intelligence and security structures can be drawn from Kenneth W. Grundy, *The Militarization of South African Politics* (Bloomington: Indiana University Press, 1986); and Kevin A. O'Brien, "The Use of Assassination as a Tool of State Policy: South Africa's Counter-Revolutionary Strategy 1979–1992," *Terrorism and Political Violence*. Part I: 10:3 (Summer 1998): 34–51 and Part II: 13:2 (Spring 2001): 107–42; Annette Seegers, *The Military in the Making of Modern South Africa* (London: Tauris Academic Books, 1996). As well, see Republic of South Africa *Report of the Truth and Reconciliation Commission* 1:2 "Historical Context: Gross Human Rights Violations in Political and Historical Perspective": www.polity.org.za/govdocs/commissions/1998/trc/1chap2.htm, and all further chapters in the Report; and National Party of South Africa, *Second Submission of the National Party to the Truth and Reconciliation Commission*: www.truth.org.za/submit/np2.htm.

3. South Africa was run with every element of society geared towards fighting the war—resulting in the total and integrated coordination of every sector of society into a nationally-managed security architecture (whose aspects would include the military, political, social, welfare, economic, etc.) to oversee the implementation of this "total national strategy."

4. Annette Seegers, *The Military in the Making of Modern South Africa* (London: Tauris Academic Books, 1996), 126–32.

5. On the evolution of the South African security establishment at the end of apartheid, see Robert d'A. Henderson, "South African Intelligence Under de Klerk," *International Journal of Intelligence and Counterintelligence* 8:1 (Spring 1995); and the author's

"South Africa's Evolving Intelligence and Security Structures," *International Journal of Intelligence and Counterintelligence* 9:2 (Summer 1996): 187–232.

6. Mark Shaw, "Spy meets spy: Negotiating new intelligence structures," in *The Small Miracle: South Africa's Negotiated Settlement*, eds. Steve Friedman & Doreen Atkinson, South African Review 7 (London, 1994): 257–59.

7. Shaw, "Spy meets spy," 268–69.

8. Participants in the discussions included the NIS, DIS, and representatives from the services of the "homelands" of Transkei, Venda, and Bophutatswana—all of which would later be integrated. Shaw, 263.

9. Republic of South Africa, *White Paper on Intelligence* (October 1994): 9–10, 13–14 [hereafter *White Paper*].

10. White Paper, 11. This code of conduct would reflect similar ones for SAPS and SANDF.

11. White Paper, 2–3.

12. White Paper, 17–18.

13. Shaw, "Spy meets spy," 269.

14. Rex Gibson, "Memoirs of an invisible man," *The Star International Weekly* (January 26–February 1, 1995): 13.

15. White Paper, 5. Most of these points arose out of the ANC's National Policy Conference statement entitled *ANC Policy Guidelines For A Democratic South Africa: A New Approach To Intelligence*, released on May 31, 1992.

16. Annexure B, subsection 4 of the White Paper on Intelligence mandates the president or minister to authorize "special activities" further to the missions of the NIA and SASS (Republic of South Africa, *National Strategic Intelligence Act* (Act 39 of 1994) (December 1994) [hereafter *NSI Act*] s2(1) and 2(2)) pursuant to the definition of the counter-intelligence mission as laid out in section 1(v) of the *NSI Act*. There is concern that this grants too much leeway for covert activities to the authorities, as has happened elsewhere (cf. the history of the US *National Security Council Act* 1947 and subsequent CIA covert activities).

17. Although the independent homelands of Transkei, Bophutatswana, and Venda had intelligence services (civilian and military), Ciskei did not; its International Research Bureau, which later became the Ciskei Intelligence Service, was disbanded in August 1991 due to (at best) questionable covert activities: Sandy Africa, "The Role, Prospects, and Expectations of the TBVC Intelligence Services during an Interim Government Period," *Strategic Review for Southern Africa: Security and Intelligence in a Post-Apartheid South Africa* 14:2 (October 1992): 79. For a brief discussion of the PASS, also known as the PAC Intelligence and Security Department, see Tom Lodge, "A Profile of the Azanian Peoples' Liberation Army," in *About-Turn: The Transformation of the South African Military and Intelligence*, eds. J. K. Cilliers and Norkus Reichardt (Nidrand: Institute of Defence Policy, 1996), 109.

18. Republic of South Africa, *Intelligence Services Act* (Act 38 of 1994) (December 1994): s3(1)(a-g) [hereafter *IS Act*].

19. Shaw, "Spy meets spy," 265.

20. Sharon Chetty, "Meeting the Government's needs is Sigxashe's aim," *The Star and SA Times* (December 20, 1995): 7.

21. Shaw, "Spy meets spy," 265.

22. White Paper, 12.

23. A further explanation of this mission was laid out in the *NSI Act*, s2(1)(a/b/c).

24. *NSI Act*, s2(3)(a/b).

25. White Paper, 12.

26. This role was further explained in the *NSI Act*, s2(2)(a/b/c).

27. Brendan Seery, "Out of the cold and into the light," *The Star International Weekly* (March 16–22, 1995): 11.

28. White Paper, 12–13.

29. This retention of senior personnel (not including those who voluntarily resigned) was mandated in section 2(b) of the Intelligence Services Act. Of the approximately 4,000 personnel included in the new civilian structures, 2,130 came from the NIS, 910 from the ANC-DIS, 304 from Bophutatswana, 233 from Transkei, 76 from Venda, and the remainder from the PASS.

30. *Electronic Communications Security (Pty) Ltd Act* (Act 68 of 2002): s7.

31. *Electronic Communications Security (Pty) Ltd Act* (Act 68 of 2002): Chapters 2, 3.

32. White Paper, 15; National Intelligence Agency, *Guiding Principles of the new South African Intelligence Dispensation* (Pretoria, 1995), 19–20; *NSI Act*, s4(2).

33. *IS Act*, s31.

34. "Fivaz announces agreement between police and intelligence agencies" and "SAPS, NIA, SASS, SANDF to fight together against crime," SAPA Reports, May 10, 1996.

35. Section 2 of the *Intelligence Services Control Amendment Act* 1999.

36. *ISC Amendment Act 1999*: s2b.

37. White Paper, 14; Republic of South Africa, *Intelligence Services Control Act* (Act 40 of 1994) (December 1994): s2(1)/(2), 3(1)(g) [hereafter *ISC Act*]. Its first chair was Lindwe Sisulu and its current chair is Dr Siyabonga Cyprian Cwele—both of the ANC.

38. www.parliament.gov.za/pls/portal30/docs/FOLDER/PARLIAMENTARY_INFORMATION/PUBLICATIONS/FIVE/chapter6.htm.

39. *ISC Act*, s4(1)/(3).

40. *ISC Act*, s4(2)(a). The IG, however, is authorized to access information detailing sources.

41. Shaw, "Spying for democracy," 2.

42. *ISC Amendment Act 2002*: s2.

43. *ISC Amendment Act 2002*: s4b.

44. Eddie Koch, "SA intelligence world in turmoil," *Weekly Mail and Guardian* (20 October 1995).

45. *ISC Amendment Act 2002*: s6.

46. Shaw, "Spy meets spy," 267.

47. White Paper, *Annexure A: "Code of Conduct for Intelligence Workers."*

48. *IS Act*, s22(1).

49. *IS Act*, s15–18, 22(2), 23.

50. This code was in addition to the more traditional sections on violations of powers and duties as found in Chapter III "Discipline" and section 22 "Offences" of the *IS Act*: Shaw, "Spy meets spy," 266.

51. *ISC Act*, s7(1)/(2),(3)–(6).

52. This was clarified in the Act that "one Inspector-General may be appointed with regard to some of or all the Services as long as the activities of all the Services are monitored by an Inspector-General": *ISC Amendment Act 1999*: s5a/b.

53. *ISC Amendment Act 1999*: s5b.

54. *ISC Amendment Act 1999*: s7.

55. *ISC Amendment Act 1999*: s8–9.

56. *ISC Amendment Act 2002*: s7(7).

57. *ISC Amendment Act 2002*: s3c.

58. *ISC Amendment Act 2002*: s7(7) and s7(11)(a).

59. *ISC Amendment Act 2002*: s7(11)(h).

60. www.nia.org.za.

61. *General Intelligence Law Amendment Act* (66–2000): s18–22B.

62. *Intelligence Services Act* (65–2002): s5 [hereafter *IS Act 2002*].

63. *IS Act 2002*: s22, s12, s26.

64. *General Intelligence Laws Amendment Act* 2003 (Bill 47 of 2003): 2(b).

65. *General Intelligence Laws Amendment Act* 2003 (Bill 47 of 2003): 8(c).

66. *General Intelligence Laws Amendment Act* 2003 (Bill 47 of 2003): 14.

67. Some of this is documented in Kevin A. O'Brien, "South Africa's Evolving Intelligence and Security Structures." *International Journal of Intelligence and Counterintelligence* 9:2 (Summer 1996): 187–232, and will be updated in a forthcoming article on the topic.

68. *IS Act*, s4(3)(a/b).

69. Gaye Davis, "Spying Allegations: Who are the silly buggers?" *Weekly Mail and Guardian*, February 3, 1996.

70. In the mid-1990s, the existence of a subcommittee on intelligence and security attached to the ANC National Executive Committee was discovered (composed of Joe Nhlanhla, Joe Modise, Sidney Mufamadi, and Bantu Holimisa). In addition, there were reported attempts by *Inkatha* to resurrect a paramilitary and intelligence capacity within both the IFP and the KwaZulu-Natal Police, using funds from Germany's Konrad Adenauer Foundation and, allegedly, the CIA: Paul Stober, Marion Edmonds, Eddie Koch and Ann Eveleth, "Inkatha's secret German war chest," *Weekly Mail and Guardian*, September 15, 1995; Jeff Stein, "South Africa's Many 'Watergates' May Spill Over on the CIA," *Baltimore Sun*, March 20, 1996.

71. Koch, op cit.

72. Indeed, in November 2001, Mbeki's office established a new presidential support unit in the Ministry of Intelligence to provide logistical backing to the presidency and former president Nelson Mandela. "'Spy unit' for Mbeki," *ZA*NOW*, February 22, 2002.

73. Interview, April 5, 1996.

74. In February 2004, Zolile Thando Ngcakani—the former head of ministerial services in the Intelligence Ministry and the man who had investigated claims by the Democratic Party in November 1999 that the NIA had planted electronic monitory devices in its party headquarters—was appointed as inspector-general of the intelligence services. "New Intelligence Inspector Sworn In," *SAPA*, February 5, 2004.

PART 4

Conclusions

12

Balancing Operational Efficiency and Democratic Legitimacy

Hans Born and Loch K. Johnson

Who is watching the spies and how is oversight of the world's intelligence services maintained? The relevance of these questions, addressed in this volume, is greater now than ever before. In the wake of 9/11 and the 2003 Iraq war, many of those responsible for overseeing intelligence in both legislative bodies and executives are currently involved in investigating the functioning of the services as well as the conduct of the political leaders supposed to task and direct the services. The mass media also reports each day on the work of permanent and special intelligence oversight committees in various countries, such as the 9/11 investigation commission of the U.S. Congress. These oversight committees deal with formidable questions: Did the intelligence services malfunction? Have political leaders misused intelligence? Do intelligence services function solely to uncritically defend or selectively supply information on policies decided by their political masters without impartial counsel from intelligence professionals? Are intelligence officials working within their mandate? Are they working within the rule of law? Do they need more legal powers, budget, and manpower for dealing with the new terrorist threats, as they themselves claim? These and other questions illustrate that oversight of the intelligence services performs an important dual role in democratic societies: keeping the services in line with their legally defined mandate and ensuring their effectiveness.

This book attempts to bring to the forefront insights, good practices, and legal procedures of democratic oversight of intelligence and security services in eight countries: Argentina, Canada, Norway, Poland, South Africa, South Korea, the United Kingdom, and the United States. The sample is composed of countries with a variety of political systems (presidential versus parliamentary), different phases of democratization (new and old democracies), superpowers and small countries (for example, the United States and Norway), as well as different geographical locations (the Americas, Europe, Africa, and Asia). In spite of all these differences, the selected countries also have common features: they are democracies; they possess external intelligence oversight committees; and their intelligence services function on a statutory basis.

Before turning our attention to the main results, the concept of democratic oversight of security and intelligence services needs some unpacking (see also chapter 1). "Oversight" is defined as a means of ensuring public accountability for the decisions and actions of security and intelligence services. It must be distinguished from control, which refers to the act of being in charge of the day-to-day management of the intelligence services. The phrase "democratic oversight" introduces important conditions regarding intelligence accountability. The added word "democratic" suggests first, that elected officeholders or representatives are responsible for oversight and, second, that the intelligence services respect the rule of law. In a free nation, both elements are essential to the oversight of intelligence services. As mentioned in chapter 1, in a democracy no single area of government activity can be a "no-go" zone for parliamentarians, including the intelligence and security services. Parliaments and government together are part of a system of checks and balances, which avoids one branch of the state dominating—with all the temptations to misuse the security and intelligence services that accompany concentrated power. The rule of law is the second important element, as a broad view on democracy implies not only a majority rule, but also respect for due process, civil liberties, and human rights. In this context, the special powers of security services—for example, interference with private property and communications—has to be subject to codification and external control.

This book focuses on oversight by parliament and the executive, as well as the legal frameworks in which they operate. It not only examines the simple question of who watches the services but also discusses how the institutions under consideration actually exercise oversight. Although important in their own right, the role of the media and the judiciary—two additional institutions of significance to democratic oversight—are only touched upon in this volume, with the exception of chapter 3 which deals with the influence of the European Court of Human Rights (ECtHR) case law on national democratic oversight systems. With regard to the services, both domestic (security) services and foreign intelligence services are included in the study. Here intelligence is interpreted as the entire cycle of planning and direction, collection, processing, analysis, and dissemination of intelligence (see chapter 4).

Taking Stock: Democratic Oversight of Intelligence Services in Eight Nations

Democratic Oversight of Intelligence: A Recent Development

The deepening and widening of democratic oversight of intelligence and secret services is a recent development. Until well into the 1970s, widely considered the first decade of serious intelligence oversight, accountability over secret agencies was considered an executive prerogative in nearly all democracies (not to mention authoritarian regimes). Elected representatives in parliaments had hardly any, and often no, authority over intelligence matters. At the time, oversight was based on executive decrees and orders, not on laws enacted by parliamentarians (although there were some notable exceptions to this practice, as in the Netherlands). This situation changed radically in the mid-1970s when, triggered by scandals and violation of basic civil rights, the United States enacted sweeping reforms with respect to intelligence, including a key role for Congress and new laws to ensure closer supervision of secret operations. Not long after, Canada and Australia followed suit. This period of New Oversight, which gained strength in the 1980s, can be regarded as the second decade of intelligence accountability. Mainly Anglo-Saxon countries started to introduce democratic provisions for intelligence supervision that established a firm legal footing for oversight, including a significant role for parliament. The end of the Cold War saw the beginning of a third decade of intelligence oversight—the 1990s—as part of the wider evolution of democracy in Central and Eastern Europe (see chapter 1).

Post-communist and authoritarian regimes were not the only ones to introduce new forms of democratic oversight for intelligence services in the 1990s. Until then, intelligence oversight had not been well developed in most Western democracies either. As a result of a political and administrative culture heavily influenced by the Cold War, most countries exhibited a broad political consensus that national security was best served if the intelligence services were left to themselves. The end of the Cold War created a window of opportunity, however, for the expansion and deepening of intelligence oversight, not only in transition states but also in established democracies (see, for example, the Norwegian case study in chapter 7).

As far as Europe was concerned, governments—both new and old democracies—strengthened intelligence oversight by way of an expanding body of case law in the European Court of Human Rights (ECtHR), as discussed in chapter 3 by Iain Cameron). In dealing with cases brought forward by citizens whose human rights had been violated by members of the security services, the ECtHR required that the legal regime of the security services had to be clear, foreseeable, and accessible. This spurred the governments of various states that are parties to the European Convention of Human Rights (ECHR—forty-six European member States in 2004, whose services mainly functioned on the basis of executive decrees and directives) to enact or improve legislation concerning their intelligence and security services. The United Kingdom, Norway, Sweden, and the Netherlands, for instance, all have made these legal changes. The growing, if modest, influence of the ECtHR on the democratic oversight of intelligence and secret services is a significant development, for it implies a slowly expanding body of pan-European legal norms for oversight beyond the nation state itself.

The politicization of intelligence is another recent development addressed in this volume (see chapter 2 by Peter Gill), in terms of the actions of the UK and U.S. governments, which led the invasion of Iraq in 2003. The governments of both countries were accused of politicizing or "cooking" intelligence to create a stronger case for war against Saddam Hussein. This selective use of intelligence, runs the argument, enabled the second Bush Administration and the Blair Administration to market a doctrine of preemptive (or, more accurately, preventive) war to block the further development and proliferation of weapons of mass destruction (WMDs).[1]

One can argue that intelligence is always politicized to a certain extent, in that intelligence is supposed to support the decisions and policy priorities of political leaders. Indeed, the collection and analysis of information is inherently meant for use in policy formulation and implementation. Otherwise intelligence would simply be irrelevant to the political leadership. As a general trend, however, an excessive politicization of the intelligence services may be partially a product of the recent democratization of intelligence oversight. The greater role for parliaments and their oversight committees in the review of intelligence activities, along with the removal of the total blanket of secrecy that historically surrounded the intelligence agencies, may have resulted in an increase in the political and public pressures on these agencies.

Democratically elected governments can no longer simply refuse to comment on intelligence issues; governments now are increasingly forced to use complex media strategies to win over both parliaments and the media to their cause, including the use of the infamous "spin doctors." The danger might be that the politicization of intelligence will lead to increased public cynicism, mistrust, and paranoia, which in turn might harm citizen trust in the intelligence services and the political system. The question remains as to whether the politicization of intelligence is caused by the processes of democratization and expanding oversight in this secret world, or the fact that political leaders have always politicized intelligence but such actions are only now visible because of the recent democratization of intelligence oversight.

The Revolution in Intelligence Oversight

The second part of this book deals with established democracies where intelligence oversight began after the mid-1970s, in other words, the United States (1974), Canada (1984), Norway (1995), and the United Kingdom (1989/1994). In all of these countries, oversight was triggered by scandals exposed by the media, in which a country's security services were found to have been spying on their own citizens. The ensuing outcry and media attention resulted in public pressure to reform and better scrutinize the way the services operated.

The U.S. case study highlights one of the most powerful approaches to legislative oversight in the selected sample of countries (see table 12.1). The U.S. Congress mandated itself to review the legality and effectiveness of the services, with authority to approve top presidential intelligence appointments, to authorize and appropriate the annual intelligence budget, and to subpoena experts and witnesses. Moreover, the congressional oversight committees in Washington, D.C., enjoy nearly unlimited access to secret information. The members of the U.S. House and Senate Intelligence Committees are not vetted by the intelligence services, as this would be a sign of congressional subordination to the executive branch. As the only legislative body in this book's sample, the oversight committees of the Congress receive prior notification of special operations, except in extraordinary circumstances (when a two-day delay is permitted). In spite of these formidable powers, however, strong congressional oversight continues to face various obstacles, such as the lack of will among lawmakers to engage actively in routine oversight tasks and the fact that Congress remains largely dependent on the willingness of the White House to submit information and keep lawmakers well informed.

In the United Kingdom, the first intelligence legislation (for the security service, MI5) was enacted in 1989, when it became clear that the British would be found to be in breach of the regulations set out by the ECHR, that is, allowing intelligence gathering to function without a statutory basis and without sufficient procedures for legal compliance (see chapters 3 and 5). In 1994, legislation for other (foreign) intelligence services followed and a parliamentary oversight committee was established (still leaving, inter alia, military intelligence without a statutory basis). It is striking that even a long-established democracy like the United Kingdom introduced parliamentary oversight for the intelligence services only in the mid-1990s. Before then, Parliament remained outside the ring of secrecy and ministers were trusted on their word. In spite of these recent innovations, the UK oversight system has some serious drawbacks. National security is not fully defined in the services' mandates, implying that the services can move into new areas of work without parliamentary consent. Additionally, the executive has the power to interfere in the work of the parliamentary committee, as the prime

TABLE 12.1

Comparison of the External and Parliamentary Oversight Bodies in the Eight Selected Countries

(1) Country	(2) First Oversight Legislation	(3) Mandate of Oversight Body	(4) Budget Control Powers of Oversight Body	(5) Type of oversight body; # Membership, Clearance, Appointment of Oversight Body	(6) Subpoena powers.	(7) Prior notification requests
(A) Argentina	1992	Reviews legality and effectiveness of the services, including citizens' complaints.	Both scrutiny and authorization powers.	Parliamentary oversight body of 14 MPs as member, appointed by Parliament. There is no security vetting.	No.	Not regulated by the law.
(B) Canada	1984	The SIRC checks legality and efficacy of the agency.	SIRC has no authorization powers, yet can comment on CSIS's budget	External independent expert oversight body of max. 5 experts as member, appointed by prime minister. Members are under oath	Yes.	No prior notification required.
(C) Norway	1995	The oversight focuses primarily on legality of the services, including human rights protection.	No budget oversight function.	External expert parliamentary oversight body; max. 7 members (non-MPs) but appointed by Parliament.	Yes.	Agencies are forbidden from consulting with the Committee about future operations.
(D) Poland	1995	Overviews, legality, policy, administration, and international cooperation of services. Effectiveness is not checked.	Commission scrutinizes the services' draft budget and its implementation.	Parliamentary oversight body; 9 MPs as member max, appointed by parliament. All members undergo security vetting.	No.	No legal duty.
(E) South Africa	1994	Its oversight purview includes legislation, activities, administration, financial management, and expenditure of the services.	The Committee does not oversee the intelligence services' budgets per se, but its purview includes financial management of the services.	Parliamentary oversight body; committee consists of 15 MPs, appointed by president. Members are vetted.	Yes	No legal duty.
(F) South Korea	1994	It examines and comments legislation, effectiveness of the Services. It holds hearings on individuals nominated for senior positions in the NIS.	The Committee has no budget powers.	Parliamentary oversight body of 12 members, put forward by political parties.	No	No legal duty.
(G) United Kingdom	(1989) 1994	Finance, administration and policy of MI5, MI6, and GCHQ with a view on efficiency. It does not check legality	Committee scrutinizes the finance together with the Public Accounts Committee but has no authorization power.	Parliamentary oversight body of 9 members drawn from both Houses of Parliament, appointed by the prime minister	No.	No legal duty
(H) United States	1974	Reviews all intelligence agencies. Approves top intelligence appointments. It checks both legality and effectiveness of the services.	Both oversight committees possess authorization and appropriation powers.	Two congressional oversight committees, consisting of 20 (House) and 17 (Senate) congressmen, appointed by House and Senate leaders	Yes, on both committees	Yes, except in times of acute emergency, in which the agencies can delay reporting for 2 days

minister appoints its members. Concerning its reports, the Committee is required by law to report to the prime minister in the first instance, who can edit the reports before they are laid before Parliament (see chapter 5 and table 12.1). As Ian Leigh concludes in chapter 5, "No independent person would recommend these arrangements as a model to other countries . . . but in a stable democratic system they work tolerably well."

Triggered by a scandal in 1976 (intelligence service personnel breaking into a press agency), Canada legislated its Canadian Security Intelligence Service (CSIS) in 1984 and established an external oversight body, the Security Intelligence Review Committee (SIRC). The SIRC was mandated to review the effectiveness of the CSIS and its compliance with the law, as well as to investigate complaints against the service and cases where security clearances were denied. The Committee's members are appointed by the prime minister and report to the minister responsible. The advantage of the Canadian oversight system is that it has an independent expert committee with security-cleared support staff and full access to the agency they monitor; therefore, oversight is less politicized than in some other nations. But the Canadian system has a downside. The oversight body only reviews activities of the CSIS and does not exercise oversight over other intelligence services in Canada. Furthermore, the oversight body has no direct linkage to Parliament and cannot alert members of Parliament until the minister does so in an annual report. Therefore, the Canadian Parliament is only remotely involved in intelligence matters. It was only in 2003 that the Canadian government acknowledged the existence of a "democratic deficit" and the great need for a parliamentary committee to oversee all Canadian services (see chapter 6).

Norway has one feature in common with Canada. In 1995, the Norwegians established an expert committee whose members are not parliamentarians. In contrast with Canada, however, the Norwegian oversight committee is strongly linked to Parliament. Its members are appointed by and report to the Parliament. Without losing any involvement in intelligence oversight, the parliament therefore delegated the oversight to experts with more knowledge and time to carry out the daily chores of program review. The Parliament's expert committee is mandated to conduct inspections (twenty per year), to deal with complaints, and to set up inquiries if necessary. As Fredrik Sejersted concludes in chapter 7 the Norwegian oversight system is "strong but within clear limits." The independent parliamentary oversight body is concerned only with the rule of law and the protection of human rights; overseeing the effectiveness of the services and their efficiency is left to the executive alone.

In summary, the issue of legislative oversight of the intelligence services became a focus in Western democracies only recently and often as a result of scandals. Today, it seems to be the norm that security and intelligence services in democratic societies are "parliamentarized." This means that the executive shares its power over intelligence with the Parliament, diminishing the chance that the executive is able to misuse the services. Not all oversight bodies have the same mandate. The Canadian and U.S. oversight bodies review both the efficiency and legality of the services. The Norwegian oversight body focuses solely on legality, and the UK's parliamentary oversight body is concerned only with effectiveness. Norway and Canada have chosen a system of independent expert review (outside Parliament), while in the United States and the United Kingdom members of Parliament and their staffs (internal experts) directly oversee the services.

The Spread of Intelligence Oversight

The fourth decade of intelligence oversight, spawned by a rising frequency and lethality of terrorist attacks at the beginning of the twenty-first century and a growing concern about inaccurate estimates of WMDs in Iraq, has led to demands for further intelligence reform in many of the countries studied in this book. High on the list of reform proposals are calls for better intelligence quality, more "actionable" (detailed) intelligence forecasts, improved coordination of intelligence agencies within and between nations, stronger norms against the selective use of intelligence ("cherry-picking") to support preordained political objectives (such as regime change in Iraq in 2003), and, last but not least, greater attention to police-patrol oversight—that is, more serious involvement of overseers in the day-to-day efforts to enhance the effectiveness of intelligence against terrorists and other threats to peace and security.

In the wake of worldwide "democratization waves" since the 1970s, the placing of intelligence services under democratic supervision in Europe was fostered by Europe's international organizations, such as the Council of Europe and the Organization for Security and Cooperation in Europe (OSCE). The third part of this volume deals with the analysis of democratic oversight of intelligence and security services in transition states beyond Western Europe: in Poland, Argentina, South Korea, and South Africa. In these countries, the introduction of democratic oversight and reform of the security and intelligence services was a long and painful process. The main reason is that the services occupied a powerful, central, and repressive role under the authoritarian regimes. They were supposed to guarantee "regime security" and placed an emphasis on securing the leadership's survival. It was their task to deter or to excise any sign of opposition. The services were instruments of raw power, and their names and acronyms frightened people. Because dictators wished to monitor each and every one permanently, the services were vast, enjoyed ample resources, and had connections to all layers of society. So, how, if at all, could these behemoth organizations be contained and put under democratic oversight?

The secret services in these regimes acquired enormous powers, even after the turn to democracy, as Andrzej Zybertowicz argues in chapter 8. To fully understand the intricate relationship between the nascent Polish democracy and that nation's intelligence services, one must understand the concept of a "security complex" in Poland. According to Zybertowicz, it consists of the main three secret and intelligence services, along with private security and detective organizations and former secret collaborators of the communist services who remain active in business, the media, and politics. In addition, the security complex includes other state institutions that are authorized to collect information, such as border guards, custom services, and the Ministry of Finance's units dealing with tax crimes. After 1989, many security and intelligence services were either closed or forced to drastically downsize their personnel. In some cases, 75 percent of the personnel were fired. Many of the former communist functionaries found their way into new services. For example, according to Zybertowicz, two-thirds of the newly established Polish security service's staff came from the old services.

The parliamentary oversight body in Poland was only set up in 1995, and its members are from both the ruling and opposition parties, with the chairman drawn from the opposition. Zybertowicz explicitly points out the danger of having many of the alleged functionaries of the former communist intelligence services active in politics, either as high-level government officials or as members of Parliament. According to him, this development brings with it the danger that the principal-agent relations may become blurred or even reversed. It can also create a situation in which the services can blackmail their principals. During the 1990s, the services frequently came forward with accusations that specific leading politicians—including a prime minister—had been spying for the former communist security services.

During the "Junta" dictatorship in Argentina, the security services were used for the brutal repression of any form of opposition and were integrally associated with human rights abuses. Since the move to democracy in 1983, relevant reforms have come a long way (as disclosed in chapter 9). The Argentinean National Congress only legalized the entire intelligence system in 2001. Having previously experienced a repressive secret services apparatus, the lawmakers explicitly forbade the services from conducting repressive activities, having compulsory powers, fulfilling police functions, or conducting criminal investigations without explicit authorization. The lawmakers also forbade the services from collecting and keeping data on individuals because of their race, religion, political, or union affiliations. The 2001 legislation also established a parliamentary oversight committee with far-reaching oversight powers (see table 12.1). Notably, secret expenditures are subject to congressional oversight and approval.

Until 1987, South Korea was a military dictatorship and could be characterized as a "national security state." The essence of a security state is that nearly all aspects of public, economic, and political life are regarded as national security issues. The military and the security and intelligence services of South Korea played a key role in upholding this security state. They controlled businesses, repressed labor and student organizations, and tightly regulated other civil society groups. As a result of its size, resources, and networks with politics and society, it was and continues to be a powerful force with a major influence on politics. After South Korea's transition to democracy in 1987, the problems with reforming the National Intelligence Service (NIS) cannot be attributed solely to weak parliamentary oversight. Intertwined with a strong executive, the role of unofficial political networks, and the politics of national security legislation, the security services are strong and cannot be checked by parliamentary oversight alone. To this day, the executive controls the services without a transparent system of checks and balances. According to Jonathan Moran (in chapter 10), one of the persistent problems facing South Korea is that the president and his family allegedly used the secret service for their own political and commercial benefits, including illegally wiretapping members of the opposition as well as journalists and businessmen. The main challenge in South Korea today is not that the secret and intelligence services are out of control, but that they are too closely controlled by the presidential office, without parliamentary checks. Moreover, executive control exists without a clear system of tasking and directing, relying instead on an informal network of politicians. The parliamentary intelligence oversight body is weak, reflecting the National Assembly's weak power base vis-à-vis the executive. The strong position of the executive and the services might also be explained by the continuous threat from North Korea. One might argue that on the Korean Peninsula the Cold War still continues, perpetuating a "security state" environment.

After peacefully shedding the apartheid regime, the reform and control of the intelligence and secret services in South Africa was not an easy task. In 2004, a decade after the democratization processes started, many transition problems still remain. According to Kevin O'Brien (chapter 11), the main obstacle is the lack of trust between individuals in politics and intelligence, between the old and the new guard within the intelligence service itself, and a lack of trust by the general public toward intelligence. Unfortunate, too, is the fact that the intelligence process already seems to be politicized, with the political leadership developing parallel independent intelligence structures.

Nevertheless, the progress in overseeing and reforming the secret services has seen some notable advances. In 1994, the ANC and the last apartheid government decided to disband the existing security services, in favor of establishing a new agency (which included former apartheid intelligence officers, ANC intelligence members, and intelligence services of other liberation movements). Further, in 1994, at the beginning of South Africa's transition to democracy, the government enacted new laws with respect to the intelligence services and their oversight. Through these laws, various means of supervision were created, such as a multi-party parliamentary oversight committee, an independent inspector-general, and a code of conduct for intelligence personnel. The parliamentary committee, whose members are appointed by the president, has a broad mandate, including the review of administration, expenditure, financial management, and functioning of the services. The committee has access to all information (except sources, methods, and current operations); it can propose new legislation; and it may order investigations and hold hearings. However, although these oversight procedures may look strong on paper, they are weak and problematic in practice. According to O'Brien, the intelligence services are not independent from the executive and can be seen as willing servants of the executive's policies and interests. Presently, the key issue is to find a balance between ANC's domination in government and the integrity and independence of the professionals working in the intelligence services.

To summarize, democratic oversight of intelligence and security services in transition states is an ongoing concern. For the most part, intelligence oversight seems to be dominated by the president or government, which gives leeway for politicization or misuse of the services by the executive. In most of the selected transition states, political neutrality of the services and respect for human rights are codified in intelligence legislation and in codes of conduct for service professionals. Independent parliamentary oversight bodies are being created. On paper these structures look very promising, but an analysis of the reality of intelligence oversight reveals that many challenges still lie ahead.

Good Practices

What makes an intelligence oversight body strong and effective? The answer to this question depends on the goals one has in mind. As previously mentioned, oversight refers to maintaining public accountability over the services, without the sense of taking over a government's responsibility for directing, tasking, and judging the priorities of the intelligence services. This process of accountability can only succeed if the overseers have the necessary legal authority and will to exercise meaningful review. Without legal powers, financial resources, and staff, an oversight body is deemed to be a "toothless" institution, no match for a government or its intelligence services. Yet, conversely, is it possible that oversight might hinder effective intelligence gathering and analysis through legislative micromanagement and a lack of responsibility for carefully protecting classified information? In this regard, some commentators have questioned the ability of overseers to keep secrets and to resist interfering with sensitive operations, sources, and methods. Based on the country studies presented here, as well as earlier research[2] one may say that an intelligence oversight body may be declared strong if has an independent status from the executive, investigative powers, access to classified documents, a committee able to keep secrets, and sufficient expertise. These five vital elements of effective oversight are addressed in the country studies and the result of the comparisons are shown in table 12.2 and discussed below.

1. *Independence.* The oversight bodies of most transition states are not entirely independent from the executive and the intelligence services, except in the case of Argentina. In these states, the oversight body has weak statutory powers, which turn the oversight body into a feeble institution unable to counterbalance the executive. In addition, the country studies in this volume show that sometimes the members of the oversight body were formerly employed by the intelligence services they oversee and are still deeply connected with the services. Concerning Western democracies, the oversight committees in Canada and the United Kingdom are appointed by the prime minister, which undermines their claims to independence. The political system of these two countries, that is, the Westminster form of parliamentary system, is known for an executive which dominates Parliament—especially with respect to foreign and security affairs. The oversight bodies of Norway and the United States are considerably more independent from the executive. Their members are appointed by the legislature and their reports are not screened by the executive (as in the United Kingdom). The most independent oversight bodies are those which have the power to review and approve intelligence budgets (as in the cases of the United States and Argentina) or which are given prior notification from the intelligence services about impending operations—even of the most sensitive nature (again, the rule in the United States). Armed with these authorities, the oversight body becomes a strong check as overseers themselves become responsible in part for the future of their nation's intelligence agencies. Although these oversight powers symbolize the sovereignty of the legislative as an equal entity to the executive, one might raise a question about whether an oversight body can become too closely involved in the conduct of intelligence activities. It is debatable whether a group of parliamentary overseers that have become co-partners for intelligence can also step back and scrutinize objectively its own decisions.

2. The term *investigative powers* refers to the notion that an oversight body

TABLE 12.2

Elements of Strong Oversight, Based on Expert Assessment of the Eight Country Studies' Authors

Country	(1) Independence from Executive	(2) Investigative Capacity	(3) Access to Classified Information	(4) Ability to Maintain Secrecy	(5) Adequate Support Staff
(A) Argentina	Independent. Members appointed by Parliament.	Committee can initiate investigation based on a complaint or on conclusions of its own work.	Full access.	No leaks or scandals related to the Committee's activities.	The Committee can hire administrative personnel—four to eight. Each member can appoint one expert adviser.
(B) Canada	SIRC's members are appointed by prime minister, after consulting with opposition. Reports to minister who reports to Parliament.	Committee decides upon its own work plan.	Full access to agency.	Staff is vetted and members are under oath.	Not sufficient resources to review all agency's functions in one year. Has established multi-year program.
(C) Norway	Yes, very independent.	Can investigate what it chooses within its mandate.	Unlimited access to all documents.	No leaks from the Committee since its establishment in 1995.	Small secretariat (One administrative assistant and two lawyers working on a half-time basis).
(D) Poland	Commission members have often been accused of being too deeply connected to the services.	Commission lacks investigative powers. Criticized for lacking own initiatives.	Very much dependent on the discretion of the services.	Occasionally Commission members have leaked information to the press.	The Commission possesses a permanent administrative staff of three people. The staff performs only administrative tasks.
(E) South Africa	Committee members are appointed by president based on parliamentary proportionally—and report to the president, who reports to Parliament.	Committee has broad and intrusive powers.	By law unlimited access to information except on sources.	Negligible—scandals have occurred frequently during the first ten years of the Committee's existence.	Ample.
(F) South Korea	The Committee reflects the weakness of the National Assembly vis-à-vis the executive.	Meager use of its investigation powers.	Access guaranteed by law, negligible performance by the Services to grant access.	Adequate.	The Committee is very small and not well resourced.
(G) United Kingdom	Behaves independently, although appointed by and reports to the PM.	Can investigate what it chooses within its mandate.	Yes, some 'sensitive' material can be refused.	No leaks from the Committee since its establishment in 1994.	Only one investigator.
(H) United States	Yes, very independent.	Yes, e.g. Joint Committee inquiry into 9/11.	Total Access.	Leaks are rare.	Ample.

can decide to inquire into whatever subject it chooses. The research indicates that the oversight bodies of the countries studied here have the capacity to initiate investigations on the basis of complaints or as a result of its own conclusions. However, in Poland and South Korea (two transition states), the respective oversight bodies rarely use their investigative powers.

3. Do the overseers have *access* to classified documents? The oversight committees in most countries have full access to secret documents, although some access is denied in the case of information related to sources, methods, and ongoing operations. Rarely, if ever, would an overseer need access to the names of agents or sensitive modus operandi—highly classified and compartmented information.

4. Are the oversight committees able to *maintain secrets*? Though in many countries the argument is used that parliamentarians cannot keep secrets and that the Parliament, as an open institution, is ill suited for discussing secrets, the country studies here suggest that oversight committees have displayed a capacity to maintain secrecy. Leaks have rarely occurred. As a matter of fact, the U.S. case study indicates that the executive branch leaks far more, for political purposes, than the legislative branch.

5. The issue of *support staff* refers to whether the oversight body has adequate personnel to conduct meaningful research and to help carry out inspection visits, hearings, and investigations. Especially valuable are experts and investigators who are familiar with intelligence and security services. The results show that most oversight bodies have limited resources and staff. Apparently, the creators of the selected oversight bodies have been hesitant to set up a counter-bureaucracy responsible for reviewing the intelligence bureaucracy.

These five points can be regarded as good practices contributing to strong democratic oversight of security and intelligence services. However, these five points only partially cover reality. Effective parliamentary oversight is based not only on authority (legal and other powers) and ability (resources and expertise), but also on the attitude or willingness of parliamentarians to be seriously involved in intelligence oversight.[3] The case studies disclose a mixed picture. According to the practice of oversight in the selected countries, parliamentarians are especially willing to be involved in "fire alarms." These are hearings or investigations into scandals or failures that stir substantial media attention. When it comes to "police patrols," that is, the conduct of frequent inspections and other "dull" routine jobs related to oversight, parliamentarians seem to be less motivated (see, for example, chapter 4 on the United States). However, this type of routine oversight is, in the end, the most valuable form of oversight because it aims at detecting errors before they become intelligence failures.

In addition to these good practices, perhaps the best practice is for democratic intelligence oversight to become a norm for all government, with a substantial role for parliament and a solid statutory foundation. The intelligence services themselves are likely to benefit from this approach, for it can contribute to the thoughtful crafting of intelligence operations and, even more importantly, provide them with legitimacy. That is a vital result in a free society.

Notes

1. The second Bush Administration and others used the phrase "preemption" as though it were interchangeable with the phrase "preventive war," although in fact the two are distinct strategic concepts. The doctrine of preventive war assumes that war with another nation is inevitable; therefore, it is better to begin the war straight away rather than wait until the adversary grows stronger. Despite its use of the term preemption, the second Bush Administration's planning about Iraq appeared to be dominated by preventive war thinking. Used more precisely, preemption refers in contrast to a nation's decision to conduct a quick strike against another threatening nation, based on reliable intelligence that the adversary is about to launch an attack [See James J. Wirtz and James A. Russell, "U.S. Policy on Preventive War and Preemption, *The Nonproliferation Review* (Spring 2003), 113–23.] Whatever definition one prefers, these doctrines underscore the increasing importance of intelligence in foreign and defense policy.

2. Compare with Lawrence Lustgarten and Ian Leigh, *In from the Cold: National Security and Parliamentary Democracy* (Oxford: Clarendon Press, 1994), and Hans Born, Philipp Fluri, and Anders Johnson, *Parliamentary Oversight of the Security Sector: Principles, Mechanisms and Practices*, Inter-Parliamentary Union Handbook nr. 5 for Parliamentarians (Geneva: IPU and Geneva, 2003).

3. Compare, Hans Born and Heiner Hänggi, *'The Double Democratic Deficit' Parliamentary Accountability of the Use of Force under International Auspices* (Aldershot, UK: Ashgate Publishers, 2004).

Index

Aberbach, Joel D., 59–60
Access to Information Act, Canada, 107, 112
accident of litigation, 36
accountability
  agency design and, 8–9
  ECHR on, 37
  issues in, 7
  McDonald Commission on, 103
  See also democratic accountability; intelligence accountability
Acevedo, Sergio, 176
Act Relating to the Oversight of the Intelligence, Surveillance and Security Services, Norway, 121–22, 124, 131
Advisory Council on Security and Intelligence, Canada, 104
Afghanistan, 61, 65
African National Congress (ANC), 201, 207
agencies
  design of, 8–9
  and Iraq invasion, 16–19
  and knowledge/power model, *16*
  powers of, 9
  as threats to democracy, 4
Agency for Internal Security (ABW), Poland, 146, 148, 150
Agency for National Security Planning, South Korea, 180, 183–84
Air Force Information Service, Argentina, 162
Aljahoe society, 185
al Qaeda, 18, 20, 61, 65, 113
Ames, Aldrich H., 61, 66
Amman v. Switzerland, 40, 42, 46
Amnesty International, 193

analysis, in intelligence cycle, 62–63
Anti-Corruption Office, Argentina, 176
Anti-Terrorism Act, Canada, 101
  adoption of, lessons from, 108–10
Anti-Terrorism Crime and Security Act, UK, 5
apartheid, legacy of, in South Africa, 199–200, 209–10, 212, 219n2
Appeals Panel, South Africa, 216
appointees, 13
appropriations. *See* budgets
Arar, Mahar, 113–14
Archer, Jeffrey, 89
Argentina
  intelligence oversight in, 160–79, *230*, 233–34
  strength of oversight in, *237*
Argentine Coast Guard Intelligence Service, 162
Argentine Federal Police, 162
Army Counter Intelligence Corps, South Korea, 183
Army Intelligence, Argentina, 162
Aspin-Brown Commission, U.S., 58, 61
assassinations, 66
auditor-general, in South Africa, 215
audits. *See* inspections
Australia
  intelligence reform in, 87
  parliamentary oversight in, 112
  and South Africa, 204
Australian Secret Intelligence Services (ASIS), 87
Australian Security Intelligence Organization (ASIO), 87
Austria, intelligence reform in, 4
Azanian People's Liberation Army, 208

List of Contributors

Dr. Hans Born, Senior Fellow, Geneva Centre for the Democratic Control of Armed Forces, Geneva, Switzerland, h.born@dcaf.ch

Dr. Iain Cameron, Professor in Public International Law, Faculty of Law, University of Uppsala, Uppsala, Sweden, Cameron@jur.uu.se

Mr. Eduardo E. Estévez, Member of Asociación para Políticas Públicas; former advisor to the Interior Security Secretariat, Ministry of Justice, Security and Human Rights, Buenos Aires, Argentina, eduardoestevez@hotmail.com

Dr. Stuart Farson, Lecturer, Political Science Department, Simon Fraser University, Vancouver/Surrey, Canada, farson@sfu.ca

Dr. Peter Gill, Reader in Politics and Security, Liverpool John Moores University, Liverpool, United Kingdom, p.gill@livjm.ac.uk

Dr. Loch K. Johnson, Regents Professor of Political Science, University of Georgia, Athens, United States, johnson@arches.uga.edu

Dr. Ian Leigh, Professor of Law, Co-director of the Human Rights Centre, Department of Law, University of Durham, United Kingdom, Ian.Leigh@durham.ac.uk

Dr. Jonathan Moran, Senior Lecturer in Criminology and Criminal Justice, University of Glamorgan, Pontypridd, Wales, United Kingdom, jmoran@glam.ac.uk

Dr. Kevin O'Brien, Senior Policy Analyst, RAND Europe, Cambridge, United Kingdom, obrien@rand.org

Dr. Fredrik Sejersted, Attorney at Law, Office of the Attorney-General, Oslo, Norway, fredrik.sejersted@regjeringsadvokaten.no

Dr. Andrzej Zybertowicz, Director, Sociological Institute, Copernicus University, Torun, Poland, ertowicz@umk.pl